Human Behavior in the Social Environment

a social systems approach

RALPH E. ANDERSON
IRL E. CARTER
School of Social Work
The University of Iowa

CHICAGO

HUMAN BEHAVIOR in the SOCIAL ENVIRONMENT

a social systems approach

Aldine Publishing Company

ABOUT THE AUTHORS

Ralph E. Anderson is presently Associate Professor in the School of Social
Work at the University of Iowa. He received his B.A. at the University of
Minnesota in 1950 and his M.S.W. at the University of Nebraska in
1953.

Irl E. Carter is Instructor in the School of Social Work at the University
of Iowa. After receiving his B.A. at Parsons College in 1955, his B.D. at
Drake University in 1960 and his M.A. (in Social Work) at the University of Iowa in 1965, he began pursuing his doctorate and is presently a
doctoral candidate in Social Foundations of Education at the University
of Iowa.

Consulting Editor
James K. Whittaker

*First published 1974 by
Aldine Publishing Company
529 South Wabash Avenue
Chicago, Illinois 60605*

*ISBN 0-202-36015-6 cloth
0-202-36016-4 paper
Library of Congress Catalog Number 73-84929*

Printed in the United States of America

CONTENTS

ACKNOWLEDGMENTS

The persons most responsible for this book, other than ourselves, are those of our students who provoked us to think more clearly, and to attempt to teach more effectively. These students, now our professional colleagues, will recognize ideas and examples that emerged from feedback between them and us.

We wish to acknowledge the contributions of Ann Cone for her careful research, and those of Beverly Sweet, whose preparation of the manuscript approached perfection.

Finally, we are grateful to the staff of Aldine Publishing Company, especially Alexander J. Morin, Publisher, for lending his encouragement and judgment. James K. Whittaker, editor of Aldine's *Modern Applications of Social Work* series, is thanked for his helpful and critical reading of the manuscript. The Aldine staff has made this a pleasant experience throughout.

INTRODUCTION

But you gotta know the territory!

Meredith Willson, *The Music Man*

This book is an attempt to map the territory of human behavior. It is intended to introduce students in the human services to ideas and theories that are fundamental to understanding human behavior. Students in social work, education, nursing, home economics, child development, and other professions providing human services require an acquaintance with a vast body of knowledge about the behavior of humans. Today it is not possible to present enough information in one book to accomplish this. In our teaching and in our students' learning, we found that we came nearest to accomplishing this task by writing this book and using it as a global map of human behavior. It designates the major levels of knowledge of human behavior and enables the student to recognize with what human system he is concerning himself. It is designed as a textbook to organize human behavior content into an understandable whole.

Along with most of our students, we have found this book useful as a large-scale map in a "survey" of human behavior. We know from experience that its utility in a particular sector of human behavior may be limited. Since this is true, "small-scale maps" are provided in the suggested readings described at the end of each chapter. These sources provide more detailed explorations of particular human systems. This book, however, serves to place knowledge of human behavior within a broad context; to remind us that one's theory and one's practice are "a piece of the continent, and a part of the main."

1

The manner in which this book and the more specialized resources fit together varies with the terrain. For example, a great many books and articles deal with organizations as systems, and it is fairly clear how the large-scale systems map and the small-scale maps of organizational behavior can be integrated. The integration of the two scales is less clear, however, as they converge in the behavior of persons—how the part and the whole relate is always at issue. One recurrent issue, for example, is whether a person should be regarded as the basic unit (the focal system), whether he is capable of being subdivided, or whether he should be regarded only as a subunit of society. There is disagreement about which scale to use, which perspective to take. Our intent is to demonstrate that these are all legitimate perspectives, to be used selectively in accord with criteria explicated in this book.

Our objectives in this book are to explain how our map is designed and to prove its utility. We have sought an "umbrella" theory under which various theoretical perspectives would fit; or, to shift the metaphor, a "skeleton" framework upon which various theories can be affixed and fleshed out toward a comprehensive theory of human behavior. In our experience, no single theoretical construction can encompass all aspects of human behavior. Courses in human behavior have had various organizing themes, including:

1. *Normal vs abnormal behavior.* This perspective provides knowledge of individual and family dynamics, which is invaluable in understanding and dealing with individual behavior but is of doubtful validity when applied to groups, institutions, communities, and societies.

2. *Developmental patterns of the individual.* This perspective includes groups, communities, and society but only from the standpoint of their effects on the development of the person. Inherent in this approach is a view of the person as an "adjuster" or an "adapter." Human behavior is seen as adjustment to social stresses. Intervention possibilities are dichotomized; *either* work toward helping the person to adjust to his social situation *or* attempt to change the social situation so that it would be less stressful to the person.

3. *Social processes.* This perspective emphasizes knowledge of the social and cultural patterns that provide the social context of development and behavior. Such understanding is essential to social planning but omits the uniqueness of the individual person and his patterns of living.

Each of these perspectives, and others, have served as a structuring theme for ordering knowledge of human behavior. Each enables scrutiny of various theories and hypotheses. Each however has limited applicability to the broadening base of practice. The explosion of social science knowledge relevant to practice in the various human services requires a more comprehensive framework than that provided by any of the previously employed organizing schemes. What is now required is an approach that will foster an integration of psychoanalytic, psychological, and developmental perspectives with the burgeoning discoveries from the many disciplines that study human behavior. We have found that social systems is that approach.

The social systems approach is probably best described as a "theory about theories," or an "hypothesis about theories," since there is not yet sufficient research to establish it as a theory of human behavior. It is a particular variation of General Systems Theory, which crosses physical, natural, and social sciences. Emerging findings in many disciplines buttress the validity of systems theories. A social systems approach has several advantages.

1. It is comprehensive. It offers more possibility for description and integration of seemingly disparate theories into a single framework than any other approach we know.

2. Even though it does not map adequately all sectors of human behavior, it does provide suggestive leads for all.

3. It has the potential for providing a common language to various professions, both within each profession and as a means of exchanging ideas across disciplines. Students interested in psychotherapy, education, community development, and administration may find social systems a useful common framework. To use a social work practice example, the psychotherapist may not be vitally interested in community development, believing that significant changes occur in individual persons; the community developer may believe that significant changes occur only when groups act; while the administrator may believe that change is real only when it is structured and solidified in an institution or program. We believe that each is partially right and partially wrong. Like the proverbial blind men examining the elephant, each has part of the truth. Yet these three social work specialists can see the relationships between and among their localities if they share a knowledge of social systems. Each might still prefer his own domain, but would be aware that it was a "part of the main." He would recognize that interactions of persons, groups, and organizations are integrally related in a common system. It is our conviction that human services have lacked such an integrative approach far too long, even though we recognize the historical reasons for the delay.

4. A final advantage is parsimony. Social systems theory allows the student to reduce the "blooming, buzzing confusion" of theories of human behavior and methods of practice to a framework that can be mastered. Herein lies the danger, of course. Through reductionism the student may be content with the global map, flying from continent to continent, coast to coast, without encountering the

precipices, mudholes, and arid wastes upon which many a theory has foundered. Systems theory cannot replace knowledge of at least some particular sectors of human behavior, in detail. People live through the processes of human interaction, not on maps.

This book attempts to describe a systems skeleton and then locate important human behavior concepts upon that skeleton. The instructors and students who use this book must flesh out the skeleton so that the approach will be directly applicable to the practice of each respective profession.

How to Use This Book

This book is, then, a large-scale map, intended to be supplemented in each particular sector of human behavior by more detailed maps. We have used it in this way with both graduate and undergraduate students. We have guided students through the courses in modular fashion, selecting theories that made sense to us and to the students, and indicating where each more detailed theory meshed with the large-scale map.

The first chapter acquaints the student with our social systems approach. The essential systems characteristics are introduced and explained. These concepts, which serve to describe the skeleton, reappear in the subsequent chapters. They are the key ideas that compose the social systems approach of this book.

The subsequent chapters are modules—they can be taught as discrete units, requiring only the first chapter as precedent. The arrangement of the chapters is one feasible way of ordering human systems, in descending order of magnitude. If instructors using this book prefer other sequences, the order can be changed or even reversed. By so doing, this course might better integrate with others being taught during the same term, or might better convey a particular theme being emphasized. Instructors in colleges of education may decide to deal with the chapter on the person prior to chapters on group or family.

We have found it advantageous to use other texts with this book to provide additional threads of continuity throughout the general map, to assure degrees both of latitude and longitude, and to provide a single small-map source for each human system examined. For continuity crossing all human systems we have used *The Autobiography of Malcolm X* and Toffler's *Future Shock*. For specific systems we have assigned, for example, Erikson's *Identity: Youth and Crisis* for the chapter on the person and Billingsley's *Black Families in White America* for the chapter on family. Again, many choices are open to the instructor.

Suggested readings, with brief commentaries on their particular utility, follow each chapter. The readings actually used will depend on the instructor and students involved and on the clock and calendar time available. If the students are unfamiliar with the content germane to particular human systems (such as family, groups), the supplemental materials should be selected with this in mind. For students acquainted with particular content, supplemental readings can give deeper insights into theoretical writings and related research.

The glossary is designed for easy reference to the key concepts used throughout this book. Although most readers will be familiar with most of the terminology, some of the concepts may be unclear. The reader should consult the glossary explanations, as these are the definitions used throughout.

This book is intended to be an open system. We assume that each instructor will add and substitute books, articles, films, or other learning aids. This flexibility allows the book to be used in graduate schools, four year colleges, community and junior colleges, and perhaps, in-service training programs.

In other words, this work comes to you incomplete. It not only suggests that students and instructors add their own input to this study of human behavior; the book *requires* it. We hope that this social systems approach to the study of human behavior will be a step toward an integrated body of social science knowledge that will reflect both the complexity of social forces and the uniqueness of the person.

chapter 1
THE SOCIAL SYSTEMS APPROACH

No man is an island, entire of itself; every man is a piece of the con-
tinent, a part of the main; if a clod be washed away by the sea, Europe
is the less, as well as if a promontory were, as well as if a manor of
thy friends or of thine own were; any man's death diminishes me,
because I am involved in mankind; and therefore never send to know
for whom the bell tolls; it tolls for thee.

John Donne, *Devotions XVII*

This well-known passage expresses the sense of the book's systems theme, a theme
that will be referred to as the *systems approach* or *systems model*. Because our
approach is in fact a loose cluster of several theories and hypotheses emerging
from various disciplines, the term *systems theory* will not be used. Some of this
eclectic body of knowledge has been validated by experiment, some is merely
logical and promising as suggestive hypotheses for investigation. Howard Polsky
classes systems theory as a metatheory, a model applicable to any dynamic, patterned activity (Hearn, 1969, p. 12). Gordon Hearn suggests that a systems
approach is particularly well suited to the profession of social work.

> The general systems approach . . . is based upon the assumption that
> matter, in all its forms, living and nonliving, can be regarded as systems
> and that systems, as systems, have certain discrete properties that are ca-
> pable of being studied. Individuals, small groups—including families and
> organizations—and other complex human organizations such as neighbor-
> hoods and communities—in short, the entities with which social work is
> usually involved—can all be regarded as systems, with certain common
> properties. If nothing else, this should provide social work education with
> a means of organizing the human behavior and social environment aspects
> of the curriculum. But beyond this, if the general systems approach could
> be used to order knowledge about the entities with which we work, per-

6

haps it could also be used as the means of developing a fundamental conception of the social work process itself. (Hearn, 1969, p. 2)

We suggest that such a conception may be useful to other professions as well.

The general systems approach seems to apply to all phenomena, from subatomic particles to the entire universe. We will confine ourselves to one part of the systems approach—social systems—which comprises knowledge about persons, groups of persons, and the human and nonhuman environs that influence social behavior and are influenced by persons. Hearn commented in 1969:

> Subsequent studies at Berkeley and Portland each made their contribution and indicated that the utilization of the general systems approach could be fruitfully employed in social work. They confirmed the belief that the entities with which we work have the properties of systems; that social workers typically work with systems at different levels in their work on a case; that one can devise a universally applicable model of the systems universe, and use it to systematize a substantial body of social work theory developed in other frameworks; and that there is a generic core in the literature of social work theory and practice. (Hearn, 1969, pp. 2–3)

The social systems model explained in the next few pages serves as the basis for the key ideas of this book. The model enables the recognition of similar or identical ideas emerging from different ancestry (isomorphs) and provides a scheme for classifying such ideas.

A. The System Model

> By far the most widely used analytical model in contemporary sociology is that of a social system. System models of various kinds are used in many fields besides sociology, so a social system can be thought of as a special case of a more general system model. A social system is not, however, a particular kind of social organization. It is an analytical model that can be applied to any instance of the process of social organization from families to nations. . . . Nor is the social system model a substantive theory—though it is sometimes spoken of as a theory in sociological literature. This model is a highly general, content-free conceptual framework within which any number of different substantive theories of social organization can be constructed. (Olsen, 1968, p. 228)

The model itself is probably most easily and efficiently introduced by the basic metaphor common to the sciences: the atomic or molecular model. The model is composed of interacting units, each with its own parts, each unit being part of some larger whole. Buckley defined a system as "a complex of elements or components directly or indirectly related in a causal network, such that each component is related to at least some others in a more or less stable way within a particular period of time" (Buckley, 1967, p. 41).

The model is not a description of the real world. It is only a way of looking at, and thinking about, selected aspects of reality. It is a map or transparency that can be superimposed on social phenomena to construct a perspective showing the relatedness of those elements that constitute the phenomena.

A social system is a special order of system. It is distinct from atomic, molecular, or galactic systems in that it is composed of persons or groups of persons who interact and influence the behavior of each other. Within this order can be included families, organizations, communities, societies, and cultures. The social system model must be validly applicable to all forms of human association.

> Very briefly, a social system is a model of a social organization that possesses a distinctive total unit beyond its component parts, that is distinguished from its environment by a clearly defined boundary, and whose subunits are at least partially interrelated within relatively stable patterns of social order. Put even more simply, *a social system is a bounded set of interrelated activities that together constitute a single entity.* (Olsen, 1968, pp. 228–229)

Having said that systems exist at all "levels" from individual persons to cultures and societies, we should specify what we see as the "basic unit" of a social system. Within sociology there has been polar divergence on designation of the unit of primary attention. The macrofunctionalists such as Talcott Parsons tend to view the totalistic system, the society, as the prime focus and to view the behavior of the system and its components as being determined by the total system's needs and goals. At the opposite pole, the social behaviorists and social interactionists such as Max Weber, G. H. Mead, Don Martindale, and Herbert Blumer, begin with the smallest unit of the system, the behavior of the individual person. In this view, the acts of the individual persons tend to cluster into patterns, or role consensus, and the social system is constructed out of these patterns. They conclude, as did Parsons at an earlier point in his theoretical evolution, that the social system is merely an agglomeration of these acts by persons. Churchman sums up this view by stating that "for the behavioral scientist . . . the 'whole system' is made up of the behaviors of the individual persons. Once individual and social behavior have been examined in detail, then one can discover in the operation of behavior the nature of the whole human system" (Churchman, p. 200). Thus of the two polar positions among social systems theorists, one is wholistic, viewing persons as units within the social system, and behaviorally determined by it; and the other is atomistic, viewing systems as the accumulated acts of individual persons.

These polarized positions are encountered in professional education and in professional practice as "social change" vs "social treatment." The social change emphasis is grounded in the macrofunctionalist view that behavior is primarily determined by the larger system. The clinical or social treatment emphasis derives its theoretical sanction from the belief that society is constructed from the behavior of its smallest units.

We take neither polar position. Our point of view is that each social entity, whether large or small, complex or simple, is a *holon.* The term is borrowed from Arthur Koestler who coined it to express the idea that each entity is simultaneously a part and a whole. The unit is made up of parts to which it is the whole, the suprasystem; and, at the same time, is part of some larger whole of which it is a component, or subsystem. Koestler said that, like the god Janus, a holon faces two directions at once—inward toward its own parts, and outward to the system of which it is a part (Koestler, 1967a, pp. 112 ff.; 1971, pp. 192–233). What is central is that any system is by definition both part and whole. We have found the concept of holon particularly useful. It epitomizes a consistent theme in this book. No particular system is determinant, nor is system behavior determined at any one level, part or whole.

The idea of holon as used in this book extends Koestler's proposition of whole–part to include certain corollaries. First, the systems approach requires the designation of a *focal* system. The focal system sets the perspective; it is the system of primary attention. Holon requires the examiner to then attend to the component parts (the subsystems) of that focal system *and* to simultaneously attend to the significant environment (the suprasystems) of which the focal system is a part, or to which it is related.

For example, a family may be identified as a focal system. If viewed as a holon, attention must be given both to its members and to its significant environment, such as schools, community, work organizations, other families, and neighborhood. To only look at the interactions among family members (the family as whole) ignores the functions of the family as part.

The "causal network" referred to in the quotation from Buckley, above, does not imply one-way causation. Causation is multiple and multidirectional. A change in any part of the causal network affects other parts but does not determine the total network. In other words, behavior is not determined by one holon (seen as whole or part) but rather by the interaction and mutual causation of all the systems and subsystems, the holons of differing magnitudes.

Consequently, we take the position that linear cause-effect relationships do not exist, and that it is not helpful to think of human behavior in that way. Alan Watts has expressed a similar position: "Problems that remain persistently insoluble should always be suspected as questions asked in the wrong way, like the problem of cause and effect. Make a spurious division of one process into two, forget that you have done it, and then puzzle for centuries as to how to get the two together" (Watts, 1966, p. 53).

Our stance, then, rather than being either wholistic or atomistic, might be described as contextual, interactional, transactional, pluralistic, or perspectivistic (Bertalanffy, 1967, p. 93). The latter term connotes that causation or the significance of an event is relative to the focus one has at the moment of assessment; that the interpretation one places upon events depends upon where and who one is, and the perspective one has upon the focal system. "What we perceive, or overlook, in the field of our potential experience depends on the framework of concepts we have in our minds" (Ichheiser, p. 2).

If one is a social behaviorist, one sees what happens to individual persons as most important. If one is a macrofunctionalist, the essential consideration is what happens to the total system (suprasystem, usually the society). Our viewpoint, a functionalist one, is that one's perspective at a particular time is what determines one's view of the nature and the importance of an event. The focal holon must be viewed in both its positions—as part, with attention to the superordinate systems, and as whole, with attention to its subordinate components. As events are viewed from other times and other perspectives, meanings are likely to change. Robert Merton stated that "the theoretic framework of functional analysis must expressly require that there be SPECIFICATION of the UNITS for which a given social or cultural item is functional. It must expressly allow for a given item having diverse consequences, functional and dysfunctional, for individuals, for subgroups, and for the more inclusive social structure and culture" (Loomis and Loomis, p. 265).

Thus the view we take here requires the specification of the focal system, the specification of the units or components that constitute that holon, and specification of the significant environmental systems. The components and environment will have meaning in their effects on the focal system. Further, to achieve an objective description of the focal system, one must state one's own position or relation to the focal system. Such a view is philosophically consistent, we think, with the basic metaphor described by Einstein, that events are relative to the position of the observer.

B. Energy

Consistent with the atomic metaphor, we suggest the basic "stuff" of a system is energy. Just as atoms and molecules are composed of energy, so also are social systems.

> The smallest molecular particle gets its dynamic movement from the fact that it consists of a negative and positive charge, with tension—and there-fore movement—between them. Using this analogy of the molecular particles of matter and energy, Alfred North Whitehead and Paul Tillich both believe that reality has the ontological character of negative-positive polarity. Whitehead and the many contemporary thinkers for whom his work has become important see reality not as consisting of substances in fixed states but as a process of dynamic movement between polarities. (May, 1969, p. 112)

What occurs in social systems are "transfers of energy" between persons or groups of persons. The energy in this dynamic process is not directly observable. Its presence is inferred from the effects upon the system and its parts. There is some disagreement among systems theorists as to whether energy is a valid concept for social systems.

Our use of energy then is analog and construct. In this sense, energy may be defined as "capacity for action," "action," or "power to effect change." As previously stated, the presence of energy is inferred from its effect on the system and its parts.

The question becomes, "Is energy an inclusive enough concept to denote the life of a social system?" We suggest it is, providing the meaning goes beyond the precise idea of active force. To again borrow from physics, the broader meaning includes both information and resources as "potential energy." The nature of both information and resources includes the capacities to activate or mobilize the system and to serve as energy sources. "The interplay of men on the job, of husband and wife, of nations at war are all social systems that involve the sending and receiving of energy/information. System action will be examined as this movement of energy/information (1) WITHIN a system and (2) BETWEEN a system and its environment" (Monane, 1967, pp. 1–2). To disqualify information as energy is to deny its reality; information is nothing if it has no potential for action. Hence we proceed on the assumption that social systems do have energy, and that energy transformation is the prime function of all social systems.

Bertalanffy's discussion may provide some clue to the answer to this dilemma (Koestler and Smythies, 1969, pp. 71–74). He says that living systems must be thermodynamically open, that is exchange energy across their boundaries; and be information carriers. We interpret this to mean that energy and information are not identical, but that they are complementary and inseparable in living systems. Both are necessary while neither is sufficient. Energy must be structured in order to be useful; information, just as its root meaning implies, gives form to the energy. Bertalanffy, however, notes that the answer is not yet conclusive. One of the first social scientists to apply system ideas to his discipline was James G. Miller, a psychologist, who wrote in 1955 that "systems are bounded regions in space-time, involving *energy interchange* among their parts" (Miller, 1955, p. 514). Sigmund Freud said of the concept of energy in 1940:

> We assume, as the other natural sciences have taught us to expect, that in mental life some kind of *energy* is at work; but we have no data which enable us to come nearer to a knowledge of it by *an analogy with other forms of energy*. We seem to recognize that nervous or physical energy exists in two forms, one freely mobile and the other, by contrast, bound; we speak of cathexes and hypercathexes of the material of the mind and even venture to suppose that a hypercathexis brings about a sort of synthesis of different processes—a synthesis in the course of which free energy is transformed into bound energy. Further than this we have been unable to go. (Freud, 1949, pp. 44–45)

The exact nature of human energy is undetermined and depends in part upon the particular system being examined. Within a person we refer to psychic energy; we could analogously refer to the social energy of a family, group, organization, or community. What is meant is the system's capacity to act, its power to maintain itself and effect change. The energy derives from a complex of sources including the physical capacities of its members; social resources such as loyalties, shared sentiments, and common values; and resources from its environment. Environmental resources may provide information, ideas, and manpower.

For example, a military organization's energy would include the men available for service, the military hardware (weaponry, transportation facilities, communications equipment) it possesses, money appropriated for its use, and public sentiment favoring support of the military (such as "support our boys" campaigns). Other energy sources might be ideological support for military activity ("we must make the world safe for democracy"), and legal or diplomatic sanction to conduct war (as provided by a declaration of war, a request by a foreign government for assistance, or a United Nations declaration, as in Korea). All of these constitute energy sources available to the military system to perform its defined tasks.

Energy for a personality system, to give a further example, could include food; the physical state of the body; intellectual and emotional capabilities; emotional support from friends, family, or colleagues; cultural sanction for one's beliefs and activities; recognition of one's status by society and one's superiors in an organization; and perhaps most important, one's own sense of worth and integrity.

At this point two essential concepts that bear on the topic of energy in the social system should be introduced. *Entropy* has to do with the tendency of an unattended system to move toward a disordered state characterized by decrease in usable energy. *Synergy* refers to a process of multiplication of energy.

> Physical processes follow the second law of thermodynamics, which prescribes that they proceed toward increasing entropy, that is, more probable states which are states of equilibrium, of uniform distribution and disappearance of existing differentiations and order. But living systems apparently do exactly the opposite. In spite of irreversible processes continually going on, they tend to maintain an organized state of fantastic improbability; they are maintained in states of *non*-equilibrium; they even develop toward increasingly *im*probable states, increasing differentiation and order, as is manifest both in the individual development of an organism and in evolution from the famous amoeba to man. (Bertalanffy, 1967, p. 62)

In other words, in social systems, the tendency is toward concentrations of energy and increasing availability of energy within the system—that is, *if* the system is viable and evolving toward greater complexity and organization.

Synergy is appropriate to open, living systems (and thus to social systems). One advertisement proclaims, "We're synergistic." "We do a lot of things at Sperry Rand. And we do each one better because we do all the rest." The concept is the opposite of entropy: An open system not only doesn't deplete its energy, it actually *compounds* energy from the interaction of its parts. Abraham Maslow credited Ruth Benedict with the first application of the idea of synergy to social interaction. She used it to denote the amplification of goal-directed activity under circumstances where there was a fit between the individual goals of persons sharing a culture and the goals of the culture (Maslow, 1964, pp. 153–164). The concepts of entropy and synergy should probably not be employed literally in regard to social systems, but rather used as analogies in describing the characteristic of certain systems.

For example, it may be apparent that a certain organization is becoming increasingly static and predictable (as we usually mean by "bureaucratic"); it could be described as characterized by entropy. Another agency may be increasingly unpredictable and fluid, with internal shifts of concentration of energy and power, resulting in "dynamic growth"; this could be described as characterized by synergy. The same analogy could be applied to a person, as well. Rigidity and maintenance of defenses could be evidence of entropy, while absorption of new stimuli and constant adaptation to the environment, with resultant stimulation of new attachments and ideas, could be evidence of synergy.

Systems require energy in order to exist and carry out system purposes. This can be simplistically diagramed as occurring through four basic system functions (Figure 1).

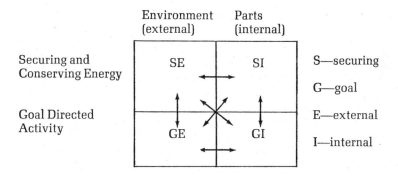

Figure 1.   Four Basic System Functions.

Functions SE and SI. The first pair of functions (cells SE and SI) pertain to the securing of energy. SE represents the function of securing energy from outside the system, that is importing energy from the environment. This function roughly corresponds to Parsons's idea of "adaptation" (Parsons, Bales, and Shils, 1953, p. 182). As diagramed here these four functions are interdependent. Consequently, the securing of energy from external sources involves GE as well. The importation of energy occurs through a transactional process between the human system and the environment. SI denotes energy from *inside* the system and requires access to energy sources from one or more component parts of the focal system. In this case GI is also operative.

A variety of possible outcomes are involved with SE and SI. If internal system energies are in short supply and energy from the subsystems is critically needed, energy-consuming frictions and conflicts among subsystems must be prevented or reduced. If the focal system has a surplus of energy available from its components, then the system can tolerate diversion of energy into subsystem conflicts. Such intercomponent conflicts may be, to focal system goals, the lesser of two evils. Diversion of energy to suppress one subsystem may be preferable to allowing the subsystem to go unchecked. An example of this is the operation of defense mechanisms of the personality. Suppression of impulses or wishes is preferable to allowing them free expression, which in turn would endanger the "survival" of the personality, that is, the focal system. Another example might be racial supremacy in a nation. Although the amount of available energy required to maintain conditions of segregation and second class citizenship for a racial minority (United States) or a racial majority (South Africa) is great and thus dysfunctional for the attainment of some goals, continuation of the system as it is may take priority because of the anticipated consequences of changing it.

Parsons refers to this function of securing energy internally as "integration" (Parsons et al., 1953, p. 182), meaning reduction of internal conflict to maximize available energies to direct toward the goals of the focal system. This phenomenon can be seen in those circumstances where a system is in danger of being destroyed or radically changed. The pulling together, tightening the ranks, and forgetting past differences found in the family, the city, and the nation when circumstances or systems threaten continued existence exemplifies this. Reduction of conflict within a personality, so as to achieve better ego orientation to reality (and thus heighten the likelihood of achieving goals), is another example.

Functions GE and GI. The second pair of basic functions (cells GE and GI of Figure 1) pertain to the use of energy, the uses to which energy is put. One of the characteristics of living systems is the purposefulness of activities. They operate in a *goal-directed* manner. This pair of functions may be called goal achievement, or in Parsons's term, "goal attainment" (Parsons et al., 1953, p. 182). As in the first pair of functions, these too are performed both internally and externally. GE refers to *outside* the system and is interrelated to SE, SI, and GI. The holon attempts to carry on transactions with the environment to achieve its own goals as whole and as part. It seeks to achieve as much reliability and control over the system-environment linkages as possible. The American Medical Association, for example, collects money and efforts from its constituent parts (the membership) to engage in lobbying activities to influence and control its environment to achieve system goals. The child mobilizes his internal resources to please his parents and achieve his goal of gaining love, status, and a position of some influence within his family system, that is, his environment.

GI refers to goal directed activity *inside* the system. Here energy is employed to subordinate the subsystems to the goals of the focal system, by whatever means possible, and consistent with the nature of the system and the surrounding environment. This is similar to Parsons's labeled function of "pattern maintenance" (Parsons et al., p. 182).

The declaration of a state of martial law in a nation is an example of goal-directed activity within the system. With system survival at stake, energies are directed inward to reduce or eliminate disequilibrium, which is perceived as threatening the continued existence of system patterns. Recent military take-overs of Greece, Chile, and Argentina are examples. A professional system requires its members to align their goals and patterns of behavior with the goals and patterns of the system. If a member fails to do so he is subject to expulsion or disciplinary measures. Social workers are regulated by a code of ethics and subject to sanctions by the National Association of Social Workers; psychologists are regulated by the American Psychological Association. A family system that holds a goal of educational achievement will direct energies of control at a member whose goals conflict.

Emphasis should be placed on the fact that these four functions are not discrete; that is, a system may perform two or more of these functions at the same time. In any exchanges between whole and parts, all partners receive some energy and have some goals met. The reciprocal nature of the transactions and exchanges should be kept in mind. If one function is predominant, the other functions are neglected to the detriment of the total system. For example, the family system that concentrates energy only on the SE function through securing and importing energy from the external environment may experience internal disintegration. This may take the form of both parents devoting excessive time and energy to jobs at the expense of internal functions. An excellent example of the condition of a person-system concentrating all energies on internal functions is Paul Simon's lyric, "I Am A Rock":

> I've built walls;
> A fortress deep and mighty
> That none may penetrate.
> I have no need for friendship—friendship causes pain.
> Its laughter and its loving I disdain.
> I am a rock . . . I am an island.
>
> Don't talk of love.
> I've heard the word before.
> It's sleeping in my memory.
> I won't disturb the slumber of feelings that have died;
> If I'd never loved I never would have cried.
> I am a rock . . . I am an island.
>
> I have my books
> And my poetry to protect me.
> I am shielded in my armor.
> Hiding in my room, safe within my womb
> I touch no one and no one touches me.
> I am a rock.
> I am an island.
> And a rock feels no pain.
> And an island never cries. . . .

C. Organization

Just as energy is the basic "stuff" and the necessary element of a system, organization is the sufficient element. A total absence of organization would mean a total absence of system. Randomly distributed energy cannot be mobilized to further the purposes of the system. A more or less closed system, a rock for instance, can only be immobile because its energy is unorganized. In order to move the rock, energy must be exerted from outside the system. A social system, to be so classified, must have a degree of organization. *Organization refers to grouping and arranging of parts to form a whole, to a putting into working order.* System organization secures, expends, and conserves energy to maintain itself and further its purposes.

Monane, in discussing the cybernetic concept of organization, asserts that it pertains to intrarelatedness, the degree of impact of a component's actions upon the action of the other components within the system. He distinguishes between high and low organization. In a *highly organized* system—the family for instance—the components are strongly interdependent; what one does is crucial for others. In systems of relatively *low organization*—for example a metropolis—components are independent and autonomous (Monane, 1967, p. 21).

The founding of a social system, the delineation of a new entity from its environment, can generally be expressed in the familiar phrases, "Let's get organized," "Let's get it together." This must be the first action of the components of a burgeoning system, to order randomly distributed energies. The Constitution of the United States organizes the component systems into a suprasystem. The Preamble sets forth the general purpose for forming a new system and then specifies system goals:

> We the People of the United States, in Order to form a more perfect Union, establish Justice, insure domestic Tranquillity, provide for the common defence, promote the general Welfare, and secure the Blessings of Liberty to ourselves and our Posterity, do ordain and establish this Constitution for the United States of America.

The various articles and amendments of the Constitution specify the conditions of intrarelatedness of the components (states and individuals) to the system. The goals of the national system as specified in the Preamble are, and must be, congruent with the goals of its components. It was precisely this organization and interrelatedness that were at issue in the Civil War (or War Between the States), and which is at the heart of President Nixon's "New Federalism." Revenue sharing, which is intended to decentralize federal control, is an attempt to restore the constitutional balance (relationships and linkages) between federal and state governments. The Watergate issue addresses itself to the balance among the three branches of the Federal government.

Organization is a concept that does not implicitly carry the message of ever increasing complexity, although complex systems with a high order of differentiation usually require complex organization. "A complex society is not necessarily more advanced than a simple one; it has just adapted to conditions in a more complex way" (Farb, 1968, p. 13).

The measure of the effectiveness of organization is its capacity to enable the fulfillment of the system's goals as well as the goals of the component elements of the system. (See discussions of effectiveness and efficiency in Chapter 3.) Effective organization enables the energies of the system to be generated and purposefully used, as well as to secure energy from the environment.

Disorganization of a system—person, family, neighborhood—does not mean totally *un*organized. It does mean *not sufficiently* organized. The system's energies are not in working order. The components of the system do not stand in sufficient relatedness to one another; energies are randomly distributed and expended. The system is tending toward a state of entropy. A vernacular term for this, in a person, is "spaced out."

In the Freudian personality system the triad of organizers id, ego, and superego need to work in harmony, with the ego dominant. If the id were dominant, energies would be directed toward goals not in keeping with the goals of the total system. If the superego were dominant, energies could not be sufficiently mobilized to fulfill total system goals.

Erikson's formulation of identity can be viewed as the expression of an organizing principle that enables the components of the personality to "get together" to fulfill the goals of the person. The "identity crisis" is defined on the bipolar dimension of "identity vs diffusion." In systems terms this could be expressed as organization vs disorganization. In the first instance the personality components are drawn together to form a working whole; identity diffusion refers to disharmony among personality components, randomization. The person diagnosed schizophrenic is seen as a disorganized system—he is not together.

The family with problems is generally a disorganized family. The members (internal energy sources—SI, GI) are operating in a system-defeating manner. Among the possible reasons for family disorganization are the following:

1. the goals of one or more members are oppositional to the system goals;
2. the elements of organization (communication, feedback, role expectations) are disrupted or unclear;
3. available energies from within the system are not sufficient for the demands on the system;
4. the family is not adequately organized to obtain additional energy from outside its own system; or
5. pressures from the environment, the suprasystem, exercise a disorganizing influence on the family system.

RECAPITULATION

The dimension of organization—the fact of organization—is characteristic of all social phenomena that can be designated as social systems. If there is no organization present, there is no system. If organization is insufficient or dysfunctional for the goals of the system, the term *disorganization* is used. Organization refers to the ordering of the energies of the component parts in some fashion that results in a whole.

Energy and the *organization of energy* are then the prime characteristics of social systems. We now describe, in more detail, aspects of social systems that follow from these prime characteristics. All systems are composed of energy interchange. Monane points out that structural and functional aspects of social systems are merely descriptions of this basic interchange (Monane, 1967, Chapter 2). Those processes of energy interchange that are slower and of longer duration and thus appear to the observer to be relatively static can be called *structural;* those processes that are of relatively fast tempo and short duration can be called *behavioral.* This is a distinction employed by John Dewey, whose discussion is worth reading (Dewey, 1966). We call these processes "behavioral" rather than functional to avoid confusion with the energy functions described earlier.

Characteristics of social systems are discussed under both the structural and behavioral headings. In addition, and to begin the discussion, we discuss system change itself.

D. Evolution of Social Systems

As with other dimensions of social systems, change and maintenance are not diametrically opposed in reality. Systems never exist in a condition of complete change or complete maintenance of the status quo. Systems are always both changing and maintaining themselves at any given time. The balance between change and maintenance may shift drastically toward one pole or the other, but if either extreme were reached, the system would cease to exist. As Whitehead once wrote, "the art of progress is to preserve order amid change and to preserve change amid order." This is similar to Erikson's "bipolarities" of personality growth and Piaget's "assimilation" and "accommodation" described in Chapter 6.

Steady state

Steady state, a systems term borrowed from physics, is the most adequate term now available to describe what Laszlo refers to as "the particular configuration of parts and relationships which is maintained in a self-maintaining and repairing system. . . . It is a state in which energies are continually used to maintain the relationship of the parts and keep them from collapsing in decay" (Laszlo, 1972, p. 37).

The terms *equilibrium* and *homeostasis* have similar meanings, but with important differences. Steady state is a state in which the whole system is in balance. The system is maintaining a viable relationship with its environment and its components, and its functions are being performed in such fashion as to ensure its continued existence. The word "steady" is somewhat confusing because it implies some kind of fixed, static balance. The balance is, however, dynamic and always changing to some degree (as just noted concerning change–maintenance). Steady state is characterized by a high degree of organization, complexity, and openness to the environment, by comparison to nonorganic systems. Equilibrium and homeostasis denote a fixed balance in which some particular adjustment is maintained, and the structure of the system is not altered significantly. Steady state does not include a fixed balance; the system can find a new balance and a new structure radically different from the previous state.

The three terms may be illustrated in three different ways. *Equilibrium* is like a teeterboard. Balance can be achieved, but the limits of being in balance are narrow. Except by acrobats on a high wire, perhaps—and the Wallenda family's tragedy illustrates that it is hazardous to attempt to move a fixed balance—no movement of a balanced teeterboard is possible. To maintain balance, it is necessary to protect it from the environment, such as wind or swaying of the tightwire.

Homeostasis denotes a more variable balance of a system; that is, the system's balance may change within some limits. Homeostasis can be illustrated by a motorcycle. Balance is maintained by movement, and by encounter with the environment. The rider has some latitude, and remains upright by leaning against centrifugal force (leaning into a curve) or altering the machine's center of gravity on a banked curve by tilting the machine. Within some limits, which are determined by weight of the machine, wind velocity, speed, and road angles, the bike maintains balance. As bike enthusiasts know, the balance is variable, but there are limits beyond which a hill climber's leather suit, boots, and helmet are advisable. *Steady state* is movement and balance like that of "Around the World in 80 Days." The balance changes, and even its structure changes. Phileas Fogg depended on transportation throughout his trip, but the mode of transportation changed from balloon to train, to ship, to raft, to foot. In each successive form, a moving balance was maintained, but to maintain movement the form had to vary with the environment.

The point of each illustration is that a system can "change its stripes." It can undergo extreme changes in order to survive. Another illustration is life itself in all the forms it has assumed to maintain ecological balance. While the forms change, it is still life.

Buckley calls these two tendencies *morphostasis* (or structure-maintaining) and *morphogenesis* (structure-changing) (1967, passim). Again, no system reaches either extreme, although it may tend toward one pole or the other. All systems must maintain a shifting balance between status quo (morphostasis) and change (morphogenesis). As this affects the relationship between civil rights and civil liberties, Ardrey has said:

> If the social contract represents a delicate balance between a degree of order that the individual must have to survive and a degree of disorder which society must have to ensure fulfillment of its diverse members, then a significant ascendancy of violence from any quarter tends radically to revise the contract. No triumph of disorder can be other than temporary. When order has been destroyed by one force, so will it be restored by another. (Ardrey, 1970, p. 254)

Steady state applies to all social systems. One example of it is Erikson's concept of "identity," which is a steady state of the personality system. Menninger's view is consistent with this. Menninger devotes an entire chapter to systems concepts to illustrate their compatibility with psychiatry, and the succeeding chapter to a discussion of the ego's function as maintainer of steady state (1963, Chapters 5, 6). What is meant really is state*s*, a complex of components that can adapt by changing its structure and hence is not the *same* from one time to another, but is *somewhat* the same. The steady state is modified consistent with the system's goals and its purposive, self-directive efforts to maintain its integrity.

Another important distinction in the terms *steady state, equilibrium,* and *homeostasis* is that equilibrium demands a minimum of stress and disturbance, and seeks minimal interchange with the environment; the quoted verses from "I Am A Rock" are the expression of a person seeking a state of equilibrium. Homeostasis also requires minimal stress and disturbance, but does require interchange with the environment. Steady state does not require minimal stress: Social systems may, in fact, prosper from stress and disturbance. Interchange is essential to the existence of steady state. Equilibrium and homeostasis imply closed and static systems; steady state denotes open and changing systems.

Table 1.   Comparison of Equilibrium, Homeostasis,
and Steady State

	Equilibrium	*Homeostasis*	*Steady State*
Stress	Minimal	Minimal	Optimal and necessary
Structure	No change	No change	Wide possibility of change
Interchange with Environment	Least possible	Limited	Necessary
Openness	Closed	Open within limits	Open

What we mean by steady state is the continuing "identity" of the system; its continuity with the previous states through which it has passed, and through which it will pass in the future.

E. Structural Characteristics

This discussion of structural characteristics is related to the preceding sections, "A. The System Model," especially the discussion of holon, and "C. Organization."

1. Boundary, Linkage, and "Open" and "Closed" Systems. In order to be identified as distinct from its environment, a system must have some limits, a locatable boundary. Consistent with our view that energy or activity is basic to social systems, we define a *boundary* as being located where the intensity of energy interchange is greater on one side of a certain point than it is on the other, or greater among certain units than among others. The intensity of energy transfer between units within the boundary is greater than the intensity of exchange across the boundary. For example, members of a family are distinguished not only by blood relationships, but also by frequency and intensity of personal contact. A neighbor would usually be considered outside the boundary, but might become "a member of the family" by participating in family activities and sharing the emotional ties of the family. An adopted child is another example of a person not related by blood who crosses the boundary and is incorporated within.

Boundaries can be defined only by observation of the interaction of the parts of the system, and the environment. Some boundaries are visible because of their impenetrability, for example the rigid personality that permits little interchange with the environment. Some religious orders have boundaries defined clearly by behaviors such as dress, marital status, and allegiance to group beliefs. The Amish are set apart by dress, modes of transportation, and style of beard. The fact that boundaries may change is evidenced in the Roman Catholic Church by the presence of a few married priests (in Europe), by changes in dress (the abandonment of traditional nuns' habits), and by some changes in group beliefs (attitudes toward birth control and ecumenical relationships to other denominations).

It is important to distinguish between the location of a boundary and its nature. Boundary does not necessarily mean barrier. A social system may have a readily discernible boundary and yet be very open to transfers of energy across its boundary. An example is the boundary of male–female.

Other boundaries are difficult to identify because interchange is frequent and intense across the boundary. For example, "who is a Jew?" is a question both unsettled and important to the nation of Israel. Which delegation from Alabama represented the real Democrats at the 1968 Chicago convention, those selected by the state's party machinery or the delegation that was more representative of the state's racial composition? More recently, the boundaries of being "American" were questioned. For some persons, support of, or opposition to, the Vietnam war constituted a boundary. Usually no single interaction defines a boundary. Obviously, more than one criterion is involved in being "American"; such behaviors as paying taxes, voting, and acknowledging "American" values and responsibilities are some other criteria to be considered. The issue of amnesty for draft evaders raises the question of such boundaries in a tangible and dramatic form.

When two systems exchange energy across their boundaries they are linked, or have *linkage* with each other. Their linkage may be for a very limited and peripheral purpose or may constitute a vital linkage, as a family's association with the economic system, for example. The parents' memberships in social clubs and civic groups may be important links to community activity and resources. Their religious affiliation may be a vital social, emotional, and ideological link as well.

Energy transfers by way of linkages are rarely, if ever, one way. Reciprocity of energy, or true exchange, is present in virtually all linkage. The church, club, or industry draws energy from its linkage to the family; hence industry's willingness to contribute to families' welfare through Social Security, United Fund drives, mental health campaigns or (increasingly) ecological improvements. (See discussion of organizations' relationships to other systems in Chapter 3.) Similarly, the church maintains its role as prime defender of family and marital stability; the linkages are vital and central.

Open and *closed* are largely self-explanatory terms. A system is receptive or nonreceptive to the movement of energy across its boundaries, or its significant environmental systems are receptive or nonreceptive. In actuality, of course, no system is completely open, since it would then be indistinguishable from its environment. Nor is a system ever completely closed—it would cease to exist. We use *open* and *closed* with these reservations in mind; what is really meant is "relatively more open" or "relatively more closed" than some other system or than some standard by which we are judging the system. A person is an open system, but from a teacher's or counselor's point of view may be less open (or more so) than is desirable for his own growth. For example, a child may be less open to interaction with his peers than he "should" be, and more open to interaction solely with his parents than is expected at his age. Community organizers might wish for a social agency to be more open to ghetto residents and less open to interchange solely with white, middle-class clientele. This latter example illustrates that it is often not sufficient to generalize that a system is open or closed. It is frequently crucial to specify "open to what?" and "closed to what?"

2. Hierarchy, Autonomy. Parts of systems are related to each other in various ways. One of these kinds of relationships is "vertical" or hierarchical, meaning that parts are ranked in the order in which energy is distributed. For example, parents in a family have greater access to the family's income than do the children. Because they receive larger shares of public good will and public resources, state universities have an advantage over welfare and penal institutions in receiving public funds. This has been modified somewhat in recent years by public reaction to campus protests; universities are perhaps lower in the social hierarchy, while community colleges have risen in access to public funds (energy).

Another hierarchy is that of power and control. Some parts control others by regulating access to resources or by regulating communication. For example, the executive officer of an organization has rank not only by title, but by virtue of controlling the allocation of responsibilities and resources. Another example was the power held by a few members of Nixon's staff due to their control of appointment schedules and communications received. Specifically, President Nixon's shake-up of the Federal bureaucracy was intended to enhance the President's control of resources and their allocation, that is, to make the hierarchy more responsive to presidential initiatives. The "gatekeeper" function is of central importance to a system. It controls the flow of information and the crossing of the system boundary, from both inside and outside.

A third form of hierarchy is that of authority. Some parts serve as sources of sanction and approval through acting as "defenders of the faith" (a phrase applied to the monarchs of England, whose status far exceed their actual power). Religious institutions serve this function, as do schools. Within a family, part of the mother's role seems to be that of imparting and representing certain values of the society; hence we observe Mother's Day with a certain prescribed reverence and respect.

A fourth form of hierarchy is by sequence, or the order in which events must occur. Some events or functions must occur before others can be seen to. One example of this is Maslow's hierarchy of needs within the person:

> needs or values are related to each other in a hierarchical and develop-
> mental way, in order of strength and of priority. Safety is a more pre-
> potent, or stronger, more pressing, more vital need than love, for instance,
> and the need for food is usually stronger than either. . . . [a person] does
> not know in advance that he will strive on after this gratification has come,
> and that gratification of one basic need opens consciousness to domination
> by another, "higher" need. (Maslow, 1968, p. 153)

Similar forms of hierarchy are found in Erikson's developmental tasks and Piaget's cognitive stages, which are discussed in Chapter 6.

There are, then, several varieties of hierarchies. Most frequently we will discuss hierarchy in one of the forms just described. We will discuss instances in which the hierarchy is one of control and power, and in which the parts are dependent upon other parts for some vital resources. The relationships in these instances will be that of subordination–superordination or submission–dominance. That is, the hierarchies most often examined will be those in which control is exerted in a "chain of command," for example, bureaucracies, communities with elected leadership, or personality in which ego functioning provides control and direction.

Not all parts, however, exist in such chains of command. Some parts are relatively autonomous from a centralized control agent. Children are relatively autonomous after reaching legal status as an adult, yet are part of their parents' family. In classic cases of "split personality" or dissociative reaction, some significant portions of the personality function autonomously without control by the ego. The military organizations of some Latin American and South American countries function largely independently of the elected political hierarchy, and are autonomous. Such autonomy in a social system may mean great power, as in the case of a military organization that is increasingly less responsible to the rest of the society, or it may mean irrelevance and powerlessness. This is seen, according to some observers, in the case of a caste or racial minority such as Black Americans or Indian Americans.

It should be noted that, as Miller says, "It is the nature of organizations that each subsystem and component has some autonomy and some subordination or constraint, from lower level systems, other systems at the same level, and higher level systems" (Miller, 1965, p. 22). In one way, this repeats what was said earlier about holons and the fact that causation is mutual; each system is both a super-ordinate whole and subordinate part.

3. Differentiation, Specialization. These terms are similar, and yet not the same. *Differentiation* means "dividing the functions" (Loomis and Loomis), that is, assigning functions to its parts. *Specialization* adds the further stipulation that a part performs *only* that function, and that no other part performs the *same* function.

Differentiation is not the same as allocation or distribution of energy, although they are certainly related. For example, assigning the GI function in the federal government to the Department of Health, Education, and Welfare is not the same as providing the necessary appropriations. Nor, for example, is the mother's relinquishment of discipline of the children to the father necessarily the same as her complete support of him doing it. She may undercut him so as to put him in a double bind whether he punishes the children or not.

Differentiation may apply to any of a large number of different aspects of system functioning. There may be differentiation by age in regard to earning income for the family. Typically, adults are expected to earn, teen-agers are expected to provide their own spending money, and the elderly and children are not expected to provide their own financial resources. In the middle class, there is differentiation by sex in regard to chores (girls are usually expected to iron clothes, not to carry papers; the mother also does ironing).

As a society becomes more complex, it becomes necessary to differentiate functions. One example is that of modern professions:

> a given profession does not come into being or continue to exist except in relation to a given level of societal development. This is clearly evident when one examines the developing societies in which social work is barely coming into its own. The reason is that these societies need to devote more attention, energy, and funds to problems of physical survival than to problems of social relationships. As these societies continue to develop and increase in affluence and aspiration, social relationships gradually begin to become important enough to warrant special attention. . . . In the event that the social structure changed and a given society at a given point in time, usually because of technological and accompanying ideo-logical changes, no longer considered social welfare or social relationships important for survival, it is conceivable that at the point social work as a profession would begin to disappear and its essential functions would either be taken over by other professions or else would not be performed at all. (Boehm, 1965, p. 641)

This could be applied to other professions as well, such as home economics, nursing, education, and various counseling fields.

Along with indicating a sequential hierarchy, this points out several facts about differentiation:

1. That as a social system becomes differentiated, at some point the need arises to reintegrate and to establish communication between the differentiated parts. The more differentiation occurs, probably the more internal exchange of energy/information is necessary. This is one of the seemingly unsolvable problems in governmental provision of human services. There has been a high degree of differentiation of function without accompanying specialization. This has resulted in much energy being devoted to communication, but in spite of that, services remain uncoordinated and random, as experienced by the consumer-citizen.

2. That differentiation may be reversible; a system may reorder its structures to perform functions more satisfactorily.

3. There are levels of differentiation according to the stages of development of the social system; the more complex, the more fully the functions are differentiated among the parts.

This leads to discussion of *specialization*. As noted earlier, specialization means exclusivity of function—as a popular song puts it, "I can handle this job all by myself." Professions stake out their boundaries (who shall administer medication, who shall give legal advice, who shall approve adoptions, who is an expert witness in court). In that sense, professions are specialities. But they are not completely specialized, in that all of them are performing integrative SI and GI functions in the society.

An example of societal specialization from ancient history is found in a manual for farmers written in the second century B.C.: "tunics, togas, blankets, smocks, and shoes should be bought at Rome . . . tiles at Venafrum, oil mills at Pompeii and at Rufrius's yard at Nola" (Lenski, p. 255). This may have been the first paid commercial in history. Occupational specialization is most pronounced in modern industrial society, but in Paris in 1313 there were already 157 different trades listed on the tax rolls (Lenski, p. 256).

As with differentiation, specialization is necessary to perform functions, but certain dangers also arise: "The more highly specialized a group's activities the more its need for the products of other groups and more important systemic linkage becomes. The ultimate of the kind of systemic linkage occasioned by cooperative specialization is reached in centralization" (Loomis and Loomis, p. 228). Loomis gives specific examples:

> There is a certain amount of risk involved in a unit's devoting itself solely to a specialized commodity or other output. The family producing and partially socializing children risks the chance that the school will not perform its function. The schools risk the chance that collective families will not provide essential facilities. The husband-father may prefer poverty on a subsistence farm to the risks of uncertain or disadvantageous systemic linkage with an outside wage-paying production unit. That the production of imperative outputs and their orderly interchange will not be a random

affair, the social systems at any one hierarchical level are systematically linked to social systems of a higher level. (Loomis and Loomis, p. 417)

Thus we have come full circle to hierarchy as an aspect of structure.

F. Behavioral Aspects of Social Systems

Behavioral aspects are those energy interchanges that are of shorter duration and faster tempo. Three of these seem to us most significant. They are related to the basic energy functions, but not identical. They are the subfunctions that seem to be most important for this book.

1. Social Control, Socialization. This activity occurs in all systems, and can have the purpose either of securing energy for the system from its components, or of achieving goals; in other words, either the SI, GE, or GI functions. This securing of energy or the expanding of it to achieve goals can be done in either coercive fashion or "persuasively." The system can secure energy or achieve goals coercively by threatening the component's survival and functioning, or its goal achievement; or "persuasively" by supporting the component's goal and encouraging its harmony with the system's goal. An example of this would be the "gentle persuasion" that a church can apply to its members to summon their efforts in supporting the church's goals, such as a building fund, yearly budget, or attendance at a revival. Or the church may employ coercive means—excommunication, or expulsion from membership—if the member interferes with the church's goals by refusing to recruit new members, or refusing to rear children in the faith.

The coercive form of control we usually refer to as "power." (You are referred to the discussion of power in Chapter 3.) Traditionally, the helping professions have espoused the persuasive approach, holding up the value of "self-determination," but in practice decisions sometimes have to be made for clients. When these decisions are forced upon the client by the threat to prevent him from fulfilling his own goals, or restrict the client's access to needed resources, the professional person is using power.

One form of social control is *socialization.* This is the induction of persons into the social system's way of life, whether the system is a family, community, or society. A bargain is struck; the system "promises" support of, or noninterference with, the person's goals so long as they are consistent with the system's goals. Deviance may be permitted so long as it does not seriously interfere with the system's goals. The purpose of socialization is to get the work of the system done; the more successful the socialization, the less control is necessary because the person's goals will be harmonious with, or identical to, the system's goals. A certain degree of aggressiveness is tolerated and sometimes valued in our society, and is expressed in approved ways. If we interfere with the society's functioning by threatening people's lives, or disrupting transportation, or preventing policemen from performing their tasks, we are liable to being controlled in some manner consistent with our "offense."

2. Communication. Communication is discussed in Chapter 2 in regard to symbols and language, and in Chapter 3 in regard to the function of communication in organizations and communities. Here we only wish to point out the necessity of communication. As Monane says, transfer of energy/information is essential in a system (Monane, 1967, pp. 42–44). Organization of a system depends upon the effectiveness of communication. Monane also says that we usually think that communication will spread emotional warmth and bring the components of the system closer together (Monane, 1967, p. 59). It may, certainly, but it is just as likely to alienate and separate people by the content of what is communicated. The point is that communication is the transfer of energy to accomplish system goals. The effect of communication depends upon the context in which communication occurs. For example, the communication "You're under arrest!" hardly seems likely to encourage affection; it expresses control. The professional who says he "communicated" with his client usually means that positive affect was conveyed. But the professional and his client also "communicate" when the energy exchange exerts control; as in "Stop it, Jimmy, I won't let you run away from the institution!"

Systems develop means to send and receive information. *Feedback* is the primary means by which systems accomplish self-direction and seek goals. Feedback is not, as the popular definition indicates, merely the echo received in response to one's actions, similar to a radar blip. In cybernetics and systems theory, feedback includes both the echo *and the adjustment made to the echo.* For example, a person or social group receives responses from the social environment and adjusts to these incoming signals. The whole process is feedback.

> Feedback mechanisms and operations familiar to social workers dealing with satisfaction-seeking human systems are: Homeostatic controls and corrective feedback; deviation-amplifying, deviation-counteracting, and deviation-reduction elements and processes, reaction-formation and over-compensation; autistic reinforcement; feelings of rejection, the "looking-glass self;" and the cycle of poverty. (Hearn, 1969, pp. 56–57)

One example of deviation-amplifying feedback is the following: A boy from a poor family wears clothing that makes a negative impression; his teachers conclude that he probably is not very intelligent. They treat him as though he is not; he responds to this, confirming their view, in order to "get along." His behavior confirms their opinion, they provide him with less attention and simpler, intellectually less demanding material. He performs at this level, and when he is tested, the tests confirm that he does not perform as well as the other children. The teacher continues to regard him as less capable than other children, and he continues to fall behind. Eventually he withdraws or is expelled from school.

Some such feedback is part of all teacher-student relationships, or all counselor-client relationships. Therapy consists, in part, of interpreting signals from the client, and feeding back to him carefully selected responses that are neutral, or positive, in order to stimulate behavior from him that is consistent with the goals of the two-person therapeutic system.

3. Adaptation. Feedback could be considered identical to adaptation. Adaptation is discussed separately to emphasize two points.

1. Adaptation is viewed by some theorists (including Parsons) as being of overwhelming importance, because systems must adjust to their environment. While it is true that there must be adjustment between systems and environment, we reject the view that the adjustment must be made only by the system, and not by the environment (our position was stated earlier in the discussion of holon). Therefore, we do recognize the importance of feedback as a mechanism of adjustment, but do not make adaptation the *primary* function.

2. Adaptation can be seen to take two forms, assimilation and accommodation. These are discussed in Chapter 6 in the section on Piaget. These two terms indicate whether the system accepts or rejects the incoming information without any change on the part of the system, or whether it modifies its structure in response to the incoming information. In reality, systems do both of these at the same time, in some mixture; as with other polarities, no system does one or the other entirely.

SUMMARY STATEMENT

This chapter introduces concepts we judge to be essential to a social systems approach to understanding human behavior. These are the fundamental ideas that will be expanded in subsequent chapters.

Before ending, one note is in order concerning the three aspects discussed in this chapter: "Evolutionary," "structural," and "behavioral" aspects are three ways to slice the same apple. They are not separate, but complementary dimensions of a system. A board that is long, wide, and thick is not three separate boards.

SUGGESTED READINGS

Bertalanffy, Ludwig Von. *Robots, Men and Minds.* New York: Braziller, 1967. The author is generally acknowledged, by himself and others, to be the "father of General Systems." This book deals with the central conceptualizations.

Buckley, Walter, ed. *Modern Systems Research for the Behavioral Scientist.* Chicago: Aldine, 1968. A comprehensive collection of the major writings of General

Systems theorists. The reader needs an understanding of the basic terminology before tackling this work.

Hearn, Gordon, ed. *The General Systems Approach: Contributions Toward an Holistic Conception of Social Work*. New York: Council on Social Work Education, 1969. A seminal monograph that established the relevance of the General Systems approach to social work. The articles by Hearn, Gordon, and Lathrope provide essential background to a social systems approach to the nature and knowledge of social work.

Janchill, Sister Mary Paul. "Systems Concepts in Casework Theory and Practice." *Social Casework* 50:2, February, 1969, 74–82. Illustrates the applicability of social systems concepts to the practice of social casework.

Koestler, Arthur, and J. R. Smythies. *Beyond Reductionism: New Perspectives in the Life Sciences*. Boston: Beacon, 1971. This is for the student who wants to delve into the complex issues inherent in General Systems. It is a report of an international symposium held in Alpbach in the Austrian Tyrol in 1968. The invitations were confined to "personalities in academic life with undisputed authority in their respective fields." They included Jerome Bruner, Von Bertalanffy, and Piaget.

Laszlo, Ervin. *The Systems View of The World*. New York: Braziller, 1972. A prelude to a major work entitled *Introduction to Systems Philosophy* (New York and London: Gordon and Breach, 1972). This is a readable inquiry into a General Systems viewpoint of a philosophy of science. The author deals with three levels of systems: suborganic (atom), organic (cell), and supraorganic human-social).

Romains, Jules. *Death of a Nobody*. New York: New American Library, 1961. One of many literary works that portrays the interlacing of human systems as they converge through a particular system, in this instance a person whose life seemed of little consequence.

chapter 2

CULTURE AND SOCIETY

‾‾‾‾‾‾‾‾‾‾‾‾‾‾‾‾‾‾‾‾‾‾‾‾‾‾‾‾‾‾‾‾

‾‾‾‾‾‾‾‾‾‾‾‾‾‾‾‾‾‾‾‾‾‾‾‾‾‾‾‾‾‾‾‾

INTRODUCTION

This section is intended to open exploration of human behavior at the broadest, most general level—that is, as species. We will examine ideas from a number of disciplines, ideas that seem particularly pertinent to social work knowledge and the systems approach. These disciplines include biology, sociology, anthropology, linguistics, psychology, and ethology.

First we should explain how we use the terms *culture* and *society*. To be consistent with the systems skeleton, we use the term *culture* in two ways. First, and generally, culture refers to those qualities and attributes that seem to be characteristic of all mankind. Culture denotes those things unique to the species *Homo sapiens* as differentiated from all other forms of life. As Jerome Bruner has said, "man represents that crucial point in evolution where adaptation is achieved by the vehicle of culture, and only in minor ways by further changes in his morphology" (Bruner, 1968, p. 74). This general usage of *culture* is employed to underscore the notion that man's evolutionary timetable is unique, in that it is through culture that man is immediately affected by, and subject to, the evolutionary principle of survival of the fittest. As Konrad Lorenz, the seminal thinker in ethology, puts it, "historians will have to face the fact that natural selection determined the evolution of cultures in the same manner as it did that of the species" (Lorenz, 1963, p. 260).

Man then is a social being, uniquely possessing culture. Cultural forms are changed, synthesized, radiated, and extinguished—not the species. This of course does not preclude the possibility of man as a species being subject to the laws of species survival as well, but the time scale is quite different for biological evolution. According to this broad definition, then, culture is to be viewed as a macrosystem, for purposes of discussion and speculation. Weston La Barre provides arguments for this position (La Barre, 1954, Chapter 1).

A *society* refers to a group of people who have learned to live and work together. Society is viewed as a holon, and within the society *culture* refers to the way of life followed by the group, that is, society. This then is the second usage of the term *culture*—that which binds a society together and includes its manners and morals, tools and techniques. With this dual meaning attached to culture, this chapter might more accurately be titled "Culture and Society and Culture."

I. SPECIES AND CULTURE

Human beings seem to have certain attributes in common regardless of time or place. These common attributes can be parsed and explicated in a number of ways. For the present purpose we will generalize these attributes under four headings: the capacity to think, the family as a biological universal, language, and territoriality.

A. The Capacity to Think

In 1948, Julian Huxley commented that "the first and most obviously unique characteristic of man is his capacity for conceptual thought, if you prefer objective terms, you will say his employment of true speech, but that is only another way of saying the same thing" (Huxley, 1964, p. 8). The capacity to think and communicate his thoughts sets man off from other forms of life. Gross impairment of these faculties is indeed a grave matter. Much of child rearing is devoted to the further refinement and development of this capacity (as is apparent in the discussion of cognitive theory in Chapter 6). Perpetuation of cultural tradition and use of the tools of the culture is dependent upon members of the culture having this capacity.

B. The Family as a Biological Universal in the Human Species

The family is biologically based and is the primary social (and socializing) unit. The *fact* of the family is a constant; the *form* of the family is a variable. Anthropological studies have convincingly demonstrated that although the family as a primary socializing unit is a universal phenomenon, there is no "normal" family form. As ethologists have learned about the mating, reproducing, and rearing patterns of a range of species they have uncovered a number of factors that seem to influence the pairings and groupings of various species. These factors include:

1. The number of offspring per mating, the reproductive rate.
2. The length of the gestation period. This influences the number of matings.
3. The length of the period of the immaturity of the young, expressed in ratio to total life span.

As the first factor reduces (smaller number of offspring per mating) and the other two factors lengthen (gestation and relative length of the time of immaturity), pair bonds and family rearing of the young increase. Among humans, the existence of the family is, of course, a necessary element for the development of culture since culture is transmitted from one generation to the next, not through the genes but through teaching (La Barre, 1954, Chapters 2, 7).

As La Barre emphasizes, the *cultural form* of family must never be confused with the *biological norm* of the family; the cultural forms vary tremendously (La Barre, 1954, p. 113). The nuclear family, consisting of the biological parents and their offspring, is only one of these forms, and *not* the most prevalent at that. The form of the family is influenced by the culture in which it exists; in turn, the form influences that culture. The human family then is a system, a holon, and has a simultaneous existence as part and whole. Its form organizes the energies of the family members, and it must engage in transactions with its suprasystems.

The following is an example of how cultural aspects influence the family system. Our economic system, with its accent on production and distribution of goods achieved through the standardization of organization of energies toward that goal, requires a mobile work force. Adaptation to this single cultural artifact has been extremely stressful to the form of the family during the past generation and has been amply discussed in both popular and technical literature. Toffler's *Future Shock* documents some of the effects of this artifact (Toffler, 1970).

The cultural bind that the resident of Appalachia finds himself in is another prime example. Gainful employment requires mobility to an industrial city, but the cultural expectations related to family and primary social group require the person's presence in time of family need. In this situation he well may desert his job to "go down home."

The main point here is that the family is universally characteristic of the human species and is necessary to the maintenance of human culture, but the form of the family varies from culture to culture and among the subcultures within a culture.

C. The Human Universality of Language

Etymologists broadly define language as any transfer of meaning, but general usage refers to the spoken and written messages. Appreciation of the universality in the broader sense—that is, any transfer of meaning—is particularly important to social workers and others who deal with persons rather than objects. Because persons with troubles often have their troubles because they rely on other means of communication without conscious intent, attunement to unspoken and unwritten language forms is essential. A person may express feelings and ideas with signals rather than with consensual symbols of communication. Consequently, such ideas as "body language" and "listening with the third ear" become important.

There are explicitly arranged language forms other than spoken and written verbal messages. A driver's examination for illiterates uses colors and sign shapes rather than the printed word. On the road, the conventions for indications of one's intent to overtake and pass another vehicle are clearly communicated through codes of blinking lights. The automobile driver can overtake a truck and signal to the truck driver his wish to pass. The truck driver, based on his better view of the road ahead, can signal the following driver either to remain where he is, or that it is safe to pass. And the variation from dim lights to bright lights communicates that the deed has been accomplished. The key to nonverbal language is the consensus of meaning attached to symbols and manipulations. An important aspect of socialization into a new system is becoming acquainted with such symbolization and learning the attached meanings. Excellent examples are the sometimes subtle and complex silent or audible signals exchanged at auctions.

There are also implicitly understood conventions and symbols that require even more consensual agreement than the explicit symbols. The initiation of a social transaction between two equals can be signaled by the shaking of hands, an embrace, or mutual acknowledgment of deference, such as bowing or removal of hats. The culturally conditioned "embracer" learns very quickly in a "handshaking" culture that the meaning of gesture is culturally defined, not universal.

Communication seems to be present in other life forms as well. The dancing flight of the bee and the singing of the bird to announce territorial prerogatives to other members of its species are well known. Such phenomena seem distinguishable from human language in respect to the thought and meaning signified. The evidence thus far is that the bee and the bird operating from instinct evolved for purposes of species survival, while the human is operating from learning that has evolved for cultural survival.

Etymologists have an interesting time with cross-cultural comparisons of word meanings and in the process provide interesting insights. For example, Mario Pei in his fascinating book *The Story of Language* has a section dealing with the symbolism of color and how symbols vary from language to language, from culture to culture (Pei, 1966). Why are we "blue" when depressed, "yellow" when cowardly, "red" when radically inclined? In Russia, red is beautiful and both "red" and "beauty" come from the same word root. White is the color of purity and innocence to Americans, but to Russians and Koreans it is the color of mourning and death. In the Russian civil war the Reds had a gigantic psychological advantage over the Whites because of the symbolic overtones. This kind of information carries implications for attempts to understand racial conflicts. Those who launched the "Black Is Beautiful" campaign were attuned to the cultural importance of color symbolism. How much of the unyielding racial prejudice is attributable to the cultural artifact of color symbolism is unknown, but it certainly must be an important factor.

In considering language and thought as species characteristics in man, the thesis propounded by Whorf and Sapir is of note. Their hypothesis is that language structures reality; the form and variability of the language determines how members of the culture will view reality and structure their thoughts (Whorf, 1956). This hypothesis is generally accepted. E. T. Hall, in developing his thesis about territoriality and its importance to man, did an analysis of the words listed in the *Oxford Pocket Dictionary*. He found that 20 percent of them could be classified as referring to space and spacial relations (Hall, 1969, p. 93).

Bruner, for one, says that the Whorf and Sapir formulation serves to set up the pins in the wrong alley. He holds that attention should really be focused on *how* language determines thought, regardless which language is being considered (Bruner, 1968). At any rate, there is a close, demonstrable relationship between culture and language. This relationship is not necessarily causal in either direction. As often cited, modern English and American language structures attend closely to the temporal plane. So in the study of grammar, tenses are of utmost importance since time is so essential to aspects of the culture. Some cultures make no provisions for tenses—the precise measurement of time is of little cultural importance to them.

Weston La Barre presents intriguing facts and speculations about language as symbolic communication (La Barre, 1954, Chapter 10). He accepts the Whorfian hypothesis and states that the structure of reality is, much of the time, merely imputed to reality by the structure of our language. As soon as the human infant learns to speak any language at all, he already has a "hardening of the categories," or "they are different, this we know, for our language tells us so."

La Barre goes on to develop the idea that language is so flexible that a word can put into semantic equation any two disparate objects in the universe. If the society accepts the equation by consensus semantically it becomes the essence of reality; if the individual does this without societal consensus he is schizophrenic, not attuned to reality. "A psychotic's truth is one 'I' make it, and cultural truth is what by unwitting vote 'we' make it; but ultimate truth still remains in the outside world of that which is" (La Barre, 1954, p. 266). Robert Merton expressed the same idea in his Thomas Theorem, "If men define situations as real, they are real in their consequences" (Merton, 1957, p. 421). Kœstler comments:

> The prejudice and impurities which have been incorporated into the
> verbal concepts of a given universe of discourse cannot be undone by any

amount of discourse within the frame of reference of that universe. The rules of the game, however absurd, cannot be altered by playing that game. Language can become a screen which stands between the thinker and reality. This is the reason why true creativity often starts where language ends. (Koestler, 1967, p. 177)

D. Territoriality

Another dimension of culture that has only recently received much attention is territoriality. This concept refers to the tendency of man, in his social systems, to seek and maintain a territory. Some authors deal with territory as primarily spacial (Ardrey, 1966; Hall, 1969), while others stress the interactional aspects (Lyman and Scott, 1967, pp. 236–245). Man's definition of his spacial and interactional territories is a paramount feature of any culture.

One simple example is the definition of territorial elements as squared or rounded. This choice seems to be simultaneously determined *by* other features of the culture as well as a determinant *of* culture. The "home territories" within a given culture give clues to other aspects of the culture. The sedentary and specialized culture with much differentiation of function tends to organize living and work spaces in squares with specialized uses. The square house has its bedrooms, bathrooms, kitchen, living room, den, and so forth. The nomadic, unspecialized culture lives in round houses (igloo, wigwam, cave, or round hut) without specialized compartments. Arranging territories in squares tends to close boundaries. The increasing use of geodesic domes as homes may signify cultural shifts in our society. Another significant feature may be newer designs of public schools in "pods," "clusters," or "modules." (For further discussion see Marshall McLuhan, *Understanding Media: The Extensions of Man*, pp. 123–130.)

The spirit of equality, fidelity, and camaraderie embodied in the King Arthur legend is symbolized by the table round. Formal dining tables are usually rectangular, while tables in small, intimate bars are round. Youth's expressions of dissatisfaction with the impersonal, highly structured role relations and specialized functions of the bureaucratic system or organization are expressed in the epithet "square." Dictionaries show that the meanings attached to this epithet by immediately preceding American generations were "justly," "fairly," and "honestly." These meanings reflected the primary purpose of the impersonality of the bureaucratic system—to protect the person from unjust and arbitrary decisions. The Paris peace talks were delayed for many months while it was decided if the talks would be conducted over a rectangular table or around a circular table. In part, this dispute symbolized crucial differences in cultural traditions between the contending systems.

Relationships are symbolized by diagramatic representations intended to concretize interactional territories (Figure 2A and B). The components in Figure 2A are arranged in a vertical hierarchy, and each component (person or department) is designated by title or role rather than by name. Specialization and differentiation are designated by these labels. In Figure 2B the components will be labeled by name (or number, to protect the innocent). The hierarchy here is represented in the circular plane and conveys positive, negative, and absent patterns of relatedness. Each of these diagrams is illustrative of interactional territorial arrangements and relationships.

It is hypothesized then that all holons have a territorial dimension. This territory may be spacial or interactional, not static, objective, or observable. It probably is a "sense of territory," and as such is congruent with the particular culture. Territoriality refers to the cultural ways man locates himself in his universe and establishes the boundaries of his various human systems. Territorial aspects of social work as a subculture are discussed in the next chapter.

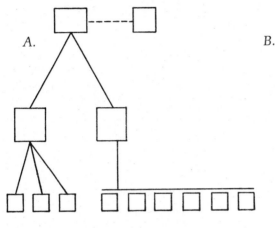

A.   B.

Figure 2.   A. *Typical Representation of*   B. *Typical Sociogram.*
              Bureaucratic Structure.

II. ANALYTICAL DIMENSIONS OF CULTURE

Definitions of culture abound and frequently conflict. Kroeber and Kluckhohn devoted 28 pages to a listing of definitions of culture. They concluded that the definition given by Edward Tylor in 1871 was as good as any. Tylor's definition was that culture is that complex whole which includes knowledge, belief, art, law, morals, custom, and any other capabilities and habits *acquired by man as a member of society* (Teicher, 1958, pp. 450–455). The italicized words represent an important qualification on occasion overlooked by enthusiastic culture determinists. Konrad Lorenz considers this qualification of the utmost importance, and states that "human behavior, and particularly human social behavior, far from being determined by reason and cultural tradition alone, is still subject to all the laws prevailing in all phylogenetically adapted instinctive behavior" (Lorenz, 1963, p. 237). Rather than choosing a definition of culture from the myriad that have been offered, or trying to form one, we will discuss five dimensions of culture.

These dimensions are expansions on what Jerome Bruner has termed "the five great humanizing forces" (Bruner, 1968, pp. 75 ff.) : toolmaking, social organization, language, management of man's prolonged childhood, and man's urge to explain his world.

These are dimensions in that they are important facets of any culture. One can approach the analysis of culture through examining these dimensions regardless of the time and place or kind of culture being studied. With a subculture within a culture, such as a peer group culture or a professional culture, certain of these dimensions may seem less applicable; but each of the five seems applicable to some extent. We are then viewing culture as the ways of doing and explaining, in a particular system.

A. Tools

Tools are amplifiers of human capacities, whether the tools are invented or synthesized. They fall into three classes:

1. Amplifiers of *sensory* capacities, for example microscopes, telescopes, telephones, clocks, spectacles, radar, conch shells, and in some cultures psychedelic drugs.
2. Amplifiers of *motor* capacities, for example hammers, wheels, the lever, and rockets.
3. Amplifiers of *reasoning* and *thinking* capacities, for example mathematical systems, logic, the abacus, the computer, and the blackboard (a major educational invention).

Tools then are devices, objects, and procedures that are extensions of man's natural capacities. The crucial, most important aspect is not the tool itself but rather its function, the use to which the tool is put. A hammer is generally assumed to be of use to pound nails and, if it is a claw hammer, to remove nails as well, but it can also be used as a lethal weapon or to prop open a door or window. Books generally are assumed to be for the purpose of reading, but they can also serve to press flowers, level the short leg of a table, or to impress other people with the owner's literary sophistication. Understanding the tools of a culture includes therefore not only understanding its seeming intrinsic or built-in purpose, but more importantly how the tools are used, what is the purpose of the user. Some years ago one of the authors worked in a small Indian reservation where the occupants had been given a refrigerator for each household and electricity was available. The purpose of food storage by refrigeration was not part of the way of life of this culture. The refrigerators were used for other purposes—for decoration in a few instances, but mostly for storage. They were perceived as attractive boxes with a door, but the "built-in purpose" was not the purpose of the users.

Peter Farb, a cultural anthropologist, has analyzed the evolution of cultures in a remarkably readable book. One of his major theses is that a new tool or technique must have a counterpart in social organization or knowledge to become functional. He uses the example of the introduction of the horse into two quite different cultures. The first of these cultures, a hunting tribe, mounted the horses and used them to pursue the buffalo. This amplified human motor capacities, making them much more efficient hunters, and rapidly the culture evolved toward one in which the horse became central. The second culture merely slaughtered the horse and ate it (Farb, 1969, p. 29).

Tools then are a key dimension by which a culture may be analyzed. They extend the uses of energies within the cultural system toward fulfillment of the system's goals. It may be equally significant and analytical of a culture that certain tools do *not* exist. For example, the absence of written languages or of the wheel are significant in some North and Central American Indian cultures.

B. Social Organization

All cultures, being social systems, have organization. They may be organized, may be in the process of organizing, or they may be in the process of disorganizing; but in any event the dimension of organization is present. As previously stated, the structure is not fixed and any analysis of structure is like a still photo. At the moment of analysis, the social organization of a culture is not what it has been nor what it will become. It is structured in the sense of a system of interacting elements, and any change in one element or single pattern of relationships affects all other elements, directly or indirectly.

Evolutionary theory, in its essence, describes the increase of complexity, whether from simple to complex biological organisms, or from simple to complex cultures. The social organization of an evolving culture becomes more complex because of an increased volume of interrelationships between the various elements of the culture. A "stagnant culture" is one in which the interrelationships are static and interaction of the cultural elements is unchanging. Some have postulated that bureaucracy will appear as an organizational system when society reaches a given state of complexity, regardless of the form of government. The bureaucracies of ancient China, Rome, the Catholic Church, the Russian monarchy, and most recently American democracy and Russian communism can all be cited as illustrations. As Ralph Nader pointed out in a speech on our campus (November 1, 1972) bureaucracy seems to have as a major function the reduction and containment of forces that might lead to change. As such, bureaucracy is probably used as a "buffering" device by all complex societies. The systems term *equifinality* applies to this phenomenon.

Certain important concepts related to social organization are commonly employed. These are the interrelated ideas of *class, status,* and *role.* All societies have schemes of ordering human interaction and ways of defining and communicating expected behaviors. As with definitions of culture, many theorists have proposed hypothetical *social class* structures. In considering the current American scene, Martin Loeb attempted to describe categories of life styles (Loeb, 1961, pp.

12–18); Hollingshead used a variety of socioeconomic indices (Hollingshead, 1949); and Kvaraceus ordered social classes by values (Kvaraceus, 1959).

T. H. Marshall, an English sociologist, has worked out a scheme based on Max Weber's writings (Marshall, 1964). The general idea is that there are three aspects operating: economic status, social status, and political power. When the groupings of these three coincide (multibonded), then social class is a visible thing. If the boundaries between the social classes are clear and closed, the result is caste. The idea of social class suggests a group consciousness on the part of members, both of their own groups and other groups, and of their general position in the social scale.

Social status does not necessarily imply the existence of groups at all. It refers to a consensus of social ranking. Status, of course, can be achieved or ascribed, but the organizing mechanisms for acquiring or granting status, as well as the recognition thereof, seem to be present in all cultures. To understand the culture it is important to know the key determinants of status.

Role relates to, and derives from status. Ralph Linton described role as "the sum total of the cultural patterns associated with a particular status. It thus includes the attitudes, values and behavior ascribed by the society to any and all persons occupying that status" (Linton, 1945, pp. 76–77). The complexity of a status is manifested partly by the complexity and differentiation of role expectations. Bureaucracy is one of the organizational forms devised to reduce this complexity. In the bureaucratic structure the role may become more important than the person occupying the status, but it is only through occupying the status that one can assume the role. Beyond the family, continuity depends less on the person's characteristics and more on the roles he occupies and interacts with.

Role expectations then are culturally defined by the system and its components, and incorporated by the persons filling the role. A culture may allow more or less latitude in deviations from the expected behaviors. Certain cultures rigidly define role behavior, but more often the rigidity or flexibility of role definition is dependent on what else is transpiring within the system. For example, there was a time in American culture when expected role behavior of a child in relation to the adults in his environment was expressed by the phrase "children should be seen and not heard." More recently children are expected to be heard, and if this role behavior is not forthcoming they are considered withdrawn or at least shy.

In a dynamic, open cultural system, role occupants are constantly seeking flexibility of role definition with or without the encouragement of the culture. As the cultural system is threatened from either external or internal quarters, strings are drawn more tightly on the expected role behaviors.

All persons occupy a complex of roles, the total number of these being influenced by the quantity of networks of interrelationships they are involved in. At any given moment a person is likely to be more actively behaving in one or another of the roles, but he does carry them all at one time. When there is excessive conflict (for him) between or among roles in their expectations, the person has troubles. Or if society finds him to be failing to fulfill role expectations, the person has troubles. In either case, society has troubles. If any significant minority of the members of the society do not do what the consensus requires for a length of time, the system is in difficulty and the survival of the culture is in question. In such instances, energies of the system must be devoted to maintaining the organization and redefining the expectations of those in the particular status.

C. Language

Here again we refer to language in its broader sense, that is as transfer of meaning. The structures of language strongly influence the content conveyed—language is composed of symbols, and the meanings are learned and transferred through social interaction. *Symbolic interaction* refers to this process. The communication of symbols and their attendant meanings represents the major form of transaction between human systems.

Most of the work of the symbolic interactionists is built on the insights of George Herbert Mead and Charles Horton Cooley (Manis and Meltzer, 1967, pp. 217–219, 139–148). Mead stated that we do not simply respond to the acts (including speech, of course) of others; rather we act on our *interpretations* of their intentions. Gestures are an important kind of symbolic communication and we respond to the meanings not necessarily as they are intended, but as we interpret them. When a gesture has a common meaning, some measure of consensus, Mead termed it a *linguistic element*—a significant symbol. Common examples include the kiss an expression of affection; the drawn-back, clenched fist as threat of aggression; the smile as an expression of pleasure; and the frown as an expression of displeasure. Because of the consensus of meaning, we attribute the quality of pleasure to the smile of the baby even though it might be an expression of gas on the stomach.

The term *generalized other* is central to Mead's formulation. This refers to a generalized stance or viewpoint imputed to others that one uses to assess and judge his own behavior. Another key concept is *self*. An individual may act socially toward himself as toward others. The self is comprised of the *I* and *me*. *I* is the impulsive, spontaneous, and unorganized energizing part of the self. *Me* is the incorporated other. The *I* energizes and provides propulsion, while the *me* provides direction, in other words, controls function. These are similar to, but in important ways different from, id and superego. The emphasis is on social rather than intrapsychic functioning.

The "looking glass self" was Cooley's construct and refers to the idea that we interpret what others think of us. It involves the following sequence: (1) the imagination of our appearance to others, (2) the imagination of their judgment, and (3) a self feeling in response to this imagined judgment—for example, pride or mortification.

The symbolic interactionists, as represented by Mead and Cooley, go far toward explaining the process of transfer of meaning. Their formulations clearly demonstrate that meaning derives from interaction between the sender and the receiver at both verbal and nonverbal levels. These are, in essence, descriptions of the feedback cycle as transacted between human systems. If there is little or no feedback from outside the focal system, then the assessment of appearance and judgment must be projected from the inside. For example, the paranoid person is not able, or is not allowing himself, to participate in this feedback cycle with outside systems, and must rely on his own imagined judgments. It was argued during the 1972 presidential election that a nation-system can find itself in this same situation, with its feedback projected from within, and therefore become isolated and chauvinistic.

Language then is the vehicle for transfer of meaning between the components of a cultural system and between one culture system and other cultures. That which is considered important enough to symbolize and communicate is as important in understanding a culture as is the understanding of the methods of communication. In this instance, Marshall McLuhan seems wrong; there is more to the message than merely the medium. Furthermore, language is a means of setting and maintaining cultural boundaries as well as a major means of organizing the energies of the system. Subcultures universally employ their own jargons or argots and one of the major tasks of socialization into a subculture is to become acquainted with the particular language used. Certainly the subculture of social work is an example, with such jargon as "personal-social needs," "relationship," and "intervention." The special language of a subculture may serve to exclude others from participation in the culture. Because it prevents interaction, this "linguistic collusion" is an effective way to close a boundary. (Incidentally, we hope that the systems approach helps prevent such boundary closure in social work.)

The importance of "screening" and interpreting symbols in working with people is abundantly clear. Much of psychoanalytic and social work literature, for example, is devoted to making the helping professional sensitive to the possible meanings of the symbols he receives from the person being helped. Theodore Reik's idea of "the third ear," in which the therapist's own emotional reactions give clues to unspoken messages being sent by the patient, is an example (Reik, 1948). Another example is psychological testing, especially "projective" tests such as the Rorschach, Thematic Apperception, or House-Tree-Person tests. In these tests the responses of the subject being tested are interpreted in order to provide clues about the subject's personality structure, and what treatment methods may be most useful in dealing with this person. In these instances, between the professional person's reception (input) of the symbols and his response (output) to them, the interpretation (processing) that occurs is formalized and takes on the character of scientific problem-solving—or at least, this is what professional schools hope their graduates are capable of doing.

In such professional techniques, obviously some standardization of language and symbols is necessary, and thus each theoretical approach, such as psychoanalysis, transactional analysis, or behavior modification, must devote much energy to training professionals in some standard terminology. This is necessary so that the results of professional efforts, and the theoretical elaboration of them, can be conveyed in some common language. Certainly the history of psychiatry is replete with examples of attempts by Kraepelin, Freud, and others to standardize terminology. Menninger lists such attempts since medicine began (Menninger, 1963, Chapters 1, 2, Appendix). A major problem for each of the developing helping professions has been the training of professionals to apply the same labels to similar phenomena, so that terms have some consensual meaning—that is, so that one psychiatrist's "schizoid" is not another psychiatrist's "passive-aggressive." Despite such efforts as the American Psychiatric Association's standard nomenclature, however, serious disagreements on interpretations of symbolic behavior do occur within that profession. Consensus of meaning with a high degree of precision is difficult to achieve; if it were not so, probably such books as this one would be unnecessary.

D. Child Rearing—Man's Management of His Prolonged Childhood

Anthropologists, sociologists and psychologists have exhaustively researched forms of child rearing in various cultures. Although most of these studies focus on the family system, many deal with other educative and socializing social systems as well. Writers in ethology compare the family of humankind with the family structure of other animals, seeking generalities and unique attributes (Ardrey, 1966; Lorenz, 1963; Morris, 1967). The human family is always found to be highly organized, in the sense Monane uses this phrase to connote intense intra-system relatedness (see Chapter 1, "Organization"). There is a predominance of sentiment in this interaction rather than only biological need gratification and response, although the two are always related. As a culture becomes more complex and differentiated, so too does child rearing become complex and differentiated and other social provisions appear. There are numerous examples in the recent evolution of American society. As the economic system required greater mobility, the extended family began to dissolve. This was accompanied by the advent of the baby-sitter. Currently the demands of the economic system and shifts in role definition of the female are leading to rapid growth of day-care centers.

New social institutions, such as day-care facilities, are accompanied by changes in family functions, but this is not necessarily tantamount to family breakdown. These new systems arise to more effectively realize the complex of values of a culture. Usually certain values are in conflict with certain other values, leading to tension and strain in the various systems. The historical development of the public school is an excellent illustration. The belief that a certain amount of formal education should be the right of every person developed over centuries in a number of places, particularly Western Europe. This was related to values such as "equality" and the "importance of knowledge." An informed citizenry became a system goal in America in the first half of the nineteenth century. As the belief became a cherished system value, held by a significant portion of the components of the system, provisions were implemented to fulfill the value. This was followed by the adoption of the "common school" in a majority of the states during the decade of the 1850s. Since then the public school as a child-rearing social subsystem has continued to evolve, becoming more complex and differentiated. The current controversy over the issue of transmission of culture, manners, and morals related to sexual behavior, and whether this should be a family or school responsibility, exemplifies the process of culture change and the inherent value conflicts.

The management of man's prolonged childhood is a major characteristic of any culture and as such must fit with other aspects of the culture and interact with these.

E. Man's Urge to Explain His World

This major dimension of a culture is often overlooked or minimized in explication of the concept of culture. Much of the energy of a culture system is expended in this dimension of human existence. Religion, philosophy, science, and superstition are some of these pursuits. The attendant beliefs, rituals, values, and theories are an essential part of a culture. This quest to explain the unexplained can be viewed as an integral aspect of the adaptation of a system to its environment.

In our culture at this time, science is the dominant means of exploring and explaining our world. (Only a few pockets of resistance hold out, such as the "No Moon" group in England, and the Flat Earth Society.) Cults that seek to explain the world through the drug experience, astrology, or numerology are examples of other kinds of belief systems. The scientific method, empirical observation, and inductive reasoning are highly valued only in certain cultures. Superstition is held in ill repute in American culture, unless it presents itself in the guise of science. One example is the dogmatic belief that scientific method, or technology, can solve all important problems, which is certainly not a proven fact. Religious organizations in this culture must be responsive to the currently accepted way of explaining the world, and so are compelled to engage in social problem-solving in the "scientific" way.

There is general agreement that man can only be understood within the context of his culture. This idea is now accepted as unassailable. Teicher states the case as it applies to social work (Teicher, 1958). Needless to say, culture is conceptualization, not a reality to be directly observed. How one applies this concept depends on one's vantage point, what one is prepared to see, and, perhaps most important, the knowledge used to interpret the observations.

Visualize the three-dimensional atomic model as a system and then consider the study of culture. If you are somewhere within the cultural system you can see some components well, others less well, and others not at all. If you are outside the system your perspective may help you better see the "big picture," but the further out you are, the more danger there is of reductionism and oversimplification. Popular adages express this dilemma—for example, "He can't see the forest for the trees."

There is no solution to this dilemma. To best understand culture in any of its forms—for example, a primitive society, an ethnic group, a peer group, or a profession—the observer must strive for objectivity if he is himself a component of the system, or strive for involvement if he is outside the system. It is through this process of reasoning that social work, education, and other human services have recently again concerned themselves with greater involvement in the "client system" and its particular culture, be it family, neighborhood, or community.

SUGGESTED READINGS

Ardrey, Robert. Any of his recent books provide stimulating reading for this chapter. Especially recommended are *The Territorial Imperative* (New York: Atheneum, 1966) and *The Social Contract* (New York: Atheneum, 1970).

Blumer, Herbert. "Society as Symbolic Interaction," in *Symbolic Interaction,* Jerome G. Manis and Bernard N. Meltzer, eds. Boston: Allyn and Bacon, 1967, pp. 139–148. This article succinctly explains symbolic interaction and reviews the theoretical foundation of this school of thought.

Farb, Peter. *Man's Rise to His Civilization as Shown by the Indians of North America from Primeval Times to the Coming of the Industrial State.* New York: Dutton, 1968. In this very readable book, with its foreboding title, Farb illustrates how cultures evolve.

Hall, Edward T. *The Hidden Dimension.* Garden City, New York: Doubleday, 1969. An extremely interesting and stimulating work that deals with the structure of experience as it is determined by culture. The particular cultural theme examined is the human use of space. (This book has been used as the "small map" for this chapter. Students have found the content directly applicable to social work situations.)

Johnson, Wendell. *Verbal Man: The Enchantment of Words.* New York: Harper and Row, 1956. (Originally published as *Your Most Enchanted Listener.*) A delightful little book exploring words as symbols and the processes of effective communication.

La Barre, Weston. *The Human Animal.* Chicago: University of Chicago Press, 1954. (The 1968 edition has minor differences.) The author, an anthropologist, examines the culture of man from an evolutionary stance. He combines findings from anthropology, psychiatry, linguistics, and human biology into a controversial thesis. His arguments are particularly thorough as he deals with family, symbolic communication, and deviant behavior. (This book has been used as the "small map" for this chapter and has generated much discussion.)

Lewis, Oscar. *Five Families.* New York: Basic Books, 1959. A detailed examination of five families within their cultural context. It beautifully illustrates the impact of culture.

Lyman, Stanford, and Marvin Scott. "Territoriality: A Neglected Social Dimension," *Social Problems* 15, Fall, 1967, 236–245. A definitive statement of a typology of human spacial arrangements. In addition to describing classifications of territory, this article well illustrates varieties of boundary definition and boundary maintenance.

Teicher, Morton I. "The Concept of Culture," *Social Casework* 34, October, 1958, 450–455. The publication of this brief article marked the introduction of the concept of culture into the literature of social work. It is as timely today as it was in 1958.

chapter 3
COMMUNITIES AND ORGANIZATIONS

___

INTRODUCTION

The logic of combining discussions of communities and organizations in this chapter is that both are macrosystems, as opposed to the microsystems of persons, families, and small groups. Both are intermediate between society and the small groupings in which intimate affective transactions occur.

Historically, sociology has had difficulty defining and distinguishing among community, organization, and society. The major distinction between community and organization that we have in mind is one made by Ferdinand Tönnies: *A community is held together by feeling and sentiment, primarily, while an organization is sustained by "rational" considerations, usually explicit in formal contracts, usually written* (Tönnies, 1957). The fact that organizations are more goal-oriented is both a cause and an effect of their rational, contractual nature—that is, in order to seek a goal, contracts are made, and then, in order to perpetuate the organization, further goals must be sought.

I. COMMUNITY AS SYSTEM

Probably the two most difficult systems to define (distinguish) with precision are community and small group (which will be discussed in the succeeding chapter). As Heraud writes, "many difficulties have surrounded the meaning and use of the term 'community,' not least of which has been the reluctance of sociologists to refine the term in ways which would make it more useful either for the concerns of social policy or for actual sociological analysis. The term has reached a "high level of use but a low level of meaning" (Heraud, 1970, pp. 83–84). Because the community is the interface between society and microsystems, it is of prime concern to nearly all social disciplines and professions. The family is a person's primary field of interaction during childhood, but in adulthood his major field of interaction will be community, or at least significant sectors of community. Such sectors include the financial, commercial, religious, educational, and legal institutions in which he participates. "At one and the same time it is an important building block of society, and it is society itself. It represents culture to the individual and as such shapes him, and it is subject to the will of the individual who as a citizen can enact changes in his community" (French, 1969, p. 5).

A. Kinds of Communities

Communities differ in several ways. First, Tönnies described kinds of communities:

1. "place" communities, which he called "locality"; this is also called geographic or spacial community. It is based upon a common habitat and ownership of adjacent properties.
2. "nonplace" communities, which Tönnies called "mind" communities. This "implies only cooperation and coordinated action for a common goal," without reference to "place" (Hillery, 1968, pp. 77–78).
3. Tönnies described a third kind of community, "kinship," by which he meant those who have blood relationships. Since this is synonymous with extended family and "primary group," discussion of this will be postponed to later chapters.

Tönnies also described communities as *gemeinschaft* and *gesellschaft*. A *gemeinschaft* community is characterized by implicit bonds that relate all community members to the others. These bonds include common values and beliefs, mutual interdependence, respect, and a sense of status hierarchy. Rules of relationship are not formalized but rest in cultural traditions and similarities of social expectations. A *gesellschaft* community, on the other hand, is characterized by bonds that are formal and explicit. Community members relate to one another through formally structured role relations within community institutions such as employment, professions, and civic organizations (Nisbet, 1966).

Examples of the "nonplace" community include professions such as barbering, symbolized by the striped pole and a license, which are protected from intrusion by custom or by law. Other examples are the academic community's jealous protection of "academic freedom," a highly abstract and symbolic territory. The press is concerned about "freedom of the press" and "the public's right to know," and the military is concerned about secrecy, as illustrated by the Pentagon Papers controversy. That all of these territories can be disputed can be seen when newsmen are jailed for refusing to divulge their sources of information, and when a man such as Ellsberg is tried for releasing the Pentagon papers. The "Black Community" is another example. Black people may share common interests in civil rights, common identification in a cultural heritage, and shared identity as exemplified by the slogan "Black is beautiful!"

Second, communities differ in the degree of attachment to a specific location. Nonplace communities have geographic ties, even though they never convene in one location at one time. For example, although the academic community does not reside in a single location, it has ties to college campuses.

Third, the kinds of community differ in the breadth of activities, interests, and needs with which they are concerned. The "place" community encompasses virtually all human interests and needs; the "nonplace" community is usually concerned with one, or a few of these. Almost every kind of human activity (in one form or another) is to be found in the place community of Chicago, but the nonplace "business community" or "academic community" concerns itself with a narrower spectrum of interests and needs.

We suggest the following composite definition of community, derived from several authoritative sources of community theory. *Community* is a consciously identified population with common needs and interests, which may include occupation of common physical space, which is organized and engages in common activity including differentiation of functions and adaptation to its environment, in order to meet the common needs. Its components include the individuals, groups, families, and organizations within its population, and the institutions it forms to meet its needs. Its environment is the society within which it exists and to which it adapts, and other communities and organizations outside itself that impinge on its functioning.

B. Energy Functions

1. For Components/Subsystems. The functions the community performs include the maintenance of a way of life (Ross, 1955, pp. 40–41) or culture (in the second usage of "culture" in Chapter 2). Another important function is the satisfaction of common needs, interests, and ambitions. A contemporary example of the recognition of common interests and needs is Malcolm X's redefinition of the community to which he belonged. He found common interests and needs unexpectedly in a new community:

> That morning was when I first began to reappraise the "white man."
> It was when I first began to perceive that "white man," as commonly used,
> means complexion only secondarily; primarily it described attitudes and
> actions. In America, "white man" means specific attitudes and actions

toward the black man, and toward all other non-white men. But in the Muslim world, I had seen that men with white complexions were more genuinely brotherly than anyone else had ever been.

That morning was the start of a radical alteration in my whole outlook about "white" men. (Malcolm X, 1966, pp. 333–334)

Further, the members of a community must be aware of its "we-ness" (French, 1969; Ross, 1955); in other words, there must be a social consciousness or "sense of" community. This assists the community in meeting the social identity needs of the persons who are its components. The community must provide them "full opportunities for personal development through social experimentation. . . . This conception falls close to Erikson's views on ego identity and ego integrity as well as to Sullivan's emphasis on a full repertory of interpersonal relations" (Stein, 1960, pp. 335–336). "A community must then provide its members with, at the least meaningful sexual and work identities if it is to ensure its own continuity as well as the psychic integrity of its members" (Stein, 1960, p. 266).

Other components such as families, organizations, and groups must also be able to identify with, and find common cause with the community's way of life, in order that energy may be drawn from them to meet the community's needs. The phrase *common cause* has been adopted as the title of a national voluntary organization with this necessity explicitly recognized. This organization mobilizes energy (funds and lobbying actions) of its components to attain agreed-upon goals.

Presthus emphasized these functions which the community performs for its components. He notes that there is

> in every community a certain ongoing network of fairly stable subsystems, activated by social economic, ethnic, religious, and friendship ties and claims. Such systems of interest, values, and power have desirable consequences for their members to the extent that they satisfy various human needs. In a sense, however, such subsystems are suprahuman, in that they tend to persist indefinitely and, more important, that their members may change but the underlying network of interrelated interests and power relations continues. (Presthus, 1964, p. 5)

2. For Environment/Suprasystems. A community must meet the needs of its environment, as well. It is clear from "central place" theory in geography and economics that place communities function as parts of hierarchical, relatively stable economic and political systems, and that alterations in one community affect other parts of the region as well (Christaller, 1966; Ullman, 1941, pp. 853–864). The rise of Chicago as a major industrial and railroad center affected the commercial and social development of communities within its region. These smaller communities adapted to Chicago as a trade center, both supplying and being supplied by Chicago's services. Communities unsuited to adapt to new economic and transportation networks ceased to exist, such as small farm villages.

Religious communities, as examples of nonplace community, have also been confronted with the need to adapt to their environment. Within the Roman Catholic Church in recent years, some orders which formerly were cloistered have moved into society, performing secular tasks such as teaching, and social welfare work in prisons and hospitals. A few orders have disbanded as their members have returned to lay status, some members in order to marry, and others to carry on secular work as part of their religious commitment.

Successful communes in the United States adapt to their environment, performing economic functions in the wider society and obtaining needed energy from other systems. Some cooperatives and communes have attempted "freak capitalism," selling and/or producing leather goods, ceramics, clothing, art work, furniture, or vegetables for the support of the community. In some communes, such as Twin Oaks in Virginia, members alternate in taking employment in nearby cities for financial support for the community. The history of unsuccessful utopian communities is replete with examples of those that attempted to isolate themselves from the social environment and thrive as closed systems. Without energy exchange with the surrounding environment, a system is bound to run down.

In general, the functions the community performs for its environment are the energy functions described in Chapter 1—giving, getting, and conserving energy. The community supplies to its environment and its components energy in the form of persons and products to be used by those systems. A community may supply students for higher education who become society's leaders, while also supplying political support for wider organizations, and taxes for state and national governments.

C. Aspects of Community System

1. *Evolutionary Aspects.* As Mumford points out, the first cities were burial places to which wandering tribes returned at certain times to perform ceremonies that ensured stability of the universe (Mumford, 1961, p. 7). From that symbolic beginning, place communities have evolved to encompass all human needs and functions. The character of a particular community is determined by its environment of other communities, and the society within which it exists, by the characteristics of its components, and by its own steady state. B. F. Skinner's *Walden Two* describes a fictional utopia (copied by several real communities) that evolved into a complex, planned community. As noted by the Lynds, Middletown evolved toward being a satellite in the regional system of a New York City; decisions about industries were increasingly made outside Middletown.

Doxiadis describes the evolution of cities through five stages, differentiated by "kinetic fields," the distance a person could travel within a certain span of time (Miller, 1972, pp. 116–119). Miller identifies the city as an organization rather than community here, but we prefer to regard the community aspects of the city as relatively more important. Doxiadis's stages are:

A-level organization. 2 by 2 kilometers, no more than 50,000 population. No more than ten minutes is required to walk from center to periphery.

B-level organization. 6 by 6 kilometers, more than 50,000 population. Examples are capital cities of empires, such as Rome, Constantinople, and Peking. Walking time was no more than half an hour; paved roads and horse-drawn carts moved people. Such cities were difficult to govern, slums grew, and mobs frequently controlled the city.

C-level organization. These cities depend on subways or elevated trains, thus extending the "kinetic field." This was satisfactory only briefly, and freeways were built to accommodate auto traffic.

D-level organization. This is the modern city, beset by the myriad urban problems we are all too familiar with.

E-level organization. This is the megalopolis, with the pathology that remains from having failed to solve the problems at the D-level (Miller, 1972, pp. 117–118).

According to Miller, the "universal city" or "ecumenopolis" is the ultimate, and would require highly centralized planning. In this system, technology would solve the problems or transportation, distribution of energy supplies, and waste collection. How the problem of retaining a sense of community would be resolved is not made clear.

The alternatives for communities are clear in a rapidly changing society such as ours. Goldsmith's poem "The Deserted Village" illustrates that this began with the Industrial Revolution. Today, ghost towns that were formerly mining camps, small farming villages, or fishing villages attest to the alternatives of disintegration if the community does not have the resources to adapt. Examples of communities that have changed steady states to survive include Iowa City, Iowa, first the state capital and then the site of the state university; and the Masonic Order, originally a craft guild, now an international fraternal order. Certainly the history of Christian denominations illustrates the evolutionary process in such communities.

In communities other than cities, no clear pattern of evolution seems to have been identified. It seems likely that to the extent that such communities resemble groups or families, their evolution is also similar.

2. Structural Aspects. Roland Warren refers to the *vertical* and *horizontal* aspects of community structure.

We shall define a community's *vertical* pattern as the structural and functional relation of its various social units and subsystems to extracommunity systems. The term vertical is used to reflect the fact that such relationships often involve different hierarchical levels within the extracommunity system's structure of authority and power. . . .

We shall define a community's *horizontal* pattern as the structural and functional relation of its various social units and subsystems to each other. (Warren, 1963, pp. 161–162; Chapters 8 and 9)

BOUNDARY

In each direction, the community's boundary may occasionally be difficult to establish. Increasingly, as Warren and other writers (Stein, 1960; Lynd and Lynd, 1937) point out, communities are subordinate to larger, regional networks and to industrial and communications centers in their economic and social decisions. Thus, the vertical boundary is difficult to determine. Within large communities, the internal structure may be composed of relatively autonomous bodies, such as corporations that function as private, independent governments (Bird, 1966, Chapter 10).

Other boundaries within the community are between institutions that differentiate tasks. These horizontal boundaries include, for example, the uniform worn. The fireman's gear is adapted to his task, but also distinguishes him from the policeman (but under sniper fire in recent years, firemen have adopted police-style protective gear). What functional purpose does the bright, fire red of the fire department's gear serve, otherwise—especially considering that red is a low visibility color? Presumably the color says, "We fight fires. Don't ask us to baptize children with our water hoses, to pick up garbage with our trucks, or to fight off crowds with our axes and poles!" Sometimes the boundaries between differentiated institutions are not so clear: Are parochial schools entitled to public funds? Should schools provide sex education? Should police conduct drug education programs? These are controversial questions in many communities.

INSTITUTIONALIZATION

The need to differentiate functions into specialized community subsystems leads to the evolution of community institutions. Such institutions usually do not originate in a single community. Since the community is an intersection between society and microsystems, the existence of church, school, and police are part of cultural prescription for communities. The form the institution takes in a particular community depends on the components and steady state of that community. Our society provides that education shall be provided by formal schools, but the form of the school varies from community to community. It may be a one-room country school, or a consolidated elementary school; it may be racially integrated or a private, all-white facility. The mode of instruction may be the Montessori method or the traditional "3 R's."

Yet single communities evolve distinctive institutions. Significant portions of the War on Poverty copied the Mobilization for Youth program in New York City; hot lines and youth crisis centers originated in a few cities; free trade zones and cooperative markets evolved within counterculture communities; and free, experimental schools have sprung up almost overnight in communities throughout the country. The process seems to be that as a need is recognized as being unmet by existing institutions, the community (or some influential component) may differentiate a new institution to fill the need, or may modify an existing institution to incorporate the service. In some communities, hot lines are part of mental health clinics, and crash pads for runaways are maintained by churches.

Community institutions pose special problems to social workers and other professionals seeking to be change agents. Institutions are systems and do seek to maintain themselves. This might be done through morphogenesis by modifying structure and function to better fulfill community needs. However, as systems they also seek to remain the same (morphostasis). Thus institutional provisions generally lag in meeting emergent community needs. As Thorstein Veblen wrote in 1899, "institutions are . . . adapted to past circumstances, and are therefore never in full accord with the requirements of the present. In the nature of the case, this process of selective adaptation can never catch up with the progressively changing situation in which the community finds itself at any given time" (Boguslaw, 1965, pp. 150–151).

SOCIAL CLASS AND CASTE

Another important facet of community structure is social class. Studies of social stratification have substantiated social class or status groupings in various communities. Hollingshead's *Elmtown's Youth* is among the most ingenious of these studies, and has been a fountainhead for others (Hollingshead, 1949; Vidich and Bensman, 1958). Some major differentiating characteristics found by researchers have been income, life style, and access to services. Diagrams of class structure vary from a diamond-shaped structure, with most persons in the middle class, to an extreme pyramidal structure with either very few poor in some wealthy suburban communities, or very few wealthy in some Appalachian communities (Figure 3).

Another differentiation within communities may be that of caste. While many Americans deny that caste status exists in the United States, it does seem to exist

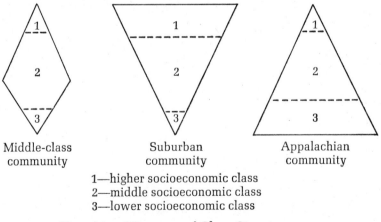

Middle-class   Suburban   Appalachian
community   community   community

1—higher socioeconomic class
2—middle socioeconomic class
3—lower socioeconomic class

Figure 3.   Diagrams of Class Structure.

if one means an impermeable boundary, a status assigned by virtue of some characteristic beyond a person's control (skin color, sex, age) from which the person cannot fully escape. Caste seems to exist for Mexican-Americans, Sino-Americans, and American Indians in many communities, and for blacks throughout the United States. Some thoughtful observers maintain that caste is a fact of life for women as well.

3. *Behavioral Aspects.* Among the most important behavioral aspects of the community is that of *social control.* The overall purpose of social control is to maintain the system, not necessarily to maintain the status quo. Social control may be exerted by the entire community through its network of values and goals, which are embodied in its institutions or in one institution. This institution may act on behalf of the entire community or it may, as sometime happens, act on behalf of some group or special interest. For example, blacks in ghettos have voiced complaints that police do not act in their behalf to protect their property or lives, but only to enforce order on behalf of white businessmen and property owners. The "web of urban institutions" that operates to enforce racial discrimination has been convincingly documented and analyzed (Knowles and Prewitt, 1969).

SOCIAL CONTROL

In nonplace communities, social control may be exerted by formal or informal sanctions. Amish men who secretly buy television sets are banished from church, and not spoken to by other Amish people for months or years (Gehman, 1970). In a professional community such as nursing or teaching, sanctions may include temporary loss of license, or a public notice that the employer is blacklisted. Such a blacklist was used during the Ocean Hill–Brownsville controversy in New York. Public schools that allegedly had violated professional codes in hiring and firing practices were blacklisted (Levine, 1969; Urofsky, 1970).

Social control is modified (but not necessarily lessened) by the overlapping memberships that community members have. Power structure and decision-making studies have revealed the interlocking positions held by some persons in the community (Domhoff, 1971). The same family may be represented on the public library board, the planning and zoning commission, the board of directors of a bank, and also operate a large business. Such overlapping memberships may lessen the effect of centralized social control, or may aggrandize it. The Lynds's 1929 study of Middletown indicated that whatever the formal arrangements may have been, the commercial leaders of the community exerted considerable social control.

A related aspect of community, and one that has received increasing attention during the past 20 years, is that of "community power." Presthus comments:

> Simply put, individuals of similar interests combine to achieve their ends, and such combinations of interlaced values and interests form subsystems of power. The community is composed of a congeries of such subsystems, now co-operating, now competing, now engaged, now moribund, in

terms of the rise and fall of local issues. Some subsystems are more powerful than others; some are transitory; others persist, one supposes, because
the interests which they institutionalize are persistent. (Presthus, 1964,
p. 6)

The classic study is Floyd Hunter's *Community Power Structure* (1953),
which is the most frequently imitated study. Hunter's basic findings have not
been challenged by any subsequent studies. He found that the powerful persons
in the community were heads of large commercial enterprises, especially banking
and finance; and that other leadership was composed of professional men, and a
few representatives of government and labor. Hunter found that within the group
of those who were powerful, a relatively small number were "policy makers," or
the "power elite" of the community. Other, somewhat different studies by
C. Wright Mills (1956, 1948, 1951), G. William Domhoff (1967, 1968), and
others largely confirm the existence of a power elite, although the dispute continues between "elite" theorists and "pluralist" theorists as to whether there is any
single, dominant power group (Banfield, 1961; Domhoff, 1967; Hunter, 1953;
A. Rose, 1967).

The process by which powerful persons exert control and how decisions are
influenced is the subject of another group of studies, which overlap the community
power studies to some extent. These "decision-making" studies largely attend to
specific cases, and examine the factors that entered into these decisions. Hunter,
Dahl, and Banfield each derived decision-making models that ranged from the
bureaucratic, pyramid model in which decisions were made "at the top," to
"mutual adaptation" models in which decisions were made by consensus in a
decentralized fashion. These two models have some relation, of course, to the
argument between the elite and pluralist power theorists. In these studies, it was
found that the political structure played an important, but not necessarily dominant
role. Decisions were made by subsystems differentiated by social class, or organizational position, or by the kind of institution being represented. The informal
decision-making structure was often as influential, or more so, than the formal
(including political) one.

SOCIALIZATION

Socialization is essential to the life of a community. Some utopian communities have been unable to maintain themselves as their members died. New
members must be secured to supply new energy, or the community becomes
entropic. Iowa, for example, faces the continuation of a trend toward higher
mean age because of the number of young Iowans who emigrate to other states.
This is serious enough that the state legislature considered requiring medical
school graduates to remain in Iowa.

Communities must enculturate the newcomer, however. The complaints of
urban northerners that Appalachian immigrants leave junk cars in the yard, throw
their garbage out the window, and tie clothes lines to their neighbors' houses
point to the difficulty of socialization to an urban setting. Some communities

have had to attempt to socialize deviant subcommunities (counterculture communes) that reject established community values, specifically norms of productivity, health, and appearance. In the face of such deviations, communities have attempted to apply social control in the form of jail sentences, compulsory socialization (enforcing truancy laws, mandatory work programs for relief recipients), or expulsion. Expulsion took the form of "warning out"—persons likely to become recipients of public assistance were told to leave the county. This was practiced in some states as late as 1959.

If deviation is not reduced or removed, communities may adapt to the deviant values by creating new institutions (as discussed earlier), just as public schools and settlement houses were created to socialize millions of immigrants from Europe, and Project Headstart to socialize racial minorities.

There are more informal means of socialization: parades and fourth of July celebrations socialize citizens into wider patriotic values. Formal ceremonies may mark induction to the community: the Jewish Bar or Bas Mitzvah, Christian baptism, freshman hazing, and naturalization ceremonies are examples. Rites of passage symbolize the socialization of a person into a new status.

COMMUNICATION

A highly important aspect of community system behavior is that of *communication*. Institutions such as churches and schools carry on some communication, but the major communications activities occur between persons face-to-face, and by public media such as newspapers, television, and radio. In British, early American, and some Sioux communities, for example, this function was performed by the town crier or his equivalent. Billboards, soapboxes, loudspeakers, sirens, pamphlets, and flyers are all means of communication used and controlled by segments of the community to impart symbols of the community's way of life. "The essence of community, as John Dewey suggested, is communication. For without communication there cannot be that interaction by which common meanings, common life, and common values are established" (M. Ross, 1955). "Communication has even more meaning in that a social system survives only as each significant component performs its particular specialty for the total system. In the social world this is not done by a unit isolating itself and following its own interests but by participating as expected in a network of relationships" (Sanders, 1958).

Components of the community system can monitor each other's performance, and are provided with directives via feedback linkages such as newspaper reports of governmental meetings, public hearings on controversial issues, and elections. In some nonplace communities, such as Synanon, specific times are set aside for mutual criticism by members. In some religious denominations and in Alcoholics Anonymous, testimonials serve a feedback function. This feedback is evident in the following comments on the use of a systems model in planning of communities:

> the use of this model in planning has demonstrated its many implications
> for the design and operational implementation of delivery systems, espe-

cially for community programs (e.g. "comprehensive community health" programs). The ecological systems approach insures that the entire process of planning for a community is rooted in the realities and needs of that community. The organized identification of the ecological systems making up a target community allows for the planned inclusion of information collection stations in each key system and at primary interfaces which provide feedback to the planning arena, thus setting up a servo-system which assures that planning will remain closely related to a changing need. (Sager and Kaplan, 1972, p. 312)

D. Social Work as a Nonplace Community

An example of a profession as a nonplace community seems relevant here. An established profession claims for itself, and is recognized by society as responsible for, a symbolic territory. Almost by definition, when a group carves out for itself a societal function or some part of the society's total stock of ideas, it becomes defined as a profession. When the societal function of instructing the young was delegated to and assumed by teachers, the next step was inevitably the formation and protection of territory by professional teachers' organizations. The same can be said of medicine, law, and the ministry, the three so-called "established" professions. It can be said as well of the newer, developing professions of law enforcement, nursing, engineering, and social work. Werner Boehm, in discussing social work, said of professions that:

> A domain of specialized knowledge must develop . . . which will furnish the theoretical underpinnings for the practice skills by which the profession expresses its function. In the absence of specialized knowledge at least the technical means—for example, techniques or skills whereby the professional is characterized and differentiated from the nonprofessional or layman—need to be specified. (Boehm, 1965, p. 641)

Boehm makes the concept of professional territory concrete: "each profession has a specific or core function and in a sense holds a monopoly on this function. . . . however, each profession shares with all other professions in society what Hiltner has called a village green, a common area that is peripheral to each profession" Boehm, 1965, p. 642). Clearly social work, psychiatry, nursing, education, and law enforcement, among other professions, share a "village green."

The major commonality among the professions is that they are sanctioned by society to bring about change that is beneficial to the social system and its components. Historically, social work has concerned itself with change among microsystems (persons, families, small groups) more than macrosystems. But it has dealt with societal and community change as well, although these have been the domains of other professional groups such as political scientists and sociologists. There are indications that social work is enlarging its territorial claims, and border disputes between professions within the same institution are common. Examples include social work and law, within the juvenile court; social work and psychiatry, in mental health institutions; and social work and educators, in the schools. Clearly there are border disputes between home economists and family counselors; between nurses and doctors; and between teachers and guidance counselors.

Boehm points to other characteristics of community that distinguish a profession: a common system of values and ethics (way of life, or culture); a group identity that holds the allegiance of the members; and social control and socialization within the profession. Clearly these are all matters of concern, currently, to a professional community that must decide its relationships to practitioners whose commitments are more radical and at the same time its relationship to society.

COMMUNITY AS SYSTEM—A SUMMARY STATEMENT

Because the term carries many meanings, *community* is an elusive concept. Meanings range from the territorial community of Robert Park and the Chicago sociologists to the almost mystical "mind" community of more recent writers. Two current critiques of the concept particularly germane to social work are those by Chatterjee and Koleski (1970) and Meenaghan (1972), which review the literature of community and conclude that the concept of community is an evolving one. Each work concludes that community is a perspectivistic idea— that is, it is futile to attempt to understand a total community, but worthwhile to select issues or problems and then define community as it is relevant to these particular concerns. Such a stance is in agreement with our use of the concept in this book. We view community as a social system, and as such to be perceived from a particular perspective. To do this it is necessary to have criteria for classifying patterns of relatedness as a system and then to further distinguish community from family, group, or organization. These criteria include the elements of the composite definition suggested earlier:

1. a system intermediate between society and microsystems,
2. consciously identified population—a sense of belongingness,
3. organized and engaged in common pursuits,
4. differentiation of functions,
5. adapting to environment through energy exchange, and
6. (most important of all) creates and maintains organizations and institutions to fulfill needs of both subsystems and environment.

A community may or may not occupy common physical space. The boundary of a community may or may not coincide with the boundary of a political subdivision—city, town, or county. Communities can, and do, interlace through the overlapping memberships of significant subsystems.

II. ORGANIZATION AS SYSTEM

Our society is an organizational society. We are born in organizations, educated by organizations, and most of us spend much of our lives working for organizations. We spend much of our leisure time paying, playing, and praying in organizations. Most of us will die in an organization, and when the time comes for burial, the largest organization of all—the state —must grant official permission. (Etzioni, 1964, p. 1)

The fact that ours is an organization society was noted by observers from virtually the first day of the United States, but social workers and other professionals have been slow to recognize this, and to take it into account in appraisal of human behavior. Otto Pollak comments: "If ever this writer were asked to propose a further development of the theoretical underpinning of social work practice, he would put the emphasis on an integration of organization theory and psychoanalytic theories of personality development" (Pollak, 1968, p. 52).

The nature of organizations has been incompletely understood, and even the most sophisticated organization theorists readily admit that there is no single definitive theory. Miller writes:

> Organization theory is a field without a large body of empirically established fact. Like medicine before 1930, management science is based largely upon case studies. . . .
> Scholars in this area would also profit from an agreement . . . as to what are the basic subsystems common to all organizations. I suggest that comparisons with the other levels of living systems can provide this. A generally accepted taxonomy of types of organizations is also desirable, and general systems behavior theory may be able to provide it. . . . (Miller, 1972, p. 174)

Definitions of organizations have ranged from whole volumes to the admirably concise but somewhat cryptic one by C. Wright Mills: "An organization is a system of roles graded by authority" (Presthus, 1962, p. 4). Probably Talcott Parsons's statement is as clear as most definitions.

> Organizations are social units (or human groups) deliberately constructed to seek specific goals. Corporations, armies, schools, hospitals, churches, and prisons are included; tribes, classes, ethnic groups, friendship groups, and families are excluded. Organizations are characterized by: (1) divisions of labor, power, and communication responsibilities. . .; (2) the presence of one or more power centers which control the concerted efforts of the organization and direct them toward its goals. . .; (3) substitution of personnel. . . (Parsons, 1960, p. 17)

This definition relies on specific examples, in part, because the organization is difficult to distinguish from society and from community. Parsons mentions differentiation, power, goals, and the substitution of one person for another as characteristic; each of these is true to some degree of societies and communities as well. Certainly *some* organizations are less characterized by these than are *some* societies and communities. Thus the differences are not in the presence or absence of these characteristics, but rather the form they take. This will be expanded on at several points, particularly in the conclusion to this chapter. Consistent with Parsons's view, characteristics to be stressed in section B in this discussion of organizations are goals, differentiation, power, control, leadership, and communication.

A. Theories of Organization

There are four major types of organization theory, to which we add a fifth, systems.

1. The Classical Model. This is sometimes called the "machine theory" because it "started with the assumption that the member of an organization was essentially a physiological unit" (Dubin, 1961, p. 28). He could be treated as a cog in the machine, so far as production was concerned. The organization, likewise, was viewed as a larger-scale machine with interchangeable parts and clearly identifiable operations. The model stressed the formal structure of the organization.

Principles of this formal organization include: (1) division of labor, with each unit performing specific tasks, (2) unity of control, that is centralized control, (3) pyramid of control, with each unit subordinate to one above it in the hierarchy, and (4) a center of authority with a top of the pyramid from which control emanates. The emphasis on control and mechanical regulation is apparent. This model further stresses the rational aspects of the organization. These two aspects, control and rationality, are the prime characteristics of this model.

Mumford has traced Organization Man to earliest recorded history.

> Behind every later process of organization and mechanization one must, however, recognize primordial aptitudes, deeply engrained in the human organism—indeed, shared with many other species—for ritualizing behavior and finding satisfaction in a repetitive order that establishes a human connection with organic rhythms and cosmic events.
>
> Organization Man is the common link between the ancient and the modern type of megamachine: that is perhaps why the specialized func-tionaries, with their supporting layer of slaves, conscripts and subjects—in short, the controllers and the controlled—have changed so little in the last five thousand years. (Mumford, 1970, p. 277)

2. The Human Relations Theory. Partly as a reaction to "machine theory," human relations theory as exemplified by Elton Mayo, Kurt Lewin, and indirectly, John Dewey (Etzioni, 1964, p. 32) stresses the *in*formal structure, and the emotional, nonrational motivations that operate in organizations. Such factors as communication, participation, and leadership are emphasized. The best known studies issuing from this school are the Hawthorne studies, including the Bank Wiring Room study (Mayo, 1945; Olmsted, 1959, pp. 25–32; Roethlisberger and Dickson, 1947). The results of these studies indicated decisively that other factors besides rational, impersonal motivation affected the production of workers.

In the best known example, now known as the "Hawthorne effect," it was found that the highest motivation for one group of workers was neither money nor working conditions, but rather the fact that they were a special group being researched! The general conclusion that sets this theory apart from the "machine model" is that workers do not function as separate, distinct units, but rather as members of groups. The influence of the small group became readily apparent. Litwin labels this the "social system" school because it stresses the systemic properties within the organization (Litwin, 1968, pp. 52 ff.). This is however far too narrow a use of "social system."

3. *Structuralist Theory*. The structuralists, who include Karl Marx and Max Weber, represent in some respects a synthesis of the above two theories in that they recognize both formal and informal structures and their interaction as significant. They agree with the classical theorists that the search for rationality is not necessarily opposed to the happiness of the persons within the organization; they differ in the balance of the two that is to be achieved.

The major difference between the structuralists and the two previous theories is that the former recognize the inevitability of conflict within the organization. "The Structuralist sees the organization as a large, complex social unit in which many social groups interact. . . . The various groups might cooperate in some spheres and compete in others, but they hardly are or can become one big happy family as Human Relations writers often imply" (Etzioni, 1964, p. 41).

This theory resembles systems theory in that it recognizes components within the organization, and that these components frequently conflict. It does not view conflict as a problem, as do the previous two theories. Lewis Coser, for example, spells out the positive contributions that conflict can make to an organization, in that it may force a confrontation that leads to a test of power (Coser, 1964).

4. *Neoclassical, or Decision System Theory*. Etzioni calls this the neoclassical school in that it, too, is concerned with the achievement of rational decision-making *whenever possible*. Chester I. Barnard, H. A. Simon, and J. G. March are the leaders in this theory development. They recognize that there is, in addition to the "horizontal" differentiation by task, a "vertical" differentiation by "levels of decisions" made. This differentiation is made on the basis of power—that is whose decisions are binding upon whom. They distinguish between policy-making and policy implementation.

Perhaps most important is the qualification *whenever possible*. This school holds that human behavior in organizations is best described as "intendedly rational" (Simon, 1945, p. 196). Thus they recognize the nonrational aspects of decision-making in organizations. Also emphasized is "search behavior," the concept that an organization does not seek endlessly for perfectly rational behavior, but instead seeks *satisfying* solutions that are "reasonably good" or "acceptable" (Etzioni, 1964, pp. 30–31).

COMPARISON OF THESE MODELS WITH SYSTEMS MODEL.

The model suggested here, although not without fault, seems to us to avoid the pitfalls of the earlier models. The systems model of organizations agrees with the decision system model that the goal is not perfection. It goes one step further by stating that goal-seeking behavior is not necessarily the primary behavior of a system at all times. Goal attainment is essential and is occurring at all times, as pointed out in the first chapter of this book. But, as Talcott Parsons says, one basic function is concentrated upon only to the detriment of other basic functions, and thus exclusive or primary attention upon goal attainment neglects other essential functions of the system.

The systems model also stresses a wider context of decision-making and organizational behavior than is pictured in other theories. It takes into account environmental influences as well as the influences wielded by groups within the organization. Conflict is seemingly better explained by the systems model in that it recognizes the inevitability of conflict within and between systems, each of which holds to the legitimacy of its own goal. Miller states the systems point of view well:

> No decision is entirely rational or satisfactory, a fact which can give administrators some solace. There is no perfect rational solution to most administrative problems. The higher the echelon, the truer this is of the issues which confront it. The dimensions along which many decisions must be made are incommensurable. Human lives are incommensurable with money. Money is incommensurable with time. Time is incommensurable with professional excellence. Yet all of these are in scarce supply to a given organization and trade-offs among them must be decided upon. (Miller, 1972, p. 79)

Control is also pictured differently in the systems model. It is, like goal attainment, exclusively pursued only to the detriment of other functions, and other functions do take precedence at times. This lends a flexibility to the systems model, and allows for understanding variant forms of organization not permitted by the classical model.

One item of comparison must be left unanswered. This is the question of inevitable alienation of the person from the goals of the organization. Classical theory assumed that rational behavior on the part of workers would prevent such alienation. Human relations theory saw such alienation as inevitable. This is similar to the entropic principle, in that organizations would degenerate into randomness and disorganization if the member's personal needs were not tended to. Structuralists and decision system theorists both recognize that rationality is struggled for; the latter theory recognizes that the struggle occurs within the context of power, and not necessarily on neutral territory. Both seem to suggest that alienation is inevitable, but that alienation carries with it the seeds of its own resolution.

5. The Systems Model. Gouldner refers to this as the "natural-system model":

The natural-system model regards the organization as a "natural whole." The realization of the goals of the system as a whole is but one of several important needs to which the organization is oriented. . . .

Organizational structures are viewed as spontaneously and homeostatically maintained. Changes in organizational patterns are considered the results of cumulative, unplanned, adaptive responses to threats to the equilibrium of the system as a whole. . . .

The focus is not on deviations from rationality but, rather, on disruptions of organizational equilibrium. . . .

The natural-system model is typically based upon an underlying "organismic" model which stresses the interdependence of the component parts. (Gouldner, 1961, pp. 394–395)

Barnard (Barnard, 1961, p. 19) and March and Simon stress the organic analogy as well. The latter carry the analogy further:

A biological analogy is apt here, if we do not take it too literally or too seriously. Organizations are assemblages of interacting human beings and they are the largest assemblages in our society that have anything resembling a central coordinative system. Let us grant that these coordinative systems are not developed nearly to the extent of the central nervous system in higher biological organisms—that organizations are more earthworm than ape. Nevertheless, the high specificity of structure and coordination within organizations—as contrasted with the diffuse and variable relations *among* organizations and among unorganized individuals—marks off the individual organization as a sociological unit comparable in significance to the individual organism in biology. (March and Simon, 1961, p. 31)

Presthus emphasizes that large organizations are similar to society as a system, in that they have specialization, hierarchy, and authority, and that they socialize their members in similar fashion (Presthus, 1962, pp. 94–95). The structural and functional characteristics of organizations as systems of human behavior, and their similarities and differences from other systems, are discussed in the remainder of this chapter.

B. Characteristics of Organizational Systems

Kahn claims that it is correct to discuss the "job to be done" by organizations, and to call this *the* function. He suggests that other activities that contribute to the overall functioning of the organization should be called "subfunctions" (Kahn, 1969, p. 145).

1. Goal Attainment. Parsons defines organizations as those systems that give primacy to goal attainment (Landsberger, 1961, p. 215). While no system gives goal attainment primacy at all times, organizations are goal-directed to a greater degree than other systems. Miller emphasizes this when he states the following definition of an organization as a "goal seeking system which has interacting goal-seeking subsystems with different goals arranged in a hierarchy" (Miller, 1972, p. 5).

What is an organizational goal? Etzioni says that a goal is "a desired state of affairs which the organization attempts to realize" (Etzioni, 1964, p. 6). In this sense, a goal may be expressed by a myth or by a rational, projected set of specific objectives—that is, it may be "maximum service to the client" or "caseloads of 50, with short-term crisis intervention allowing for attention to 50 percent more clients than at present." The goal expressed by either is a future state of the agency in which its assigned purposes are being fulfilled. These goals guide the organization in its activity; they legitimize or fail to legitimize specific actions undertaken or contemplated by the organization.

Etzioni's conception of goal is similar to the "ego ideal" of the person in some regards, and to the self toward which one strives in Sartre's form of existentialism or Maslow's "self-actualization." In fact, Argyris says that research "points up quite clearly that the importance of the organization as an organism worthy of self-actualization is now being recognized" (Argyris, 1961, p. 71).

Two aspects of goal attainment should be distinguished. *Effectiveness* refers to the degree to which the organization achieves its goals; *efficiency* refers to the manner in which it is done, specifically the amount of energy and resources necessary to achieve a goal. The former is part of the GE and GI function of systems; the latter is part of the SE and SI functions. Efficiency in an organization requires reduction of conflict (or friction) within the organization; thus some internal control of the utilization of energy is necessary for goal attainment. One example would be the coaches' encouragement of team spirit with its implied reduction of intrasquad animosities in a football team, so that its points (or goals) may be scored.

As several theorists point out, goals are not static. Goals can be *displaced;* that is, other goals can be substituted for them. The most frequent form of this is making ends of means. For example, efficiency in public welfare is a means to effective service to clients and society, but all too often efficiency in the form of economy through accounting for each dollar spent becomes an end in itself. When this occurs the completed forms become more important than the clients they represent. Another example is the accusation by many university students that universities have displaced education with research, resulting in lower-quality instruction.

Other forms of goal change are *succession,* in which an organization achieves its initial goal, and establishes another; or the goal disappears and the organization turns to new goals. Examples of this include those private welfare agencies that began as adoption agencies in an era when there were more abandoned children than now, and whose goals have become treatment of emotionally disturbed children or family treatment. Both Christmas Seals and the March of Dimes established new goals after attaining their original goals.

There may also be goal *multiplication.* The Red Cross, which began as a service on the battlefield to soldiers, broadened its goals to include services to soldiers' widows and orphans, and eventually to disaster relief. There are, of course, advantages and disadvantages to such goal multiplication. Among possible advantages are that synergism may increase the effectiveness of an organization, and recruitment may be easier because workers enjoy variety. Disadvantages include shortage of energy, or conflict between goals. An example of the latter might be the conflict between the child welfare worker's concern for the unwed mother's future, and the welfare department's desire to economize by allowing the child to remain with its mother.

2. Differentiation. This is more pronounced in organizations than in other social systems. Differentiation is the prime sociological characteristic of modernization, according to Etzioni (Etzioni, 1964, p. 106). Modernization means essentially that modern society is a society of organizations.

> Differentiation . . . makes possible the formation of "artificial" social units, deliberately designed for the efficient service of (specific) functions. . . .
> Moreover, we now have secondary differentiation in each sphere—i.e., the emergence of subspecialties each with an organizational structure geared to its own needs. Thus the vocational high school is different from the academic high school, and a mass-production corporation differs from a small business. (Etzioni, 1964, pp. 106–107)

Durkheim pointed out that differentiation of tasks within an organization was not all good; that if the worker did not see and understand the activities parallel to his own, and was not "horizontally" related to it, he was nothing but "an inert piece of machinery." He must "keep in constant relations with neighboring functions. . . . not lose sight of his collaborators, that he acts upon them, and reacts to them. He is, then, not a machine" (Durkheim, 1961, p. 43). That differentiation may lead to such isolation of the components of a system is apparent in offices and factories where there is no exchange between clerical and professional staff or between production and management.

3. Power and Control. In the definition of organizations by Parsons given earlier in this section, the existence of one or more "power centers" that control the organization's efforts is acknowledged. Robert Bierstedt states it even more emphatically: "Power supports the fundamental order of society and the social organization within it, wherever there is order. Power stands behind every association and sustains its structure. *Without power there is no organization and without power there is no order"* (Bierstedt, 1961, p. 246). One characteristic of organizations as distinct from other systems is the explicitness of power; it is largely visible and institutionalized. But what is power?

A widely used definition of power in political science Robert Dahl's: "A has power over B to the extent that he can get B to do something B would not otherwise do" (Dahl, 1957, pp. 201–215). Similarly, Bierstedt says:

> Power is the ability to employ force, not its actual employment, the ability to apply sanctions, not their actual application. Power is the ability to introduce force into a social situation; it is the presentation of force. Unlike force, incidentally, power is always successful; when it is not successful it is not, or ceases to be, power. Power symbolizes the force which *may* be applied in any social situation and supports the authority which is applied. Power is thus neither force nor authority but, in a sense, their synthesis. (Bierstedt, 1961, p. 243)

What we mean by force, in systems terms, is the application or deprivation of energy so as to affect the functioning of another system. Force should not be taken to mean only physical force; moral force or Gandhi's Truth Force qualify as well. Since power is an energy function, it is finite. In other words, energy expended to influence the behavior of others may deplete the power potential.

Miller's definition is more terse. "In my conceptual system I use the word *power* as the ability of a system to elicit compliance from other systems" (Miller, 1972, p. 66). We will define power, then, as the system's potential to achieve its goals by the application of energy (or the deprivation of energy) to another system or component so as to affect the functioning of another system or component. The degree of effectiveness of power depends upon the extent to which the target system is affected, and the extent to which the goal is achieved. One example is the use of federal funds for Appalachian development. The goal was social and economic change; the result was an improved highway system and some new courthouses, which benefited the residents of the county seat towns and the politicians. A great deal of energy (funds and propaganda) was expended, but although there were some substantial achievements, they were not the ones originally intended. In this instance the federal government's power to achieve its goals was shown to be ineffective. If the federal government's covert goal was *political,* its power to achieve its goals through the political system of Appalachia was quite effective. Power must thus be measured by its objectives, not simply by the magnitude of its effects.

We consider power and control to be similar, except that *control* suggests longer duration and wider influence over another system than does power. This is similar to Miller's term *influence:* "*Influence* is a more pervasively exercised power relationship. It exists whenever one system is able to bring about significant alterations in the actions of another system over which it may or may not have the right to exercise authority" (Miller, 1972, p. 68). Further, power may have other effects than control. The application of power could release control, as might happen in casework or some other form of social work intervention.

> the success of an organization is largely dependent upon its ability to maintain control of its participants.
>
> All social units control their members, but the problem of control in organizations is especially acute. Organizations as social units that serve specific purposes are artificial social units. They are planned, deliberately

structured; they constantly and self-consciously review their performances and restructure themselves accordingly. (Etzioni, 1964, p. 58)

The problem of control is especially apparent in the following example, reported from Vietnam by correspondents Horst Faas and Péter Arnett.

> A reporter was present at a hamlet burned down by the U.S. Army's 1st Air Cavalry Division in 1967. Investigation showed that the order from the division headquarters to the brigade was: "On no occasion must hamlets be burned down."
> The brigade radioed the battalion: "Do not burn any hamlets unless you are absolutely convinced that the Viet Cong are in them."
> The battalion radioed the infantry company at the scene: "If you think there are any Viet Cong in the hamlet, burn it down."
> The company commander ordered his troops: "Burn down that hamlet." (Miller, 1972, p. 69)

Implicit in this effort to control is the expectation at each level that some control must be exerted in order to limit the activities at the next lower echelon; but with each descending level, the latitude allowed was enlarged. Miller suggests that such distortions may have accounted for the My Lai massacre of Vietnamese civilians in 1968, which resulted in trial and conviction of some participants, and a review of the manner in which such orders were given. Parsons included this "construction and reconstruction to seek specific goals" in his definition of organizations. Control is based upon goals and the degree to which they are being achieved.

There are three forms of control, as Etzioni describes them: physical control, material rewards, such as "goods and services," and symbolic rewards (Etzioni, 1964, pp. 47–59). Symbolic rewards are in many ways the most significant, in that one's sense of who one is and what value one has is derived from symbolic interaction with others, as noted in the previous chapter. Symbolic rewards are most likely to be used by the systems with the least coercive power or material rewards—religious denominations are perhaps the prime examples. The casework relationship is an example, when it does not involve money grants; what is offered is acceptance and esteem. Going to a psychiatrist might symbolize prestige as well, for some people.

In this light, social work, nursing, or education can be regarded as means of social control, in that they assist an organization such as the school, hospital, prison, or army to increase the person's commitment to it or control his behavior.

   4. Leadership. Leadership may be either formal or informal. Leadership includes power and control used to achieve organizational ends and make means effective. *Command* is defined as the use of power to insure compliance, while *leadership* is defined as a "continually creative function involving constant appraisal." The distinction is really that between power and authority, or "authority of position," and "authority of leadership" (Dubin, 1961, p. 350). "Authority of position depended upon centrality in the organization's communications system— it was determined by a structural decision—while authority of leadership was dependent upon the superior ability of the leader" (Zaleznik and Jardim, 1967, p. 217).

In other words, command derives from the organizational position, from the role and status, while leadership derives from the personal characteristics of the leader. But leadership is not solely dependent upon these personal qualities:

> No single set of personal traits essential to the performance of managerial jobs has yet been established to the general satisfaction of psychologists and personnel experts. Different combinations of qualities may carry different men equally far. The qualities needed depend on some extent on the nature of the job and of the organizational environment in which the job is placed. (Gordon and Howell, 1961, p. 161)

This illustrates the mutual multicausation that is part of systems theory. Leadership depends also upon the linkages the leader has with those he leads; he is limited by this interdependency. "If a system once accepted destroys that mutual adaptation of behavior of leaders and followers—either because it reaches ineffective decisions, or destroys leadership or divides followers—then disorganization, schism, rebellion, or conformance to a new system ensues" (Barnard, 1961a, p. 357).

Robert Townsend, former president of Avis ("We Try Harder"), comments that a leader can permit conflict within the organization

> up to a point. A good manager doesn't try to eliminate conflict; he tries to keep it from wasting the energies of his people. . . .
> If you're the boss and your people fight you openly when they think you're wrong—that's healthy. If your men fight each other openly in your presence for what they believe in—that's healthy. But keep all the conflict eyeball to eyeball. (Townsend, 1970, p. 39)

Again, if systems are untended, entropy results.

It should be added here that leadership, like power, is not only hierarchical, but lateral. Leadership occurs at all levels; groups do operate within organizations and leadership emerges from these. In some organizations, such emergence of leadership at lower levels is deliberately cultivated; the usual manner in which this is done is decentralization of decision-making. In essence, this is the concept behind the Creative Federalism or New Federalism as espoused by Governor Rockefeller of New York and President Nixon—decentralizing the decisions of government and returning initiative to lower levels, state, city, and county governments. The mechanism for accomplishing this is revenue sharing.

C. Structure: The Bureaucratic Situation

The term *bureaucratic situation* is borrowed from Presthus, who uses it to describe the total environment provided by large organizations (Presthus, 1962,

p. 4). We use it in the same sense, knowing that not all organizations are characterized by what is usually referred to derogatorily as bureaucracy.

Bureaucracy is a phenomenon contemporary with industrialization. Its primary theorist is Max Weber. Weber's primary concern was power: the distribution of power, control of power, the legitimation and use of power, and the satisfaction derived from membership in the organization. It is clear from Weber's writings that organizational structure is intended to permit and regulate the exercise of power.

The principles of bureaucracy are:

1. a clear-cut division of labor corresponding to a high degree of specialization in tasks;
2. a hierarchy of office in which each officeholder or employee is under the control and supervision of a higher one;
3. a consistent system of abstract rules in which tasks must be performed to assure coordination through uniformity of work results;
4. impersonality in the conduct of the office;
5. career employment within the organization; and
6. machine-like efficiency (Pollak, 1968, p. 51).

These are, of course, characteristic of the machine model. To these should be added that:

7. transactions are reported in writing and carefully checked and filed; and
8. ideally, positions are filled by persons fully trained and experienced to the degree required by that office (Washburne, 1964, pp. 41–42).

These principles are intended to protect the integrity of positions at all levels; like the feudal contract between lord and vassal which spelled out mutual obligations, these bureaucratic prescriptions detailed the rules for interactions. Blau says that "authority is strictly circumscribed and confined to those directives that are relevant for official operations. The use of status prerogatives to extend the power of control over subordinates beyond these limits does not constitute the legitimate exercise of bureaucratic authority" (Blau, 1956, p. 29).

Such rationality as is demanded by these rules and regulations is, as the human relations school pointed out, unrealistic. There are limits to rationality—"the capacity for self-denial which the rational organization requires cannot be developed within it; it depends upon the more encompassing social relationships that exist in the traditional family or charismatic movement" (Etzioni, 1964, p. 53).

There must be a basic commitment to the organization that is only partially rational. It inevitably involves emotive factors such as loyalty and sentiments about the worth of the organization and about oneself as a part of it. Such commitments, values, and feelings do not originate with the organization; they must begin in other systems.

> The citizens of modern societies are socialized to shift constantly among various social units such as the family, the community, and the work unit. . . . Tensions generated in one unit are released in another by changing partners . . . and by shifting back and forth between social units in which rational, efficient behavior is demanded (a form of behavior which is particularly taxing) and those in which the norm is non-rational (which is comparatively relaxing). (Etzioni, 1964, p. 73)

An organization member's estimate of his own value, and that of his organization, are greatly affected by the opinion of members of the other social systems to which he belongs. *Life* magazine once ran a feature concerning people who switched careers in middle-age, often because the work they were doing was not valued by their acquaintances (*Life,* Vol. 68, No. 22, June 12, 1970, pp. 50–56). (Ironically, *Life* itself has now terminated publication.)

Many writers have described the effects of bureaucratic organizations on the personalities of their members. Some have suggested a "bureaucratic personality." Etzioni describes the features of this personality: he (1) is accustomed to shifting between social units, especially the family and the organization; (2) has high toleration for frustration and the ability to defer gratification; and (3) has the psychic urge to achieve material and symbolic rewards (achievement orientation). Etzioni added this note about the relationship between organizations and other systems:

> The major credit for this convergence of personality and organizational requirements . . . must go to the modern family and the modern educational system, both of which produce the type of person who will make a good organization man. The middle-class stress on the values of punctuality, neatness, integrity, consistency, the accent on conformity, and above all achievement, are the foundation. . . . The organization's effectiveness . . . is due more to the social environment which provides the "right" kind of participants than to any deliberate efforts by the organization to shape personalities according to its needs. (Etzioni, 1964, p. 110)

The organization values the kind of personality that puts the organization's goals above its own; to the extent that the organization can enforce this, it has power over its members. Erich Fromm and others have shown that this is unhealthy behavior that encourages alienation because it is manipulative (Fromm, 1962, pp. 446–452). Presthus says this may result in "a subtle corrosion of integrity" (Presthus, 1962, p. 18). The reader is referred here to Erikson's definition of integrity (Erikson, 1968, p. 139).

D. Evolutionary Aspects

Are there alternatives to bureaucracy? Perhaps not in an industrial society for large numbers of people. Some organizations have attempted other forms of decentralized structures, with autonomous units that allow freedom and control to line workers (Bennis, 1969, pp. 44 ff.). Douglas McGregor's Theory Y reorganizes structure to delegate authority in a downward direction (McGregor, 1960).

Toffler suggests that we are currently witnessing the breakdown of bureaucracy and that it will in turn be supplanted by "Ad-hocracy" (Toffler, 1970, pp. 124–151). Ad-hocracy denotes an organizational scheme congruent with an era of accelerated change, wherein people are brought together on a task basis and disband once that task is completed. Toffler credits Bennis with first predicting the demise of bureaucracy and the rise of new forms of organization. Bennis comments:

> I anticipate an erratic environment where various organizations coexist at different stages of evolution. Rather than neat, linear, and uniform evolutionary developments, I expect that we will see both more centralization (in large-scale instrumental bureaucracies) and more decentralization (in delivery of health, education, and welfare services); both the increase of bureaucratic-pragmatic and/or revolutionary-charismatic leadership; both the increase in size and centralization of many municipal and governmental units and the proliferation of self-contained minisocieties. (Miller, 1972, p. 122)

According to one of Miller's hypotheses, increasing size generates greater variety of subsystems; the proliferation Bennis describes would seem to follow. Miller comments that organizations, unlike organisms or some groups such as a nuclear family, may outlast the lives of the original members. Because organizations can replace components and learn from experience, it may be true that the longer an organization lives, the better its chance for survival (Miller, 1972, p. 130). Miller further comments that old organizations are resistant to change, but that research is so far inconclusive. It would seem, for example, that the United States government has survived as the world's oldest democracy (excluding Great Britain, which is technically a monarchy) because of its ability to modify its internal structure and its adaptation to its environment. But, as Bennis indicates, the trends are mixed. The 1972 general election, for example, indicated public dissatisfaction with the speed of change; racial reforms were occurring too fast for some, but tax reform was occurring too slowly; centralization of power in the executive branch was feared by many, who cited the president's revenue sharing as organizational decentralization, and by others who cited control of prices and wages as organizational centralization.

One reason for the mixed nature of organizational change is the rapid diversification and expansion of major corporations during the past generation. As Miller describes it:

> Organizations are subsystems, components of subcomponents of societies, sometimes of more than one society. . . . International and supranational systems, such as General Motors and Interpol, have organizational components which exist in more than one society. . . . Organizational com-

ponents can also be inclusions in societies other than the one to whose subsystem structure they belong, e.g., Japanese marketing organizations in Australia and Canada. (Miller, 1972, p. 5)

Thoughtful analyses (including some by science fiction writers, notably Isaac Asimov) have suggested that the governments of the future may not be nation-states. Instead, international conglomerates may rule, and in some cases, more rationally. One hint that this speculation has some foundation is the comment by a former Secretary of Defense and president of General Motors that "What is good for General Motors is good for the U.S.A." (later satirized by Al Capp in "Lil Abner" as "What's good for General Bullmoose is good for the U.S.A."). It may well be that unless governments become equally adaptable, other organizations may absorb these functions as well. One authority comments:

> The internationalization of production has brought with it many new problems along the national-corporate interface. The lack of a consistent set of rules regulating the relationship between national governments and corporations, particularly in areas such as antitrust regulations, ownership rights, capital repatriation, labor relations, tax laws and the issuance of securities has been costly, particularly for poor countries. (L. Brown, 1972, p. 200)

While the future of organizations is unclear, and events seem mixed in their implications, Miller may be correct that organizations increase their potential for survival as they accrue longevity. The most successful organizations seem to be those that can adapt rapidly to a changing environment—altering goals and functions (as when the March of Dimes took on new research targets after polio was curbed), or altering structure (as aerospace industries have done with autonomous, shifting units that dissolve or merge as the specific task demands, or as a corporation that absorbs or sheds subsidiary companies according to its financial, research, or market needs does.)

Not only commercial organizations will be subject to the necessity of change. Miller suggests that persons may work for more than one organization; that part of one's time will be spent at one organization, part at another. This is a counterpart to Toffler's "modular" relationships between persons (Miller, 1972; Toffler, 1970). Such "plugging-in" would permit fairly rapid modification of organizational structures and necessitates greater professional identification beyond the particular organization that employs a professional. In fact, a significant number of professionals are presently related to two or more organizations, serving as consultants or part-time service workers. Many of these are regular employees of one organization, and moonlight or act in consultant roles in other organizations. It seems likely that this will become more common in the future. Perhaps, as Miller suggests, this will be the norm. If so, knowledge of organizations and how to work with, or within, them will be essential to effective professional practice.

III. COMMUNITIES AND ORGANIZATIONS: COMPARISONS

Probably the most succinct statement of the differences is Edward O. Moe's:

The community is a system of systems. A community, even a small one, includes a great many different institutions and organizations. . . . These organizations and groups are social systems and they are part of the social system of the community.

The community is not structurally and functionally centralized in the same sense as a formal organization. The great range and diversity of the needs, interests, goals and activities of the people of the community are met through a variety of separate institutions and groups—no one of which holds a completely dominant position in relation to the others.

The community as a social system is implicit in nature as compared with the explicitness of a formal organization. (Moe, 1966, p. 400)

The last point requires some elaboration here, and in part II of the next chapter. As noted at various points in the preceding discussion of organizations, the organization is artifically formed, rather than being natural in the same sense as families and other systems. March and Simon recognized that organizations are more highly coordinated and centralized than any other human system. Organizations are far more explicit in their functions and structures than other social systems. Organizational roles are more highly elaborated, stable and defined (even written) than other systems. These explicit mechanisms are necessary to permit predictability and control.

Thus we return to the theme that organizations, far more than communities, are goal-oriented; to maintain this concentration they must correspondingly give attention to control of the components. Thus social control is crucial in organizations. This cannot be sustained without supportive relationships with the society, communities, families, institutions, and persons among whom they exist.

SUGGESTED READINGS

Bennis, Warren G. "Post-Bureaucratic Leadership," *Trans-Action* 6, July/August, 1969, pp. 44 ff. An essay arguing that the nature of bureaucracy is such that it cannot accommodate to the acceleration of the pace of social change. Consistent with Toffler's views in *Future Shock*.

Blau, Peter. *Bureaucracy in Modern Society.* New York: Random House, 1956. A rich source for a societal view of bureaucracy.

Domhoff, G. William. *The Higher Circles.* New York: Vintage Books, 1971. One of the most thought-provoking of the studies of power structure. Presents a strong argument for the existence of a power elite in our society.

Etzioni, Amitai. *Modern Organizations.* Englewood Cliffs, N.J.: Prentice-Hall, 1964. An excellent, concise examination of theories of organizations and processes within them. Chapters 5 through 10 are especially recommended. (This has been used as the small-scale map for this chapter.)

Hillery, George A., Jr. *Communal Organizations: A Study of Local Societies*. Chicago: The University of Chicago Press, 1968. A superb, exhaustive examination of theory of the community. Should be read by anyone undertaking serious study of this system.

Miller, James G. "Living Systems: The Organization," *Behavioral Science* 17, 1, January, 1972, pp. 1–182. This is a chapter of Miller's forthcoming book. Miller is almost certainly the most generative systems theorist today. This exhaustive study of the organization is erudite and imaginative, with extensive illustrations of each hypothesis Miller extrapolates from his transsystem grid. Recommended for students who have some acquaintance with systems ideas.

Warren, Roland. *The Community in America*. Chicago: Rand McNally, 1963. A well-written general text on community. "The American Community as a Social System" (pp. 135–167) is particularly congruent with this chapter. Also recommended are Warren's *Perspectives on the American Community* (Chicago: Rand McNally, 1966), a collection of articles, and *Truth, Love, and Social Change* (Chicago: Rand McNally, 1971), essays relevant to social work practice in communities.

chapter 4
GROUPS

Nothing is harder to stop than a freely and fully united band of human beings.

Milton Mayer, *On Liberty: Man v. the State*

It is within the group that the power, basic and immense, human beings have over one another occurs: the power of acceptance or rejection.

Gisela Konopka, *Social Group Work*

INTRODUCTION

The human group is a social system that has received, and deserves, extensive investigation. The term *group* includes those patterns of association and activity in which persons engage most of their "selves" on a day to day basis. A holon composed of individuals and small constellations of persons, it is a component of its environment. To be a group it need be more than simply an aggregate of individuals; it has a unique wholeness of its own. As Lewin phrased it, "The whole is *different from* the sum of its parts: it has definite properties of its own" (Marrow, 1969, p. 170). (Note that the words "different from," not "more than," are used.) Thus the human group is to be viewed as a system; distinguishable from its environment, having the properties and functions of a system, and providing the connectiveness between its components and its environment.

The group also fulfills the basic character of social systems as exchanges of energy. Maslow's use of the term *synergy* (borrowed from anthropologist Ruth Benedict) has been applied to groups by Hampden-Turner:

> Synergy involves the resolution of the selfish/unselfish dichotomy by making the enhancement of the Other the precondition or result of personal enhancement. . . .
>
> Further evidence for synergy came from the supervisors' reports on

their work groups. There was a substantial increase in groups which reached decisions by mutual agreement and in reports that "differences in opinion are directly confronted and discussed to productive solutions." (Golembiewski and Blumberg, 1970, pp. 51–52)

Since the discussion of groups in this chapter is from a social systems viewpoint, a cluster of persons can be considered a group *only* if it fulfills certain specific criteria. Donald Campbell suggests that rather than starting with the assumption that aggregates are systems subject to analysis it is advisable to subject such aggregates to empirical examination to see whether they do in fact have the properties of systems. If the subject of such examination is not found to possess such properties, that is, cannot be established as a holon, then the analysis should be properly carried out at the next lower level (Campbell, 1958, pp. 14–25). A group with *a high level* of systems properties might be analyzed largely with group concepts, *a moderate level* with group and individual concepts, and *a low level* with individual concepts. In other words, a gathering together of persons does not a group make. The expression "the group jelled" conveys a point in time or process when an aggregate of persons became an entity, a group, distinguishable from its environment and different from the sum of its parts. This leads to two questions.

What are the significant properties of a group as system or entity?

What differentiates a group from an organization or community? (The family is dealt with in the next chapter as a distinctive form of group.)

The remainder of this chapter is addressed to these two questions.

I. DIMENSIONS OF GROUPS

There are as many kinds of groups as there are observers, leaders, and therapists. Rather than attempt a comprehensive taxonomy, we will discuss a few important dimensions that have been used to classify groups. These dimensions are polarities. Any given group, at any given time, theoretically could be placed on each of these continua.

Instrumental vs Expressive. Drawn from Parsons's formulation, this dichotomy is similar to others that are frequently used: "task vs sentiment," "goal achievement vs group maintenance," "task-oriented vs group-oriented," and "guidance behavior vs sociable behavior" (Olmsted, 1959, p. 135; Parsons, 1964b, pp. 79–88). The distinction is usually understood as being between a particular, articulated, time-limited objective and a diffuse, unarticulated, enduring group harmony. Further, the distinction is usually taken to imply that a "goal" or "task" is adaptive, that is, related to the environment; while "expression" or "sentiment" is related to interactions of the components of the group.

It seems to us that the distinction is best understood as a distinction between two steady states toward which the group could evolve. The first steady state is one in which some fairly clear, specific objective, with specific results for "vertical" relations (that is, group to suprasystem), has been accomplished (Warren, 1963, p. 161). The other steady state is one in which the objectives are fairly diffuse and unspecific with the general result of integration of components; that is, "horizontal" relations (Warren, 1963, pp. 161–162).

Consequently, in our view, "instrumental vs expressive" activities or orientations are intended to move the group toward one of these two steady states. Probably "adaptive vs integrative" would be more accurate. Bales agrees with this: "The social system, in its organization . . . tends to swing or falter indeterminately back and forth between these two theoretical poles: optimum adaptation to the outer situation at the cost of internal malintegration, or optimum internal integration at the cost of maladaptation to the outer situation" (Weisman, 1963, p. 87).

These are polarities, and are not mutually exclusive; that is, the "adaptive" steady state focuses *more* attention on goals and tasks, but deals with integration also, though to a lesser extent. The "integrative" steady state, conversely, does not exclude some adaptive activity. For example, the Supreme Court must spend some time mediating between the justices' personal feelings at times. A sensitivity group must decide upon meeting dates, and when termination should occur. Reginald Rose's play *Twelve Angry Men* illustrates the successive steady states of a jury as it alternately focuses upon the court's demand for a verdict and the members' needs (Rose, 1955). Whittaker's *We Thought We Heard the Angels Sing* provides a vivid picture of a group adrift on a raft for three weeks undergoing successive steady states (Whittaker, 1943).

It is this variability that makes the group difficult to characterize, as contrasted to the family, which is predominantly integrative, and the organization, which is predominantly adaptive. The community is largely made up of groups, and shares their indeterminate character; indeed, it is sometimes difficult to distinguish between communities and groups. We suggest this guideline: *The greater the breadth of influence upon its members and the more diffuse its goals, the more the group resembles a community.* Correspondingly, an organization has more specific goals and less breadth (see the final section of Chapter 3.)

Carl Rogers lists several kinds of "intensive group experience" and briefly describes them; we will only list them here.

> T-group
> Encounter group (or basic encounter group)
> Sensitivity training group
> Task-oriented group
> Sensory awareness groups, body awareness groups, body movement groups
> Creativity workshops
> Organizational development group
> Team building group
> Gestalt group
> Synanon group or "game"
>
> (Rogers, 1970, pp. 4–5)

Rogers includes other, less clearly identifiable groups. What Rogers seems to be listing are groups that are "intentional" in the same sense that some communities are "intentional," that is committed to specific outcomes or ideologies.

Vattano identifies two other kinds of groups, similar to those listed by Rogers in that they are self-help groups; these are community organization groups, and welfare rights groups. They differ from the groups mentioned previously, in that they "are primarily concerned with the failures and inadequacies of the environment and social institutions" (Vattano, 1972, p. 12). Community organization groups include those employed by Saul Alinsky and his Industrial Areas Foundation, and by Mobilization for Youth in New York City. Vattano judges these to be similar "in the emphasis on the power of organized people to work out their own destinies" (Vattano, 1972, p. 13). Welfare rights groups developed within the past decade in response to specific issues. Initially guided by professionals, the groups evolved their own natural leadership, in order to pursue specific goals, "to protect the civil rights of recipients who are threatened by the welfare system's abuses, humiliations, and deprivations" (Vattano, 1972, p. 13).

To the extent that the groups identified by Rogers and Vattano are aimed toward specific goals, they partake of the nature of organizations. In fact, many such groups probably are components of organizations, and might be considered as such with nearly as much accuracy as calling them systems in themselves. These examples clearly demonstrate that groups range widely in character. Some resemble families or communities and some resemble organizations in their position on the "instrumental vs expressive" continuum. Northen has commented that the use of groups to problem-solve is a major emphasis at a certain stage of group development; at this stage, perhaps, all groups move toward the instrumental end of the continuum (Northen, 1969, pp. 189 ff.).

Primary vs Secondary. Olmsted equates this dichotomy with "instrumental vs expressive," calling it "primary-expressive" vs "secondary-instrumental" (Olmsted, 1959, p. 133). This is logical, and we agree with this usage; but some further precision is advisable. A group may be essentially expressive or integrative, but be of minor significance to the members. The afternoon coffee klatch is a good example. It is predominantly expressive. If it is important to its members, it is clearly a primary group; but if it has little importance to them, it should be considered secondary. One criterion, then, is the breadth of influence the group has upon its members, and particularly its influence upon their affective functioning.

Another way of saying this is that if members react to each other more as role occupants than as persons, it is a secondary group. As these roles become more formalized, and the group becomes more goal-specific, and narrows its range of influence, the closer the secondary group comes to being an organization.

Narcissistic vs Generative. This polarity is similar to Parsons's polarities of "self vs collectivity" and "particularism vs universalism" (Parsons, 1964b, pp. 58–67). The dimension is self gratification of one or more members vs wider commitment to the group's goals. Mills notes that this dimension is similar to Freud's pleasure and reality principles, to Erikson's concept of "generativity," and to Redl's typology of authority relationships (Mills, 1967, pp. 120–122).

The importance of this dimension of groups is that it explains the ability or inability of some groups to survive. Mills states that in narcissistic groups, "no provision is made for internal and external adjustments as protections against threat or the realities of the passage of time. . . . they tend to be rigidly structured. . . . Their principle of organization is narcissism, which in itself opposes the social arrangements necessary for resolution of the critical issues of their system" (Mills, 1967, p. 121). In other words, they violate the principle that no function can be concentrated upon to the exclusion of others. Evolutionary capacity is nullified by inability to change structure—that is, a closed, morphostatic system. A "generative" system, like a generative person, is engaged in mutually constructive interchange with its environment. (See Erikson's seventh stage, in Chapter 6.)

In summary, these dimensions that have been used to classify groups indicate that groups share important properties of systems: adaptation, integration, goal-seeking, structural maintenance, and structural change. Groups have important similarities to, and differences from, other systems.

II. ASPECTS OF GROUP AS SYSTEM

A. Evolutionary Aspects

Analysis of any specific group requires much attention to its evolution; more so, perhaps, than with any other system except family. This is true because groups and families are more dependent upon particular persons and thus more likely to be affected by changes in personnel than other systems. Since this is so, the formation and disintegration of a group are more likely to occur during a single observer's (or member's) lifetime than other systems; it is thus more subject to observation and analysis.

Accordingly, less attention has been given to structure and more to "process" in groups; and in social work practice, to problem-solving as the most significant aspect of process. Because of this, the equilibrium or steady state of the group has received much emphasis. In group work practice it has been almost a dogma that all aspects of groups are subordinate to the maintenance of equilibrium. In our discussion of other systems, we have had to establish that they *were* systems, and to establish that *steady state* was a valid term to apply to them. With groups, the problem is the converse; so much has been researched and written on the group as a system, and upon group "equilibrium" or steady state in particular, that the problem is to establish that any other aspect of the system is of equal importance.

1. Steady State.

The group is like an organism—a biological organism. It forms, grows, and reaches a state of maturity. It begins with a set of constituent elements

—individuals with certain personalities, certain needs, ideas, potentialities, limitations—and in the course of development evolves a particular pattern of behavior, a set of indigenous norms, a body of beliefs, a set of values, and so on. Parts become differentiated, each assuming special functions in relation to other parts and the whole. . . . As a group approaches maturity it becomes more complex, more differentiated, more interdependent, and more integrated. (Mills, 1967, p. 13)

This is a detailed way of describing a group's steady state. More general means are to describe its "identity," or its "culture." Erikson might protest this usage of "identity," but Mills describes groups as having some of the same qualities as Erikson describes in persons; this is discussed later. Olmsted observes:

Each group has a sub-culture of its own, a selected and modified version of some parts of the larger culture. The significance of these sub-cultures lies not so much in what they add to the larger culture as in the fact that without its own culture no group would be more than a plurality, a congeries of individuals. The common meanings, the definitions of the situation, the norms of belief and behavior—all these go to make up the culture of the group. (Olmsted, 1959, p 84)

Two of the components of a group's steady state merit discussion here: consensus and goal attainment, since they seem to be obverse aspects.

CONSENSUS

Homans defines "norms" as "what ought to be, and only this. They are part of culture, but not all of it" (Homans, 1950, p. 125). Culture includes, in addition, what *is* done. Northen's definition of norm is more complete:

A norm is a generalization concerning an expected standard of behavior in any matter of consequence to the group. It incorporates a value judgment. It is a rule or standard to which the members of a group are expected to adhere . . . A set of norms introduces a certain amount of regularity and predictability into the group's functioning. (Northen, 1969, pp. 33–34)

The steady-state implications of "regularity and predictability" are obvious. Sherif explored the concept of group norm, and found that when individuals are placed in groups, their individual norms tend to converge into a group norm (Cartwright and Zander, 1960, pp. 23–25). This was illustrated in the Bank Wiring Observation Room study, in which the workers had explicit expectations about the production norms and pressured others to conform (Roethlisberger and Dickson, 1947). Another example was Shils's finding that soldiers observed group norms about supporting their "buddies" (Mills, 1967, p. 4 n.). As Bill Mauldin put it in *Up Front,* combat units "have a sort of family complex":

New men in outfits have to work their way in slowly, but they are eventually accepted. Sometimes they have to change their way of living. An introvert or recluse is not going to last long in combat without friends, so he learns to come out of his shell. Once he has "arrived" he is pretty proud of his clique, and he in turn is chilly toward outsiders. (Cartwright and Zander, 1960, p. 165)

The norm was cooperation; the underlying value was survival.

Consensus is "the degree of agreement regarding goals, norms, roles, and other aspects of the group" (Shepherd, 1964, p. 25). When this agreement is carried further into mutual satisfaction of important needs by the group members, it is "symbiotic" (Cartwright and Zander, 1960, p. 81). When such agreements and need satisfactions operate to bind members to the group, it has "attractiveness," or "valence," and the result is "cohesiveness" of the group.

Such cohesiveness gives rise to "solidarity," which is "the stabilized mutual responsibility of each toward the other to regard himself as part of the other, as the sharer of a common fate, and as a person who is under obligation to cooperate with the other in the satisfaction of the other's individual needs as if they were one's own" (Bales, 1950, p. 61).

This has also been called group "bond." Grace Coyle described group bond as being of three levels:

1. conscious purpose, for example sociability or friendship;
2. assumed or unavowed objectives, such as achievement or status, ego expansion, courtship (especially among adolescents), and class rise;
3. unconscious, including sanctioned release of aggression, escape from reality, and sublimation of erotic impulses. (Coyle, 1948, Chapter 4)

The narcissitic group as Mills described it is most likely to have a bond at this unconscious level.

Consensus and cohesiveness, then, are *expressive, integrative,* and *primary* aspects of the group.

GOAL ATTAINMENT

The other component of steady state that should be discussed is *goal attainment* (Parsons, 1964) or goal pursuit (Mills, 1967, p. 108). In contrast to consensus and cohesiveness, goal attainment is *instrumental, adaptive,* and *secondary.*

Northen uses the term *purpose,* saying that "every group has a purpose for being. Purpose means any ultimate aim, end, or intention; objective or goal usually refers to a specific end that is instrumental to the purpose" (Northen, 1969, p. 19). Her discussion of these terms leads us to conclude that "purposes" mean those goals the suprasystem assigns to the group; while "goals" mean those ends sought by the system itself. We prefer to use the same term, *goals,* for both, to maintain consistency within the systems framework.

Locomotion is the name given to the group goal pursuit by Kurt Lewin and the Group Dynamics theorists.

The concept of locomotion may be interpreted as Group Dynamics' chief intellectual device for dealing with task- or problem-oriented activity in the group. It is generally treated as a characteristic of groups rather than individuals; group process is thus represented as a movement toward (or away from) the group's agenda. (Olmsted, 1959, p. 115)

The term is one to which Sorokin particularly objects, but the idea is consistent with the systems view. Groups move within an environment, or field, to achieve goals that are mutually defined and valued by the group and its relevant environment.

Goal-seeking behavior has effects upon group consensus and cohesion.

The prospect of working together toward a common goal brings people together on new and special terms. If we assume that their earlier relation was for the sake of individual gratification, we can assume that it is now oriented toward the shared idea of a goal. . . . [which] *tends to disrupt the existing structure of emotional and normative relations* and to require a redistribution of energy, affect, and action. In this sense, the demands of entering into instrumental roles . . . introduces the classic conflict between self-oriented pairs (or cliques) and the group as a whole. . . . The conflict creates what we call the *intimacy* issue. (Mills, 1967, p. 108. Emphasis ours.)

Mills holds that this issue forces the member to distinguish between affective and goal-seeking behavior, divide his activity between the two, receive separate rewards for each, and have the option of a variety of affective and nonaffective relations. That is, his value as a worker is not dependent upon his value as a lover (or vice versa) (Mills, 1967, pp. 108–109). This is role differentiation, and permits the person to engage or disengage from intimacy depending upon the instrumental or expressive nature of the particular activity.

2. Stages of Evolution. Several formulations of group evolution have been suggested; each would require full discussion. We will simply present here a brief sketch outlining the evolutionary process in groups. The steps are:

1. The group adapts to its environment; in response to this adaptive behavior, members develop activities, sentiments, and interactions. These adaptive components are the group's external system.
2. The group develops activities, sentiments, and interactions beyond the necessary adaptive behavior, through its goal-oriented behavior; these become the internal system.
3. As the internal system elaborates, it develops bond, cohesiveness, norms, roles, and statuses.
4. In feedback fashion, adaptation is affected by the environment and the developing internal system.
5. The group in turn modifies the functioning of its members. (Weisman, 1963, p. 87)

Homans carries this further, and describes the development of the internal system as "elaboration." At some point, however, a countertrend occurs in which members' behaviors and sentiments become more alike. Homans describes this as "standardization," and as we show later, this is a form of social control (Homans, 1950, pp. 109–110, 119–121). If social control fails, or if adaptive and integrative functions fail, the group may disintegrate or merge into other units. For example, a task force may dissolve and each member go back to his own department or organization; or a friendship group may merge into a larger group, such as a church group or fraternal group.

We have attempted to synthesize a scheme of group evolution from several sources (including Garland, in Berstein, 1965; Mills, 1967; Sarri and Galinsky, in Vinter, 1967; Trecker, 1955). The scheme focuses on the internal development of the group; little reference is made to the environment. Table 2 presents this scheme in abbreviated form. An excellent scheme of group development has been presented by Bennis and Shepard; it is compatible with our scheme here, but based on somewhat different theoretical premises (Bennis and Shepard, 1956, pp. 415–437).

In our survey of group process literature, two major phases, with several sub-phases, seem to emerge. A third phase may or may not occur; if it does, the result is a loop back to some earlier stage and subsequent redevelopment of the group, or the result may be disintegration or termination. None of these phases is presented here as discrete or absolute. This is a highly general synthesis, which—to refer again to the introduction to this book—corresponds to the reality of groups in the same manner that a map corresponds to mud, rocks, and clear running water.

PHASE I

During the first major phase, exploration of each other occurs among the members. The activity of the members in this phase is similar to the "inclusion" stage identified by William Schutz: "In the inclusion stage . . . the member confronts questions dealing with his individual membership in the group. He asks: Do I want to be part of this group and do the other members want me to be part of it? Who else is here? Should I become intensely involved or marginally involved? Can I trust my real self to the others?" (Galper, 1970, p. 72). Such questions are answered by probing each other. A summary description of a group of unemployed fathers receiving aid to families with dependent children (AFDC) says:

> Perhaps one of the most surprising phenomenon was the members' en-
> thusiastic discussion of their problems. During the initial and early middle
> phases of the group the members expressed much anger and despair.
> However, they also stated they did not realize that anyone else (includ-
> ing the agency) was interested in their feelings or difficulties. By the fifth
> meeting they began to verbalize their identification with the group and
> soon used the group as a place to try out new behavior and social skills.
> (Green, 1970, pp. 3–4)

Carl Rogers has identified and described the phases of encounter groups. His phases are similar to what we intend here. He offers them not as "high-level abstract theory. . . . [but] merely to describe the observable events and the way in which, to me, these events seem to cluster" (Rogers, 1970, pp. 14–15). Rogers describes "patterns or stages," the first five of which seem to us to fit within our first major phase. His first five stages are:

1. *Milling around.* . . . there tends to develop a period of initial confusion, awkward silence, polite surface interaction, "cocktail-party talk," frustration, and great lack of continuity. . . .

2. *Resistance to personal expression or exploration.* . . . some individuals are likely to reveal rather personal attitudes. This tends to provoke a very ambivalent reaction among other members of the group. . . . only gradually, fearfully, and ambivalently do they take steps to reveal something of the private self. . . .

3. *Description of past feelings.* . . . expression of feelings does begin to assume a larger proportion of the discussion. . . .

4. *Expression of negative feelings.* Curiously enough, the first expression of genuinely significant "here and now" feeling is apt to come out in negative attitudes toward other group members or the group leader. . . . This is one of the best ways to test the freedom and trustworthiness of the group. . . . Another quite different reason is that deeply positive feelings are much more difficult and dangerous to express. . . .

5. *Expression and exploration of personally meaningful material.* . . . the event most likely to occur next is for some individual to reveal himself to the group in a significant way. . . . A process which one workshop member has called "a journey to the center of self," often a very painful process, has begun. . . . Such exploration is not always an easy process, nor is the whole group receptive to such revelation. (Rogers, 1970, pp. 15–20)

Evident in Rogers's description of "process patterns" are the characteristics shown in Phase I in our scheme. Discussion of symbols and meanings may take the form of tentative exploration of what structure is possible, what "freedom" means in this group, and how others interpret what the leader says. The interpretation that members arrive at determines the group's *valence* (Lewin's term), or attractiveness. Members begin to share their *life space* (again Lewin's term), to permit others to enter their interactional, personal territory, their "bubbles." Strean has recently employed *life space* in his approach to casework; it clearly is applicable to groups (Strean, 1972).

Some agreement among group members that feelings, thoughts, and behaviors are to be tolerated (though there may be some reluctance, as Rogers suggests) permits open discussion of the group's emerging "culture"—as we defined it in Chapter 2, "the way we do things." As members give assent to, and sanction for, group "we-ness" they accommodate (in Piaget's terminology) to each other. Lewin describes this as group movement or *locomotion;* in systems terminology, they are approaching a *steady state.*

Table 2. Group Evolution

Phases	Cognitive Aspects	Affective Aspects	Behavioral Aspects
I. Components' goals predominate			
Exploratory; "matching"	Discussion of symbols, meanings	Checks for feelings, values; "valence"	Observes behavior of others; tentative participation
Affiliation (approach-avoidance)	Attempt to find common meanings, symbols	Expression of feelings	Interaction and reaction in overt behavior; territory shared
Commitment	Limited agreement on symbols, meanings, norms	Development of group bond; satisfaction of individual's feelings; group values emerge	Beginning of modification of behavior to conform; mutual accommodation; locomotion
II. Group purposes predominate			
Socialization	Internalization of developing group culture; accommodation of schemas	Same as Cognitive	Roles defined and agreed to
Social control	Standardization; acceptance of group views; subordination of idiosyncratic views	Subordination of idiosyncratic feelings; reinforcement of those which "match"	Group prescription of behavior; reduction of deviance; differentiation of roles and territories
Stability (internal)	Enforcement of group views; codes and stated purposes; "right thinking" and developed symbol systems	Enforcement of group values; statements expressing solidarity and allegiance; traditions	Rituals, offices, hierarchy

Table 2—Continued

Group goal pursuit (external) ↕	Problem-solving; decision-making; thought exclusively focused on goal and means to achieve it; "Brainstorming"	Elevation of values which support goal; devotion to them, excluding other values, both personal and group	Focus on specific group goal; sacrifice and joint effort
Intimacy; cohesiveness	Exchange with each other to the exclusion of others; "private" group views, beliefs, actions		

III. *Components' goals predominate*

Conflict	Dissensus on norms, goals, evaluations; selectiveness of evidence	Disaffection; return (or remaining) to predominance of individuals' sentiments; "hidden agenda" predominates	Antagonistic behavior; violation of roles, territories, boundaries; failure to observe rituals, hierarchy

RETURN TO EARLIER PHASE OR:

Disintegration or termination (subgroups or complete disassociation)	Maintenance of divergent views; ideological combat	Hostility; defensiveness; feelings of betrayal; anger	Alliances; power struggles; "splitting" from the group; betrayal to outsiders

NOTE: Arrow indicates that these subphases may be reversed in sequence.

PHASE II

In this major phase, the emphasis shifts, as Schutz describes it, from "inclusion" to the "control" stages. "In the control stage he asks: Now that I have decided to be a member of the group, what power will I have in it? Who is in charge and how do I find this out? What does the group want of me?" (Galper, 1970, p. 72). The group of unemployed fathers cited earlier faced this stage:

> One of the most important dynamics of the group was the attempt of each member to obtain, retain, and offer acceptance. It was during the middle phase that the members' behavior and perspective began to change. They became more oriented toward planning and appeared more patient. Many moved from an outlook of pessimism and depression to one of optimism, which the leaders continually reinforced. (Green, 1970, p. 4)

The group norm shifted from one affective state to another; and the group, largely at the leaders' urgings, apparently enforced this mood shift among its members. The affective shift was accompanied by a cognitive shift (planning) and behavioral shift, patience, implying respect for each others' territory, and differentiation of roles.

Rogers's stages 6 through 10 are not applicable to all types of groups, but illustrate group evolution in encounter groups.

6. *The expression of immediate interpersonal feelings in the group....* Examples would be: "I feel threatened by your silence." "You remind me of my mother...." "I like your warmth and your smile." ...

7. *The development of a healing capacity in the group....* in which a number of the group members show a natural and spontaneous capacity for dealing in a helpful, facilitating, and therapeutic fashion with the pain and suffering of others....

8. *Self-acceptance and the beginning of change....*

> ART: (Crying) Nobody else is in there with me, just me. I just pull everything into the shell and roll the shell up and shove it in my pocket. I take the shell, and the real me, and put it in my pocket where it's safe. I guess that's really the way I do it.... And here—that's what I want to do here in this group, y'know—come out of my shell and actually throw it away.
> LOIS: You're making progress already. At least you can talk about it....

9. *The cracking of facades.* As the sessions continue, so many things tend to occur together that it is hard to know which to describe first.... As times goes on the group finds it unbearable that any member should live behind a mask or front.... Gently at times, almost savagely at others, the group *demands* that the individual be himself.... In Synanon, the fascinating group so successfully involved in making persons out of drug addicts, this ripping away of facades is often dramatic....

10. *The individual receives feedback.*

> JOHN: (To Alma) .... You remind me of a butterfly. (Laughter)

ALMA: Why is that? . . . why do you say a butterfly? . . . .

JOHN: Well, to me a butterfly is a curious thing. It's a thing you can get up pretty close to, as you might say, as a new friend, but just about the time that you get up to it and pet it or bring it closer to you and look at it, it flits away.

ALMA: (Laughs nervously). . . . (Rogers, 1970, pp. 21–29)

In these five stages, Rogers has described in encounter groups the elements we have included in Table 2 under major Phase II, "Socialization." Members have taken the group norms "to heart"—they have internalized them. They have begun to sort out roles of "facilitator" (not always the group leader), "conciliator," and so forth. They "heal" each other and restrain other members who seem to violate the group norm of "caring" for each other. Those members who express "caring," or negative feelings, interact within the group's norms of behavior. Intimacy and cohesiveness are achieved as thoughts, feelings, and behavior are expressed among themselves that do not include others. In one "Family Seminar" discussion group at our school recently, for example, the members voted whether to allow two "outsiders," members of another discussion group, to join them. The vote was negative; the two outsiders, although they were fellow-members of other courses with some of this group's members, left. They acknowledged the right of this group to maintain its own intimacy and cohesiveness, however rejected they may have felt.

The notable disparity between our scheme in Table 2 and Rogers's stages is that Rogers deals little with group goal pursuit. This is understandable, since Rogers's groups are primary groups oriented toward relatively diffuse goals, and the achievement of goals outside the group process itself are of minor importance.

> To me the group seems like an organism, having a sense of its own direction even though it could not define that direction intellectually. . . . I have seen the "wisdom of the organism" exhibited at every level from cell to group.
>   . . . . The group will *move*—of this I am confident—but it would be presumptuous to think that I can or should *direct* that movement toward a *specific* goal. (Rogers, 1970, pp. 44–45)

Our scheme does deal with specific goals assigned by the environment of the group, but only to note that this may be part of group process for some groups.

PHASE III

Phase III can occur at any point in group process; it does not necessarily follow Phases I or II. When it occurs, however, it is a crisis in the life of the group; the group will either loop back to an earlier stage (similar to regression in individuals) to resolve the issue, or resolve the issue in some fashion so that it can proceed (analogous to Erikson's description of the resolution of growth crises).

Rogers describes well, in stages 11 through 15, some of the most intense encounters that can take place in groups.

11. *Confrontation.* There are times when the term feedback is far too mild to describe the interactions that take place. . . .

> NORMA: (Loud sigh) . . . . Any real woman that I know wouldn't have acted as you have this week, and particularly what you said this afternoon. That was so *crass! !* It just made me want to puke, right there! ! ! And— I'm just *shaking* I'm so mad at you—I don't think you've been real once this week! . . I'm so infuriated that *I want to come over and beat the hell out of you! !* (Rogers, 1970, pp. 31–32)

Here it is apparent that the group Rogers describes could possibly have disintegrated, or reverted to an earlier stage. Positive resolution can occur, however. The manner in which it occurs and the results are described by Rogers:

12. *The helping relationship outside the group sessions.* . . . When I see two individuals going for a walk together, or conversing in a quiet corner, or hear that they stayed up talking until 3:00 A.M. I feel it is quite probable that at some later time in the group we will hear that one was gaining strength and help from the other, that the second person was making available his understanding, his support, his experience, his caring. . . .

13. *The basic encounter.* . . . This appears to be one of the most central, intense, and change-producing aspects of group experience. . . . Such I–Thou relationships (to use Buber's term again) occur with some frequency. . . . "when a negative feeling was fully expressed to another, the relationship grew and the negative feeling was replaced by a deep acceptance for the other" . . . .

14. *The expression of positive feelings and closeness.* . . .

15. *Behavior changes in the group.* . . . The tone of voice changes, becoming sometimes stronger, sometimes softer, usually more spontaneous, less artificial, with more feeling. Individuals show an astonishing amount of thoughtfulness and helpfulness toward each other. (Rogers, 1970, pp. 32–36)

It is apparent from this description that this is compatible with Schutz's term for the third stage, following *inclusion* and *control;* the stage of *affection.*

If such positive outcomes as Rogers and Schutz describe are not forthcoming, however, conflict may result in disintegration or termination. Lewis Coser raised the question, "if conflict unites, what tears apart?" His answer is that "not all conflicts are positively functional for the relationship, but only those which concern goals, values or interests that do not contradict the basic assumptions upon which the relation is founded" (Coser, 1964, pp. 73, 80). It could be assumed, then, that if members of one of the groups Rogers describes did not take the healing role, or offer mutual support, the conflict would indeed concern the basic function of encounter groups, that is, to provide an experience of confrontation and caring. The group would terminate, in all likelihood, or break up into subgroups, as indicated in the disintegration subphase of Phase III of our scheme in Table 2.

Northen suggests several efforts to resolve conflict. They include:

> *elimination,* that is forcing the withdrawal of the opposing individual
> or subgroup, sometimes in subtle ways. In *subjugation,* or domination,
> the strongest members force others to accept their points of view. . . .
> Through the means of *compromise* . . . each of the factions . . . give up
> something to safeguard the common area of interest. . . . An individual
> or subgroup may form an *alliance.* . . . Finally, through *integration,* a
> group may arrive at a solution that is both satisfying to each member
> and more productive and creative than any contending suggestion. It is
> this latter process that, according to Wilson and Ryland, "represents the
> height of achievement in group life." (Northen, 1969, pp. 42–43)

We would, of course, agree with this; and this is very close to the same sense
in which we mean *integration* as a basic system function. Odd Ramsoy, a Norwegian sociologist, has investigated the conflict inherent between system and
subsystem in social groups (Ramsoy, 1962). He observes that a group as an
entity must be tending toward adaptation and integration. The members thus
always face the dilemma of making choices that favor system or subsystem. He
postulates that conflict between part and whole decreases as the integrative problems of the common inclusive system outweigh each subsystem's adaptive problems
and goal problems. Ramsoy, as others before him, concludes that *conflict can be
reduced through concentration on a supraordinate problem.* This occurs most
readily when the problem is an external threat. In the presence of a foreigner there
are no subgroups.

Conflict then can provide the occasion for a redressing of the necessary balance
between adaptation and integregation. As an outcome of group process, it means
that components (group members individually) and system (the entire group)
have both satisfied needs and goals, in synergistic fashion. This is, indeed, the
height of achievement in the evolution of any system.

B. Structural Aspects

1. Boundary and Autonomy. As with all systems, the boundaries of a group
are determined by the group and its components, through interaction among the
members and with the environment. Persons define themselves as members, and
are defined by others as being members of the group. For example, segregation by
race or sex is usually prescribed by society, while separation into religious denominations is largely a matter of personal choice.

Groups have greater or lesser degrees or autonomy from their environment. A
delinquent group such as Whyte's Norton gang was relatively autonomous from
its environment, with few direct controls or supports (Whyte, 1955). The group
of workers studied in the Bank Wiring study was much less autonomous, being
subject to a high degree of control by the organization (Roethlisberger and
Dickson, 1947). The boundaries of both groups were clear; the Norton gang's

boundary was less permeable. Another example of permeability is Mauldin's description of combat soldiers, cited earlier in this chapter. A group, as any other system, must have discernible, locatable boundaries.

2. *Differentiation, Hierarchy, and Role.* As previously noted, differentiation of roles occurs as part of elaboration in the evolution of groups. These roles are ranked by the group according to both their adaptive and integrative functions. In addition, the person filling the role is evaluated; members of the group may respond to either the role or the person, or to both. As noted, in secondary groups members tend to respond more to roles than to persons. When such rankings reach a consensus among the group members, the group may be said to be stratified (Bales, 1950, p. 77).

Some roles become standardized within the group, and persist regardless of the person occupying the role; some roles are common to most groups. Some examples are: the *scapegoat,* who serves as the recipient of group hostility; the *clown,* who may be either the butt of humor, or the donor, and who serves an important expressive function; the *peacemaker,* to whom the group turns for conflict reduction, an important integrative or social control function; and the *idol,* who sets some moral or social standard for the group.

The roles that have received the most research attention are the various forms of leadership. The two most common identified are the task (instrumental or adaptive) leader, and the social-emotional (expressive or integrative) leader (Olmsted, 1959, p. 69). The latter is sometimes called the sentiment leader. Homans has formulated several rules for leadership:

1. The leader will maintain his own position.
2. The leader will live up to the norms of his group. The higher the degree of conformity, the higher will be the member's rank.
3. The leader will not give orders that will not be obeyed; he would "lose face" if he did so.
4. In giving orders, the leader will use established channels.
5. The leader will listen.
6. The leader will know himself. (Homans, 1950, pp. 425–440)

While this seems to be a recipe for leadership, the steps describe common expectations for the leader role.

The fact is that leadership in a group may be at one time abrupt, forceful, centralized, with all communications originating with the leader, and at another time slow, relaxed, dispersed, with much communication back and forth between leader and followers. Each mode is acceptable, appropriate and authoritative, but each in different circumstances. (Homans, 1950, p. 419)

In other words, energy exchanges between the leader and the rest of the system determine which form of leadership is functional to the group system.

C. Behavioral Aspects

1. Adaptation. This has been discussed under "steady state," earlier. It remains here only to restate that all group behavior has some bearing upon securing and expending energy externally (SE and GE functions), whether explicitly designed to do so or not. As Homans put it, "adaptation is the name we give to the parallelism between what successful operations on the environment may require and what the organism itself creates. Adaptation is as characteristic of the group as it is of other organisms" (Homans, 1950, p. 155). Berrien, in his discussion of groups as systems, states that adaptation is fundamental, in that systems must "produce some service or product acceptable to another social system" (Berrien, 1971, p. 120).

An important component of adaptation is leadership, as already mentioned, but specifically, the problem-solving and decision-making activity inherent in the task leadership role. These components have received much attention in group research, and in research on organizations, in particular. As noted earlier, problem-solving has received prime attention in social group work practice. Mills prefers to refer to task leadership and decision-making in the wider context of

> an *executive system;* i.e., the set of all executive orientations and processes as they are distributed and organized among and performed by group members. Any member, regardless of position or office, who performs executive functions . . . participates in the executive system. . . .
>
> The executive system is the group's center for assessment of itself and its situations, for arrangement and rearrangement of its internal and external relations, for decision-making and for learning, and for "learning how to learn" through acting and assessing the consequences of action. . . . The executive system is a partly independent, autonomous center where information about the role-systems . . . is processed. (Mills, 1967, p. 93)

In our view, it is, more accurately, an executive *subsystem,* which serves the function of goal attainment. It seems appropriate here to note that this is analogous to the "ego functions" in the personality system.

2. Socialization. Socialization is, of course, integrative behavior within the group, intended to furnish energy to the group, and to reduce the likelihood of conflict. The attractiveness or "valence" of the group is based upon the various levels of goals discussed earlier.

The use of small groups to facilitate socialization is widespread—examples are the pledge group in the sorority and the basic training unit in the army. Much like the family, the small group can serve readily as a transition into wider systems. Socialization into the group itself is based upon some match between the person's needs and the group's offering; a good example is the frequent use of groups by adolescents for security, opportunities to meet friends, and to learn the cultures of both youth and adult life stages.

The process of socialization may be of three kinds, according to Kelman:

1. compliance, in which the person conforms without believing or accepting the group's view;
2. identification, in which the person adopts the group's view through making the group part of his own identity; or
3. internalization, in which the group's view is adopted because it "solves a problem for him." The group's view agrees with his own. (Shepherd, 1964, pp. 48–50)

In this process, the person may engage in various games (as Eric Berne calls them) or role strategies aimed at achieving his ends (Berne, 1966; Thibaut and Kelley, 1959; Goffman, 1961). The adaptation of the person and the integrative behavior of the system must reach some mutually acceptable bargain, or the process of socalization will fail.

3. *Social Control and Social Conflict.* The process of standardization is related to social control. Among other ways, a group achieves an identity or steady state by shaping its members' behaviors in certain ways. The application of sanctions in one form or another is social control. As noted earlier, social control is exercised by the entire group through various means. The major means of control is energy applied to, or withheld from, a member. One example is the traditional Roberts' Rules in formal meetings; if members do not conform to its usage, they may not be recognized, that is allowed any verbal interchange with the entire group, or may be ejected from the group. An extreme example would be forcing members to accept certain roles, such as worker, hunter, or mate, in order to survive. A more subtle example might be that junior members of the United States Senate are expected to "be seen but not heard"; and in most offices women staff members are expected to make coffee for the entire staff. The play *Twelve Angry Men* (Rose, 1955) illustrates the various forms social control can take in a group, from threat of violence to ridicule and "putting down" a member. Ibsen's *Hedda Gabler* and Ayn Rand's *Fountainhead* are two of many literary examples of individuals' violation of group norms, with varying success.

An important part of social control in groups is conflict and the management of conflict.

Group experience *is* conflict. It is a response to the reality that there is a shortage of what people need and want. . . . To organize, a group must coordinate one part with another, and in doing so must limit the freedom of some parts. . . . And further, groups accept and reward some members more fully than others, and this inequality creates yet another type of conflict. . . . Change, which occurs at every moment, is determined both in direction and in quality by the manner in which conflicts are resolved. Response to conflict determines the new state of the system. (Mills, 1967, pp. 14–15)

We agree, except that Mills seems to view groups as entropic, rather than synergistic. Probably the most complete statement of the dimensions and uses of social conflict in groups is found in Coser's *The Functions of Social Conflict* (Coser, 1964).

4. Communication. Communication is a basic process in groups. We have previously defined communication as "transfer of meaning or energy" by any means. According to this definition, virtually all group activity could be considered communication, rendering the term so broad as to be meaningless. Rather, we mean communication intended to accomplish adaptation, integration, social control, or goal attainment (in other words, the SE, SI ,GI, and GE functions) for the system.

Bales's interaction process analysis theory of groups is based upon communication, and the analysis of units of communication into a few categories, such as "shows solidarity," "shows tension release," "disagrees," and "shows antagonism." Tabulating the number of units exchanged during a given time and their distribution by categories, allows some index of group process to be derived. This is a highly popular means of group analysis (Bales, 1950).

Other theorists, especially those with backgrounds in information theory, have focused upon communication as the basic process in groups. Satir's conjoint family therapy, and Berne's transactional analysis can both be fairly said to focus upon communication.

Frequently the purpose of such communication is to allow the group members to improve their communication skills within the group, and then to transfer these skills to other systems. One example is a group of unwed pregnant girls and their parents. This group provides:

> the means whereby families may learn new, more appropriate communication behavior. . . . In some instances, family members learn how to communicate better when the therapists and the group decode messages that are sent and inappropriately received in a family system. In other instances, good communication among the therapists in the group's presence serves as a positive model. (Papademetriou, 1971, p. 88)

SUMMARY

It seems clear, from the wealth of research on groups, that groups do have the properties of systems, and have the same basic features. The implications of this for counseling professions are that groups are orderly, and that interventive methods can be devised that are even more effective than those used in the past, if general guidelines for system intervention are observed.

SUGGESTED READINGS

Marrow, Alfred J. *The Practical Theorist: The Life and Work of Kurt Lewin.* New York: Basic Books, 1969. A biography of Lewin written by a former student and colleague. This traces the evolution of group dynamics from its roots in Gestalt holism to the development of training groups.

Mills, Theodore M. *The Sociology of Small Groups.* Englewood Cliffs, N.J.: Prentice-Hall, 1967. A good introductory text, especially for students who have some acquaintance with the literature on small groups. (This has been used as the small-scale map for this chapter.)

Olmsted, Michael. *The Small Group.* New York: Random House, 1959. An introduction to the study of small groups. Includes some classic studies and summary reviews of major theorists. Especially useful to students who have no background. (This has also been used as the small-scale map for this chapter.)

Rogers, Carl. *Carl Rogers on Encounter Groups.* New York: Harper & Row, 1970. Interesting first-hand description of the encounter group process; includes Rogers's distillation of his years of clinical experience. Good for teaching some of the intimate details of this therapeutic tool.

Rose, Reginald. *Twelve Angry Men.* Chicago: Dramatics Publications Co., 1955. A play about the interactive processes among jurors deliberating a capital case. Dramatically illustrates the shifts between individual and group goals; demonstrates that a group is indeed different from the sum of its parts. Can be readily used for role playing.

chapter 5

FAMILIES

All happy families resemble each other; each unhappy family is unhappy in its own way.

                                        Leo Tolstoy, *Anna Karenina*

INTRODUCTION

A separate chapter is devoted to the family as a social system because the family is the single social unit in human society inextricably interwoven with all other systems. As noted in Chapter 2, the family assumes, or is delegated, primary responsibility for socialization into the culture and thus is charged with major activity to insure the survival of man, the animal who survives by means of his culture. As discussed in Chapter 3, the community mediates between family and society. Because the family can and should be viewed as a special instance of the small group, most of Chapter 4 is applicable to family. In every phase of the person's life cycle, family is of central importance in definition of social expectations and in provisions of the resources necessary for growth.

The approach to the family in this chapter will be consistent with the systems model presented earlier. We construe the family as holon with attention to the system itself, its components, and its significant environment. Family fulfills the requirements for designation as a human system.

I. APPROACHES TO FAMILY ANALYSIS

We will forego until later in this chapter the dubious pleasures of establishing our definition of family in favor of a brief examination of a few selected approaches to understanding the family. Family scholars have made Herculean efforts to organize the conceptual frameworks that have been created to analyze the family (see, for example, Hill and Hansen, 1960; Nye and Berardo, 1968). Our intent here is to summarize only those approaches we find most congruent with the purposes of this book.

A. The Family as a System of Roles

This is an important theme in the literature of family analysis. Roles are conceived as embodying the cultural expectations for behavior, and the family is the arena wherein these roles are learned and carried out. Goode, a sociologist, begins his textbook on the family:

> In all known societies, almost everyone lives his life enmeshed in a network of family rights and obligations called role relations. A person is made aware of his role relations through a long period of socialization during his childhood, a process in which he learns how others in his family expect him to behave, and in which he himself comes to feel this is both the right and desirable way to act. (Goode, 1964, p. 1)

In psychoanalytic thought the resolution of the oedipal conflict is dependent upon the existence of appropriate role models and the assumption by the child of the appropriate roles. Lidz, a psychiatrist, states:

> The family is recognized as a biologically required social institution that mediates between the biological and cultural directives of personality formation, and a social system in which the child assimilates the basic instrumentalities, institutions, and role attributions that are essential to his adaptation and integration. (Lidz, 1963, pp. 75–76)

Feldman and Scherz, social workers, write:

> The family operates through roles that shift and alter during the course of the family's life. Roles can be explicit or instrumental; they can be implicit or emotional. . . . The healthy family carries out explicit and implicit roles appropriately according to age, competence and needs during all the different stages of family life. The disturbed family experiences serious difficulty in the management of roles. (Feldman and Scherz, 1967, p. 67)

The family system of roles must be examined both structurally and functionally. Parsons's earlier formulation of the family as social system differentiated between instrumental and expressive role functions on a sexual axis, that is, the male-father role as breadwinner and adapter to the environment, the female-mother role as social and emotional provider. In his critique of Parsons's view, Rodman stresses the fluidity of the distribution of the instrumental and expressive roles within the changing American family (Rodman, 1966, pp. 262–287). Rodman cites evidence from Parsons's writings to support his conclusion that the feminine role in general has broadened from the "pseudo-occupation" of a domestic pattern to include role choices of "career pattern," "glamour pattern," and "good companion pattern"; and that society sanctions a feminine role combining these role patterns (see Margaret Adams's comment on this, later in this chapter). Parsons and others have held that the masculine instrumental role has also shifted because of the changes in occupational roles. The family business or family farm formerly located and consolidated the instrumental functions in the father and reinforced his paternal authority; the father's modern organizational membership diffuses and dissipates it.

The family as determinant and perpetuator of role expectations has long been at issue. Engels in 1902 argued that the family is a bourgeois device designed to enslave women: "The modern individual family is founded on the open or concealed domestic slavery of the wife" (Engel, 1902, p. 65). More recently C. Wright Mills stated in the same vein: "In so far as the family as an institution turns women into darling little slaves and men into their chief providers and unweaned dependents, the problem of a satisfactory marriage remains incapable of purely private solution" (Mills, location unknown).

The role system perspective on the family, especially the dysfunctional family, is a dominant one in social work literature (Feldman and Scherz, 1967; Perlman, 1968). Far more attention is devoted to adult family roles as necessary to family integrity and functioning than to child family roles, although the purposes of adult family roles as explicated are largely parental. Certainly the "normal" family roles are emphasized in the literature of child development.

B. The Family as Cause or Effect

This is a second major approach. As Nimkoff explains, the family can be seen either as "dependent" variable or as "independent" variable (Nimkoff, 1965, pp. 37–73). In the former instance, the family is responsive to the demands and dictates of the larger social systems. It adapts, or more precisely accommodates, to the goal requirements of the society it exists within. The nuclear, mobile family emerges because of the requisites of the economy; it relinquishes its functions to other social institutions due to pressures exerted upon it by its environment. The government influences by prescriptions and proscriptions; for example, compulsory school attendance, abortion laws, and court decisions that place the "welfare of the child" above the rights of the parents. The family is seen as existing to fulfill the cultural dictates of its society as that society seeks to perpetuate itself.

The family as independent variable is seen to be cause rather than effect. The family initiates change and society accommodates to these changes. Examples of this dynamic are less frequently cited in the literature on family. One example is sociologist Elise Boulding's view that:

> the family is a potentially powerful contributor to the generation of alternative images of the future. During the "quiet" periods of history—the times of relative stability, when few demands are made on the adaptive

capacities of individuals or groups—and also in periods of severe repression, the futures-creating capacities of the family may remain undeveloped. In periods of rapid social change, when each age group represented in the household has experienced critically different stimuli and pressures from the larger society, the futures-creating family is held together by strong social bonds. (Boulding, 1972, p. 188)

In this sense of creating alternatives, the family is independent variable. It generates social change, according to Boulding, in that the family is a "play community"; play may be one means by which culture is created, and thereby alternative societal futures may be imagined. Clearly the position of the family as the system interfacing between individual and society allows it to perform this function.

The controversy over abortion laws exemplifies the family initiating change, requiring social accommodation, in that family planning, in order to liberate the parents and maintain living standards, requires that society provides sanction and means for birth control. A recent Supreme Court decision gives legal sanction to abortion as a means of birth control.

Although few family theorists opt for either extreme, dependent or independent variable, most do see the family as determined by societal changes rather than the reverse. A typical position is expressed by Goode:

> Because of its emphasis on performance, such a system (industrialization) requires that a person be permitted to rise or fall, and to move about wherever the job market is best. A lesser emphasis on land ownership also increases the ease of mobility. The conjugal family is neolocal (each couple sets up its own household), and its kinship network is not strong, thus putting fewer barriers than other family systems in the way of class or geographic mobility. In these ways the conjugal family system "fits" the needs of industrialization. (Goode, 1964, p. 108)

Our opinion is, of course, that the family is both independent and dependent variable, since it is a holon. From this perspective, we agree with the view of "the family as a workshop in social change" (Boulding, 1972, p. 187).

C. The Family as Evolving System

This is a dual approach to family inquiry. One focus is on the developmental cycle of *a* family, while the other is a focus on the evolutionary cycle of *the* family as a social institution.

Various attempts have been made to delineate the developmental stages in the life cycle of a family. Nye and Berardo describe some of these, and combine them to illustrate their compatibility (Nye and Berardo, 1968, pp. 198–222; see especially Table 1, pp. 208–209). The general direction of family stages is from the point of marriage, to and through expansion stages, to and through contraction stages. The more thoroughly formulated of these attempt to account for the related growth tasks for all family members, not just the children. These are grounded in assumptions of a nuclear unit, childbearing, and a marriage that will continue until the death of a spouse. Thus the family stages are, in fact, applicable to only a limited number of actual families.

Elise Boulding describes the evolution of *a* family:

> Family life is a swiftly moving series of identity crises as members of various ages are socialized into new roles. At the same time, the image of the family as a whole, as conceived by each family member, is subject to the same set of identity crises. The pre-schooler may face the crisis of becoming a kindergartener at the same time that his parents face the crisis of narrowing horizons that hits adults in their late twenties when the future no longer seems wide open, and his grandparents face the crisis of retirement. The teenager trying to decide whether to enter one of the many subcultures and counter-cultures open to him may have parents who face both the empty-nest crisis of unrealized aspirations as the zenith of career activities is passed, and grandparents who face the crisis of no longer having sufficient health to live independently in their own apartment. (Boulding, 1972, p. 186)

This is, of course, similar to the role-system approach to the family system, but suggests a cyclical process through which a family passes.

Carle Zimmerman is acknowledged as the best known advocate of a cyclical theory of *the* family. He begins with the premise that the family and society constantly interact and cause changes, each in the other. Other social institutions (particularly the church and government) vie with the family for control of the family members. Drawing on historical data, Zimmerman proposes a three-phase family typology and suggests this is a repetitive cycle.

1. "trustee" family—the living members are trustees of the family name, family property, and family blood. The family itself is immortal, there is no conception of individual rights, and individual welfare is ever subordinate to the family group.
2. "domestic" family—an intermediate type that evolves from the trustee family. As the state gains in power, family control over its members is weakened. The state shares this power and control with the family and creates the concept of individual rights to be maintained against family authority.
3. "atomistic" family—the power and scope of family authority is reduced to an absolute minimum and the state becomes essentially an organization in the sense that the family no longer mediates between its members and society. This leads to rampant hedonism, feministic movements, childlessness, and youth problems. (Leslie, 1967, pp. 223–230)

He judges the present day American family to be well into the third phase, the "atomic age" in yet another sense. Zimmerman does not find the "present decay of the family" unique. He documents similar family dissolution just prior to the fall of Greek and Roman civilizations. Since the family is the primary humanizing force in man's life,

> [modern] inhumanity lies close, in a basic causal sense to the decay of the family system. Indeed the familial decline may well be the primary causal agent in the sapping of the universal capacity for human sympathy. Juvenal held this opinion when he wrote of "the decline in the capacity to weep." (Zimmerman, 1947, p. 76)

> The consequence then of a declining family system is that the controls of society come more into the hands of men who, in the words of Bacon, have no "hostages to fortune," and who do not possess judgments biased by an immersion in fundamental humanism. (Zimmerman, 1947, p. 77)

Zimmerman deplores the popular view of the family as ever evolving to higher and better forms. He recommends open recognition and understanding of the current state of family decline and hopes that a "creative minority" will come forward to reassert the values of familism.

D. The Structural Approach

This approach to the family has received the attention of a host of investigators. In fact, any attempt at family analysis addresses itself to certain family forms and excludes others.

The majority of American observers of the family accept the two-generation nuclear family as the norm; this is particularly true of those interested in the child rearing aspects of the family. The "normal" family is seen to be composed of two parents and their minor children. Voiland and associates note "the rise of prominence of the family of procreation—father, mother, children—as an independent unit. This primary family group has, indeed, become the structural norm of our culture. There are many manifestations of this fact" (Voiland and Associates, 1962, pp. 46–47).

Parsons has characterized the present day American family as "the isolated nuclear family," isolated especially residentially and economically from families or orientation. He sees this as a natural consequence of the specialization and differentiation of the complex social system of America today. He does qualify the degree of isolation. "I think it very important indeed, that there is much accumulating evidence that the extended family is an exceedingly important resource to fall back on in case of emergency or trouble, for financial support and for emotional support and help in planning and all sorts of things of that kind" (Parsons, 1964a, p. 17).

Billingsley draws on the formulations of Parsons and Bales to establish a typology of forms for categorizing Negro family structures. The refinements he introduces through his three categories and twelve types have broad applicability (Billingsley, 1968, pp. 15–21).

1. The *nuclear* family includes three types; the incipient, consisting only of the marital pair; the simple, consisting of the marital pair and minor children; and the attenuated, containing only one parent and minor children.

2. The *extended* family includes three types, wherein other relatives are added to the nuclear household.

3. The *augmented* family includes six types of family situations, wherein unrelated family members are incorporated into the household.

Boulding classifies the second and third types, extended and augmented, under the heading "expanded family" in order to "emphasize the commonality between the biologically related extended family and the household as a voluntary association" (Boulding, 1972, p. 188). She places all family forms on a continuum from one isolated householder to a cluster of persons either biologically or voluntarily associated. She correctly points out that there is no hard and fast line between the expanded family and the "intentional community," that is a community organized for specific social or ideological purposes. Given the variety of social experimentation being attempted today, such an elastic definition of family is very useful.

The study of kinship networks and relationships, particularly in the work of social anthropologists, has yielded additional insights into the variety of family forms. Raymond Firth commented:

> The study of kinship is a perennial theme for the social anthropologist. An understanding of the kinship system in any society is essential as clues to the working of some of the most fundamental relationships— sexual, marital, economic in that society. It also may be of prime importance in the process of socialization, in developing patterns of reaction to authority and in providing important symbols for the moral evaluation of conduct. (Nye and Berardo, 1968, p. 19)

Rodman discusses kinship responsibilities in the United States and concludes that in many respects this is a neglected dimension in family studies (Rodman, 1966, pp. 179–185). Cultural guidelines for determination of allegiance to kinsmen are ambiguous and often conflicting. Although the nuclear family norm would seem to dictate primary kin responsibility to wife and children, conflicting claims do arise. The parent of today in an isolated nuclear family may have been the child of yesterday in a closely-tied extended or nuclear family. For such a person the transfer of allegiance and emotional involvement from his family of orientation to his family of procreation may be a monumental task, as indicated by frequent letters to "Dear Abby" from wives and mothers-in-law about the son-husband's responsibilities to each. The unenviable status of the aged in our society and the guilt felt by their adult children are products of this dilemma. The unenforceable "relative responsibility" laws in public welfare are another reflection of this situation.

Alternative family forms are increasingly being suggested as possible substitutions for traditional forms, especially to replace the nuclear family norm. These include group marriages (Constantine, 1970, p. 44), homosexual marriages (Mabee, 1965, pp. 491–493; West, 1967), communal families (Hostetler and Huntingdon, 1967; Neuman and Wilhelm, p. 3), and marriages continued only by renewable vows. Moore argues that the family in any of its traditional forms is dysfunctional in modern industrial society (Moore, 1958).

E. The Functional Approach

This is another dominant theme in family studies. Usually functions are looked at in tandem with family structures in acknowledgment of the fact these two aspects cannot readily be separated, not even for purposes of objective study. There are inherent difficulties in functional analysis of family, not unlike the problems in looking at the functions of any other social system. The pitfall is, of course, to reason circularly that a pattern or value is "functional" to the given system and the proof of functionality is found in the fact of its existence.

The family is generally acknowledged to exist universally to perform certain functions necessary to the survival of the species. Generally these functions are enumerated as procreation and child rearing, implying that the family has major responsibility for these societal imperatives. Beyond this level of generality there are divergent ways of describing and explaining family functions and the relationships of these to the broader social systems.

Parsons applies his functional prerequisites of goal attainment, pattern maintenance, integration, and adaptation to the family system. As stated earlier he stresses the instrumental and expressive role functions within the family constellation and how these are allocated to the family members, especially on the sexual axis. He accounts for the changing functions of the American family through emphasizing the system characteristics of differentiation and specialization. As the macrosystem becomes increasingly complex, the family as a component system becomes increasingly specialized in the functions it performs for both the larger system and the family components. Parsons says that "when two functions, previously embedded in the same structure, are subsequently performed by two newly differentiated structures, they can *both* be fulfilled more intensively and with a greater degree of freedom" (Rodman, 1966, p. 264). The core functions remaining in the family are the maintenance of the household and the intimate personal relations of the members of the household.

As specialized institutional arrangements evolve to provide for socialization of children into the culture, the family relinquishes functions and becomes increasingly specialized. This relinquishment of family functions particularly affects women, leading to the broadening of the female role. Margaret Adams, a social worker, has commented on the transfer of "nurturant" roles for women from the family to professions. She describes the process by which women are channeled into social work, nursing, teaching, secretarial work, and certain other professions, as "the compassion trap." She says:

the proliferation of the helping professions into a complex array of welfare services took many of the more highly specialized aspects of the nurturing and protective functions out of the home. . . . In addition, when one or both parents were out of the home for a substantial part of the day, they had to delegate their acculturating functions. Thus the synthesizing role traditionally discharged by women in the home was translated to a wider sphere and spread its influence through a broader range of activities. Instead of (or in addition to) keeping the family intact and maximally functional, women became involved in housekeeping tasks on behalf of society at large and assumed responsibility for keeping its operation viable. (Adams, 1971, p. 72)

Parsons has noted the emergence of specialized peer groupings which evidently are assuming functions previously performed by the family. These are differentiated on an age axis. Examples include the aged, adolescents, and young adults. Recently Kenneth Keniston has proposed a "new" stage of life, which occurs *outside* the context of either a family of orientation or a family of procreation.

We are witnessing today the emergence on a mass scale of a previously unrecognized stage of life, a stage that intervenes between adolescence and adulthood. I propose to call this stage of life the stage of youth. . . (Keniston, 1970, p. 635)

What characterizes a growing minority of postadolescents today is that they have not settled the questions whose answers once defined adulthood: questions of relationship to the existing society, questions of vocation, questions of social role and life-style. (Keniston, 1970, p. 634)

This "youth" stage is clearly related to Erikson's sixth stage, that of intimacy vs isolation (see Chapter 6). If the family is not adequate in assisting young adults in resolving this crisis, then they must look to other institutions, or create new ones; or, conceivably, simply fail to resolve the crisis in massive numbers. Toffler's *Future Shock* suggests possible outcomes if such failure does occur, and what alternative institutions might assist (Toffler, 1970).

Feldman and Scherz take the position that the rapid changes accompanying technology and industrialization have disrupted the traditional family functions that provided for the survival and socialization needs of its members. Other institutionalized provisions must then be created to substitute for or augment the family.

Thus, schools supplement learning conducted within the family; clinics, hospitals, rest homes and other facilities provide health care; foster care is available for children and adults who cannot be provided with needed care at home; family counseling is extended when marital discord or parent-child relationships indicate the need for the intervention of an outside authority; juvenile courts and correctional institutions assist with severe problems needing control. (Feldman and Scherz, 1967, p. 53)

This functional position is congruent with Zimmerman's description of the atomistic family form.

Lidz finds the family performs three sets of discrete but interrelated functions

(Lidz, 1963, pp. 44–46). For the children, the family provides physical care and nurturance and at the same time directs their personality development. For the spouses, it furnishes the means to personal fulfillment and stability. For society, the family takes responsibility for enculturating new members. Lidz suggests "it is possible that these functions which are fundamental to human adaptation cannot be fulfilled separately at all and must be fused in the family" (Lidz, 1963, p. 45).

Magorah Maruyama finds the extent of family function specialization alarming. Dr. Maruyama coined the term *monopolarization* to describe the state of affairs wherein the child's relationship to adults is confined to a mother or a father, or more precisely, to *one set* of parents (Maruyama, 1966, p. 133). Monopolarization is seen as a metassumption of theories of personality and of many Western philosophies. The totality of the child's relationship to his parents sets narrow parameters for his development and invests undue responsibility in the parents.

Dr. Maruyama recommends dilution of this relationship through increased interfamily contacts and integration of persons who are not in the family circuit. This could be accomplished through the formation of voluntary adult-child communities, without any necessity of major reforms in family structure (Maruyama, 1966, p. 147). However, many communes have deliberately attempted to create alternative family structures. One writer reports that "today's communes seek a family warmth and intimacy, to become extended families. A 50-person commune in California, for example, called itself 'The Lynch Family', a New Mexico commune 'The Chosen Family', a New York City group simply 'The Family' " (Kanter, 1972, p. 54). Kanter also points out that exclusivity of parenting was avoided in successful nineteenth-century communes by separating children from their parents, creating a "family of the whole" (Kanter, 1972, p. 55).

F. Classification and Description of Family Dysfunction

This is the final approach to be considered here. A small number of investigators have sought to formulate diagnostic categories to analyze family disorganization. Feldman and Scherz classify families as adequate, chaotic, neurotic, and psychotic (Feldman and Scherz, 1967, pp. 47–51).

Adequate Family. This family has a history of reasonably mature adaptations to the ordinary problems of living. It comes to the attention of a social agency when an externally induced crisis, such as the death of a parent, an acute illness, or sudden loss of income, befalls it. This family will soon develop a way of coping with the stress and establish a new steady state.

Chaotic Family. Such families have a characterological set of problems. They are confused about role expectations, are unpredictable and impulsive, and have little sense of direction and family goals.

Neurotic Family. Anxiety is ever present and there is a sense of unhappiness and uneasiness. The family may perform many tasks well but have great difficulty with one. The extent of impairment of family function depends upon a range of factors, including the residual problems activated by the current stress.

Psychotic Family. This family may well develop a psychotic member or may operate in bizarre ways, or it may have a psychotic core, that is, evidence psychotic symptoms in some respects but not in others.

Based on research findings of a study conducted by Bradley Buell and Associates of multiproblem families in a number of communities, a scheme for diagnosis of family dysfunction was presented by Voiland. The following is a summary of this system of family classification (Voiland and Associates, 1962, pp. 115–289).

The Perfectionistic Family. Such families place undue importance on being without fault and avoiding open friction. Excessive self-reproach for imagined failures is characteristic of both parents and children. An external event or stress mobilizes anxiety and uncertainty in the adult family member; someone is not measuring up to the perfectionistic standards of behavior and achievement.

The Inadequate Family. Next on the continuum is this type of family with its overreliance on others for encouragement, direction, and support to resolve problems the average family can resolve for itself.

The Egocentric Family. The parents possess predominant character traits of self-centeredness and opinionated attitudes. It is the aggregate effect of parental narcissistic needs, directly or vicariously expressed, which sets the tone of this family. Problems of children in such families are denied, or the parents each blame their spouse.

The Unsocial Family. The family lacks social rapport and connectiveness with other people and their environment. Generally more than one family member is personally maladjusted to an extent warranting the attention of social and legal institutions.

These four types of families are then further categorized according to manifest problems: child rearing disorders, child disorders, marital disorders, financial disorders, and adult disorders.

These two diagnostic frameworks, and others that attempt the same thing, add an important perspective to family theory, which is especially helpful to those who work with troubled families.

II. A HUMAN SYSTEMS VIEW OF THE FAMILY

The family has come to be viewed as a system by many observers. Perhaps most notable among these, in their relevance to social work, are family therapists. One of the outstanding researchers of family therapy, Jay Haley, says:

What family therapists most have in common they also share with a number of behavioral scientists in the world today: There is an increasing awareness that psychiatric problems are social problems which involve the total ecological system. There is a concern with, and an attempt to change, what happens with the family and also the interlocking systems of the family and the social institutions in which the family is embedded. The fragmentation of the individual into parts, or the family into parts is being abandoned, and there is a growing consensus that a new ecological framework defines problems in new ways and calls for new ways in therapy. (Sager and Kaplan, 1972, p. 270)

For purposes of the following discussion we will treat the family as a social system (holon) possessing the characteristics of a social system but distinguishable from other social systems by its goals, functions, and climate of feeling. The family is defined both by its members and by the culture and community within which it exists. Lidz's functional viewpoint, referred to earlier, points to the functions performed by the family as system, subsystem, and suprasystem. The family provides the opportunity for intimate social interaction for all of its members. It is also the base of personal security for all its members.

To begin with, any discussion of family structure must necessarily start from the perspective of some individual. The inclusions and exclusions of the family system must be from some particular perspective. If that perspective is the legal status of a person for inheritance purposes, it is quite different from a perspective for purposes of establishing who are the members of a household.

A family then is to be construed as patterns of relatedness as they converge in a person. These patterns may be identical to those of another member of his family, but could be unique to him. Those relationships of the person that can be classified as family relationships will be delineated within the remainder of this chapter. The characteristics of family will be grouped under the familiar headings of structure, behavior, and evolution. For consistency we will use the subtopics introduced in Chapter 1.

A. Structural Characteristics

As with any social system, *organization* is of prime concern. Family organization is distinguishable from other systems by its high level of intrarelatedness. Since it is the smallest social and interpersonal system there is an intensity of interdependence among its components. "The family is a unit, and the actions of any member affect all; it has characteristics superordinate to those of its individual members; it subserves societal functions; it constitutes a milieu as well as a group of persons" (Lidz, 1963, p. 7).

The effectiveness of family organization is the extent to which its goals are fulfilled—the goals of its members and the goals of society. Goal attainment is paramount. If societal goals are not fulfilled the family may be dissolved by legal decree, as when children are removed or divorces granted. This action does not necessarily dissolve the family as an interacting system. Malcolm X clearly describes the difference. After his family was dispersed by the court, "separated though we were, all of us maintained fairly close touch around Lansing—in school and out—whenever we could get together. Despite the artificially created separation and distance between us, we still remained very close in our feelings toward each other" (Malcolm X, 1966, p. 22).

Society, the family, and family members may all share goals for the family of economic independence and close family affection but be in conflict about the priorities to be assigned to each of these goals. These conflicts may occur when people find it necessary to leave familiar territory to find employment. A Kentuckian told this story to one of the authors:

> A man died and was being shown around Heaven by St. Peter. Off in one corner of Heaven they saw a group of people with suitcases. The man asked who these people were and St. Peter replied, "Oh, they're from Kentucky; they go home on weekends."

In order to achieve goals the family must, through its organization, secure and conserve energy from both internal and external sources. The members of the family must contribute energy for the family system as well as import energy for their individual purposes. The following dialogue between the mother and sons (about the father-husband) is illustrative of this dependence of the family upon energy from its members and from the environment. It is from the play *Death of a Salesman.*

LINDA: No, a lot of people think he's lost his—balance. But you don't have to be very smart to know what his trouble is. The man is exhausted.
HAPPY: Sure!
LINDA: A small man can be just as exhausted as a great man. He works for a company thirty-six years this March, opens up unheard-of territories to their trademark, and now in his old age they take his salary away.
HAPPY: (Indignantly): I didn't know that, Mom.
LINDA: You never asked, my dear! Now that you get your spending money someplace else you don't trouble your mind with him.
HAPPY: But I gave you money last—
LINDA: Christmas time, fifty dollars! To fix the hot water heater it cost ninety-seven fifty! For five weeks he's been on straight commission, like a beginner, an unknown!
BIFF: Those ungrateful bastards!
LINDA: Are they any worse than his sons?

(Miller, 1949, pp. 56–57)

The *boundary* of a family is behavioral and is evidenced by the intensity and frequency of interaction among its components. The intensity of sentiment interchanges is especially distinctive as compared to other small groups. It is within the interactional boundaries of the family that the member participates in a particularly *close network of feelings, both positive and negative,* with a minimal sense of needing to put up a front. The common expression "I feel at home" conveys something of this feeling of freedom to be oneself.

This exchange between Martha and George from *Who's Afraid of Virginia Woolf* illustrates closeness through negative feeling.

> MARTHA: You've really screwed up, George.
> GEORGE: Oh, for God's sake, Martha!
> MARTHA: I mean it ... you really have.
> GEORGE: You can sit there in that chair of yours, you can sit there with the gin running out of your mouth, and you can humiliate me, you can tear me apart ... ALL NIGHT ... and that's perfectly all right ... that's O.K. ...
> MARTHA: YOU CAN STAND IT!
> GEORGE: I CANNOT STAND IT!
> MARTHA: YOU CAN STAND IT!! YOU MARRIED ME FOR IT!!
> GEORGE: That is a desperately sick lie.
> MARTHA: DON'T YOU KNOW IT, EVEN YET?
>
> (Albee, 1963, pp. 152–153)

Family boundaries change as members come and go. Extended kin, close friends and neighbors, or foster children may be absorbed within the boundary of a given family. Even physical presence is not the measure of participation within family boundaries. A person may be related by birth or marriage and living in the same household, but yet not be within family boundaries because he is not part of the interactional network, the bond that coheres. On the other hand, the family member in the hospital, away at school or military service, or incarcerated may well remain within the family boundary as defined above. Again a quotation from Malcolm X is illustrative. Malcolm describes his activities:

> I'm rarely at home more than half of any week; I have been away as much as five months. I never get a chance to take her anywhere, and I know she likes to be with her husband. She is used to my calling her from airports anywhere from Boston to San Francisco, or Miami to Seattle, or here lately, cabling her from Cairo, Accra, or the Holy City of Mecca. Once on the long-distance telephone, Betty told me in beautiful phrasing the way she thinks. She said, "You are present when you are away." (Malcolm X, 1966, p. 233)

Maintenance of family boundary occurs on both sides of the boundary. The family frequently excludes nonmembers—"It's a family argument"; "the family vacation." Society supports family boundaries through assigning the family priority on occasions highly charged with sentiment—weddings, funerals, and religious holidays. Cultures decree special occasions to reinforce family sentiment and interchange, such as Mother's Day and Father's Day. Business organizations permit employees leave for illness of immediate family members and for funerals of members of the extended family.

As is true of all social systems, families require exchanges across boundaries.

The term *monopolarization* referred to earlier in this chapter expresses concern that the specialized nuclear family tends toward entropy because of insufficient sentiment exchanges with its environment.

Differentiation and *specialization* are concepts applicable to the family. We have already alluded to the fact that the family has become a highly specialized cultural component uniquely responsible for meeting the security and sentiment needs of its members. The narrowing of family functions can be understood as a result of differentiation within American society. Other institutions such as social welfare services that provide income maintenance, health care, emotional support, and day care, have grown up to specialize in functions previously fulfilled by the extended family.

Within the family, differentiation and specialization are reflected in role allocations. So that the family can meet societal expectations and continue as an economic household, particular family members are breadwinners by mutual consent of the family members. Differential role expectations are commonly determined by age and sex, but these are uniquely refined in each family system. A particular family may reposit much of its unresolved or unacknowledged tensions in one family member who then specializes as the "problem" family member. The concept of the family scapegoat is a case in point. Bell and Vogel have elucidated the conditions that lead to a child becoming the family scapegoat.

> The parents are fraught with internal conflicts and ambivalence but each consciously expressed only one side of the ambivalence thus forming a set of overt polarization and mutual avoidance. A marriage cannot survive under these conditions so an appropriate object is selected to symbolize the conflicts and draw off the tension. The emotional disturbance of the child is simply the effect of internalizing the conflicting demands placed upon the child by his parents. In the short run he receives rewards from his family when he accepts his special role. The scapegoating mechanism may be functional for the family group through enabling its continued existence but be dysfunctional for the child's development and his adaptation outside the family. (Vogel and Bell, 1960, pp. 382–397)

A fourth aspect of family structure is its *territoriality*. Family territory has both a spacial and behavioral dimension. The concept of home territory is notably descriptive of family territory since the occupants have a profound sense of "place" and belongingness (Lyman and Scott, 1967). The family consolidates around, and finds its identity through, the achieving and maintaining of territory. Behavioral territory was earlier described in the discussion of boundary; this is the interactional territory of feeling-closeness. Physically the family also occupies territory. The architect, the contractor, the city planner, the mail carrier, indeed the garbage collector, all exist as societally supported occupations to serve and maintain the family within its spacial territory. This territory is signified by the house or apartment number; it may be further marked by posts, fences, and hedges.

The family territory may encompass a village, town, or neighborhood. "In ancient imagery, the center of his territory is a man's 'house,' be it a home or a farm, a firm or a family, a dynasty or a church; and his 'city' marks the boundary of all the houses associated with his" (Erikson, 1969, p. 176). Society requests and requires families to be territorially based, to be oriented in space. Society's primary means of establishing social identifications are the answers to two questions: "Name?" "Address?" Or, less formally, "Where are you from?" which actually means "What was the place of your family of origin?" This societal concern with family territoriality is clearly expressed in the following quotation. "Show me a man who cares no more for one place than another, and I will show you in that same person one who loves nothing but himself. Beware of those who are homeless by choice" (Southey, 1959, p. 508).

B. Behavioral Aspects

Social control and socialization are characteristic functions of the family. The family is always a subsystem of its society and as such participates in the socialization processes of that society. It would be defensible to classify all socially defined dysfunctional families as failing to meet the requirements for socialization of its members. Socialization as used here may be defined as "the process by which the young human being acquires the values and knowledge of his group and learns the social roles appropriate to his position in it" (Goode, 1964, p. 10). A central task of the family is to assure that its members are sufficiently acculturated to participate in the other societal subsystems that enable attainment of societal goals. For example, Project Headstart was instituted to supplement families that were not fulfilling this expectation as societally defined—to socialize the children, and, if necessary, the parents as well.

Furthermore, the family is expected to control its members, to prevent them from engaging in deviant behavior, which seriously interferes with attainment of the system's goals. Witness the recurring idea that parents should be held accountable for the delinquent behavior of their children, and legal efforts to enforce this.

Billingsley emphasizes the fact that the socialization charge is doubly difficult for the Negro family. In addition to the pressures that affect all families in America, the Negro family must cope with three additional facts of life:

   a. the peculiar historical development,
   b. the caste-like qualities in the American stratification system which relegates all Negroes to inferior status, and
   c. the social class and economic systems which keep most Negroes in the lower social classes.

The American Negro family must teach its young members not only how to be human, but also how to be black in a white society. (Billingsley, 1968, p. 28)

No doubt the breadth of the socialization job allocated to the family has narrowed through some aspects being assumed by other social institutions, particularly the school, but the primacy of family influence in personality development remains relatively intact.

Communication is increasingly emphasized as both the keystone of family interaction and the key to understanding family dynamics (see, for example, Bell, 1964; Satir, 1964). All family behavior is influenced by its style and effectiveness of communication. Communication is here used to denote the exchange of meaningful symbols, vocal and gestural. It refers to the transfer of energy to accomplish system goals. The discussion of communication in Chapter 1 applies exactly to the family system.

A family can be seen to have a characteristic communication style. These characteristic patterns of interaction operate within the boundaries of the family and in transactions with external systems. Don Jackson has emphasized that the "redundancy principle" operates in family life. "The family will interact in repetitious sequences in all areas of its life, though some areas may highlight these repetitions (or patterns) more quickly and systematically than do other areas" (Jackson, 1970, p. 121). An individual family then has a unique system of communication patterns, which strongly influence the behavior of its members.

The concentration of a few writers on body language has extended the reservoir of concepts capable of exploring family communication patterns (Birdwhistell, 1970; Fast, 1970; Hall, 1961; Scheflen, 1972). Communication practices are especially crucial to any understanding of family because of the importance and intensity of feeling exchange.

Communication in the family is extremely complex and subtle because of the number of functions served by the family. One energy exchange can convey any number of meanings. An example might be a parent's directive to a child to do what the teacher says. Included in this could be several messages:

1. you *ought* to obey authority (to meet societal expectations);
2. but you *ought not* to be required to submit to unjust orders (to meet the child's needs);
3. nevertheless do what she tells you to do (to avoid conflict with the environment);
4. keep out of trouble (and avoid conflict between parent and teacher, that is, between family system and environment);
5. because if you don't you'll get it from me (meet parents' needs in order to satisfy the child's need for security).

The child is expected to understand and respond to all these messages.

A recent book on marriage focuses on the "open marriage," and on communication in such a marriage, using "communication" in a broad sense as we have used it here. The book describes the open marriage as one in which there is free energy exchange between partners and between them and their social environment:

> in synergy one and one makes three, not just two. It is this special effect, this enhancement, that makes it possible in open marriage for husband

and wife to exist and grow as two separate individuals, yet at the same time to transcend their duality and achieve a unity on another level, beyond themselves, a unity that develops out of the love for each other's growth. In a synergistic, cooperative way, each one's individual growth enhances and augments the other's growth, pleasure and fulfillment. . . . the more both partners grow, the more stimulating and dynamic each one becomes for the other. (O'Neill and O'Neill, 1972, p. 261)

This statement refers to the marital partners and, similarly, we suggest that a synergistic family may exist, one in which members communicate (verbally and nonverbally) in such fashion as to stimulate and support each other. This feedback permits members to become fuller individuals and, at the same time, permits the family to become richer and more meaningful and supportive for the members.

Adaptation is an essential family function. Family is a system of accommodation to social change. Because the family has consistently had the capacity to change its structure and function to adapt to marked changes in its environment, it has survived wars, industrial and technological revolutions, and traumatic disruptions in social conditions that made traditional patterns of coping obsolete. The family calls upon the energies of its components and exchanges energies with its significant environmental systems.

Another necessary adaptive mode of the family is its assimilation of exterior stress as experienced by its members. Although other social institutions such as religious and fraternal organizations also fulfill this function, the family is expected to be the primary system wherein a person can relax (unwind), divest himself of his externally adaptable role behaviors, and be himself. If a family cannot so assimilate stress and enable a person to be himself, or if a person cannot allow this to happen, substitutes must be found. Perhaps the emergence of sensitivity and encounter groups are a replacement for a defunct family function (see Chapter 4).

A family is considered maladaptive when it cannot adapt to the changing demands placed upon it by its environment and its members. If it is too unchanging (morphostasis) and devotes an undue proportion of its available energies to maintenance of existing structures, it will not be able to cope with external requirements. In essence, it maintains its previous functions and is thus dysfunctional. If on the other hand it is in a constantly unstable state of transition, it does not furnish the degree of stability its members require for repair of ego insults and for the chance to merely be oneself in an atmosphere of feeling-closeness. This leads to the final system aspects of the family.

C. Evolutionary Aspects

Steady state is characteristic of the family system, which needs to be simultaneously changing and remaining the same. The family exists through its life cycle with ever-changing requirements from its members and from society. The well-adapted marital pair, for example, must modify its mode of functioning with the advent of their first child. A family may operate to its satisfaction and to that of society while the offspring are dependent, but run aground when the children need emancipation from their family of orientation. As Pitrim Sorokin points out, "any system changes incessantly during its existence: among all its properties something new is incessantly introduced and something old is incessantly lost from moment to moment of its existence. In this sense any socio-cultural process is ever new and unrepeated" (Rodman, 1966, p. 253).

The steady state of a family is maintained in various ways. James Framo describes a family in therapy:

> Family therapy observations have revealed how the symptoms of one member often serve useful and necessary functions for the others, how the underlying system reciprocity is revealed by symptoms appearing in a previously asymptomatic member when the symptomatic one improves, and how a marriage may rupture when the symptoms which had been built into the relationship are no longer present. (Sager and Kaplan, 1972, pp. 288–289)

He says further:

> Generally speaking, symptoms are maintained or reduced to the extent that they serve relationship system functions and are an integral component of a bonding force in the relationships. . . . Of course, changes occur in people and in symptoms in circumstances other than formal psychotherapy, most often when the context changes, that is, when the symptoms no longer have meaning in a given relationship system in time. (Sager and Kaplan, 1972, p. 294)

Haley aptly describes some of the morphostatic operations within the family, such as "mutual secondary gain," "monitoring," "open sharing," "scapegoating," and "vicarious participation." These occur in a "circular feedback system. Interpersonal conflict affects intrapsychic conflict, and vice versa." (Sager and Kaplan, 1972, p. 304)

All that was said about steady state in Chapter 1 applies to the family. Often the family in crisis is in a situation of disruptive transition from one form of steady state to another. At such times a family *may* be more open to use of energies from outside its own system, more amenable to interventive efforts. Erikson's definition of crisis applies to families as well as individuals (see Chapter 6).

SUMMARY

The family is a critical human system. It serves unique, although always changing, purposes for its subsystems (family members and combinations of family members) and suprasystems (society and parts of society). A social system view of the family provides a skeletal frame that can include, but not substitute for, the various perspectives on the family that have been offered. Each of these perspectives is valuable in its contribution to a particular aspect of the family.

We suggest that the family is best defined from the viewpoint of the person within it. The definition should include those relationships that are "family" for him—that is, a person's family are those with whom he interacts and performs the family functions within the given society. In many crucial ways the family is the principal intersection between the culture and the individuals within the culture, the point of most interaction and change. While discrete aspects of the family may each be better explained by one of the family theories we have examined, a systems view best explains the changes the family undergoes and the relationships which are cause and effect of those changes.

Postscript

No discussion of the family can be considered complete without some prognostication. It seems to be both a right and an obligation to fantasize about the future of the family. It is a cliché to call attention to the current "state of flux" of the family, or to view with alarm "the dramatic upheaval" of the American family. We would only predict that in the near future a wider range of family forms (including some of those mentioned earlier) will be sanctioned, and the definition of family roles will be on axes other than primarily the sexual one. Since the family is an interdependent part of the fabric of culture, it will influence and be influenced by changes in other social institutions. We anticipate that the family will continue to have its unique position at the point where the person and his culture meet.

SUGGESTED READINGS

Ackerman, Nathan W. *The Psychodynamics of Family Living: Diagnosis and Treatment of Family Relationships.* New York: Basic Books, 1958. A readable, interesting psychoanalytic approach to family diagnosis and treatment.

Billingsley, Andrew. *Black Families in White America.* Englewood Cliffs, N.J.: Spectrum, 1968. A systems approach to the family that has been used as the small-map text for this chapter. Billingsley has drawn on experience of blacks to supplement and revise sociological analyses of the family.

Goode, William J. *The Family.* Englewood Cliffs, N.J.: Prentice-Hall, 1964. A basic family text, excellent for an overview. This could well serve as the small-map text for this chapter for students who have not had previous family studies.

Handel, George. "Psychological Study of Whole Families," *Psychological Bulletin* 63, 1965, 19–41. An excellent review of the development of "whole family" approach (systems) and research on family. Solid, comprehensive. Appears as Chapter 6 of *Man, Woman, and Marriage: Small Group Processes in the Family,* Alan L. Grey, ed. (New York: Atherton, 1970), pp. 116–152.

Jackson, Don. "The Study of the Family," in *Family Process,* Nathan W. Ackerman, ed. New York: Basic Books, 1970, pp. 111–130. An approach to understanding the family, drawing heavily on social systems concepts.

Nye, F. Ivan, and Felix M. Berardo. *Emerging Conceptual Frameworks in Family Analysis*. New York: Macmillan, 1968. An ambitious attempt to summarize various perspectives for viewing the family system. Especially useful is Chapter 2, "The Anthropological Approach to the Study of the Family." Also includes the systems perspective.

Sager, Clifford, and Helen Singer Kaplan. *Progress in Group and Family Therapy*. New York: Brunner/Mazel, 1972. Oriented to systems approach, which Chapter 1, "Analytic Group Therapy and General Systems Theory" by Helen E. Durkin makes explicit. Excellent; current experience and research. Much on applications of systems model. Many case examples.

Voiland, Alice L. and Associates. *Family Casework Diagnosis*. New York: Columbia University Press, 1962. A detailed explication of the diagnostic system derived from the St. Paul Project and other studies of multiproblem families.

chapter 6

THE PERSON

I. THEORETICAL APPROACHES

This chapter deals with the person as a human system and introduces concepts of human growth and behavior deemed most important for the thesis of this book. To begin with, we examine three of the major theoretical approaches to human behavior as embodied in representative theorists. Next, we examine the life cycle of the person as the evolution of this human system. The three approaches to be examined are the psychosocial (Sigmund Freud, Erik H. Erikson), the behavioral (B. F. Skinner), and the cognitive (Jean Piaget).

A. Psychosocial Approach to Human Behavior

The psychosocial view of human behavior is introduced first because this will be the major theme of the content dealing with the life cycle. The other approaches, behavioral and cognitive, will be minor themes.

FREUD

Sigmund Freud was born in Moravia (Freiburg, now in Czechoslovakia) in 1856 and died in London in 1939. From the age of 40 he was a prolific writer with interesting subjects to write about and a fine literary style. His works are studied not only by students of psychology and psychiatry but also by those interested in literature and religion.

The quantity and breadth of his writings are staggering. His most influential and widely read works are: *The Interpretation of Dreams,* published in 1900, which first set forth the kernel of his views of the indispensable techniques of psychoanalysis; *The Psychopathology of Everyday Life,* published in 1901, which sought to establish the purposefulness of all behavior through analysis of slips of the tongue and trivial errors; *Three Contributions to the Theory of Sex* (originally entitled *Three Essays On Sexuality*), which provided the foundation of his theory on neurosis, the need for repression, and the nature of libido. The *Introductory Lectures to Psychoanalysis* (1916 and 1932–1936) synthesized the theory of each of these eras. *An Outline of Psychoanalysis* (1940) is considered by many the most concise and lucid statement of his general theory. Stone's biography engagingly recounts the struggle Freud underwent in the pursuit of his studies (Stone, 1971). It documents the growth of the psychoanalytic movement and the resistance of the "human behavior establishment" to the heresies being propounded.

Freud's work (like that of anyone else) must be viewed in its historical-cultural context. Many persons who disclaim the Freudian contribution do so in violation of this principle. Because his models were taken from the physical science and mechanics of the time, his system employs the terminology of "forces" and "resistances." *Libido* is described as a relatively fixed quantity of energy present in every individual, related primarily and essentially to his sexual drive. In his later writings Freud added the concept of *Eros,* which broadened the energy metaphor to include desires not accounted for by the sexual drive.

Lindzey and Hall state that Freud, brought up under the influence of the strongly deterministic and positivistic philosophy of nineteenth century science, regarded the human organism as a complex energy system (1957, pp. 29 ff.). At that time physical scientists were saying that energy must be defined in relation to the work it performed (this is consistent with the discussion of energy presented in Chapter 1). Because the phenomena that interested Freud were of a psychological nature, it was reasonable for him to give to this form of energy the term *psychic energy.*

Freud was, then, occupied with the construction of a framework to explain the structure, function, and evolution of the psychic apparatus. The structural concepts of *id, ego,* and *superego* provide the form and organization with which to process, contain, and direct the energies (libido) of the system. Personality is viewed as dynamism (the psychodynamics of behavior), not unlike the structural systems of hydrodynamics and thermodynamics. The use of the force-resistance models continues in current conceptions of stress and adaptation, conflict theory, and some theories of social change.

Almost all of the Freudians and so-called neo-Freudians (including Erikson) employ concepts and theories relying on this approach to structure and function, with certain modifications based on later advances of knowledge. The ego defense mechanisms are, in essence, substructures employed to deal with forces either through the erection of resistance blocks as in repression, suppression, and denial, or through channeling of forces toward other objects as in projection, displacement, and sublimation.

A number of the Freudian insights are especially germane to the human services and to this book. These will be introduced briefly and then expanded upon in the discussion of the life cycle of the human system.

1. The form and structure of the unconscious is a crucial concept in Freudian thought and represents the organic, the impulses, and perhaps the species (Whyte, 1962). Throughout his 40 years of study, Freud focused primary attention on the exploration of the nature of unconscious man. This is a central theme originating in his first work, *Studies In Hysteria*, published in 1894. Awareness and some understanding of the unconscious have long been of importance—to a greater or lesser extent—in the body of social work knowledge (Hamilton, 1944; Hollis, 1972).

2. The discovery of infantile sexuality (Freud, 1949, p. 26) is fundamental to the psychosexual view of human development and has traditionally been a part of the mainstream of social work knowledge.

3. We interpret the id-ego-superego triad as both structure and function of the human personality system as formulated by Freud. The Freudian psychic triad is a system that tends toward closure since the dynamics are largely intrasystem, with the goal being a homeostatic state.

   Social work and other counseling professions have largely attended to the ego aspects of the triad. In the past, as well as the present, the focus of social service ministrations has been the ego—for example, evaluation of ego strengths, techniques of ego support, and attempts to parse and understand ego functions. The concept of id is seldom encountered in the literature of the various counseling professions, and superego only a bit more frequently.

4. The Freudian construct of the *oedipal conflict* is central to his theory and the theory of most neo-Freudians. The functional or dysfunctional resolution of the oedipal conflict serves as the prototype for the subsequent intimate interpersonal relationships and the establishment of a sense of sexuality. Although most neo-Freudians hold that the oedipal conflict is strongly influenced by the cultural form of the family, they continue to view it as a central concept. In Freudian thought, the resolution of the oedipal conflict also was the wellspring of the superego.

5. The *pleasure principle* and the *reality principle* are frequently encountered in the literature of human services, although not

always so designated. It will be recalled that the pleasure principle seeks immediate gratification of impulses while the reality principle postpones immediate gratification for greater deferred gratification or gratification of a higher order. This "dynamic duo" has been applied to a range of phenomena that concern social workers and appears either explicitly or implicitly in literature ranging from child rearing to social class.

These then are some of the highlights of Freudian theory that have been incorporated into human services literature. *From the social systems viewpoint the psychoanalytical formulation can be seen as a model constructed to account for the sources of energy in the personality, the transformation of energy into behavior, and the topography of the structures employed for transformation of energy.* Neo-Freudians have carried forward the earlier formulations with their own particular emphases.

ERIKSON

Erik H. Erikson was born of Danish parents in Frankfurt, Germany, in 1902. He attended the humanistic gymnasium and began to prepare himself for a career as an artist. As an artist-tutor in Vienna he became acquainted with persons in the emerging Psychoanalytic Institute. He acquired psychoanalytic training, working most closely with Dorothy Burlingham and Anna Freud. Interestingly, he also earned a certificate from the Maria Montessori School and was one of the few men with membership in the Montessori Academy. In 1933 he emigrated to the United States, where he still lives (Maier, 1965, pp. 12 ff.; Coles, 1970).

Erikson's major work has been to create and extend a conceptual framework for the total life cycle of humans. His scheme was originally set forth in *Childhood and Society,* published in 1950. Major revisions, refinements, and expansions were published in *Insight and Responsibility* (1964) and *Identity: Youth and Crisis* (1968). He has also pioneered in the field of psychohistorical biography with his two monumental works, *Young Man Luther* (1958), and *Gandhi's Truth* (1969). He was awarded the Pulitzer Prize for his work on Gandhi.

Erikson's eight ages of man are used as the organizing theme for this chapter for two reasons. First, his seems to be the only extant theory of human development that encompasses the total life span. Second, his psychosocial approach to human development is particularly in accord with the human services with their simultaneous attention to the individual and his environment. A few of the key ideas of the Eriksonian formulation of the life cycle are enumerated to introduce his thinking.

1. Erikson's view of the life cycle is based on the epigenetic principle. *Epigenesis* ("epi" means "upon," "genesis" means "emergence") means that one developmental stage occurs on top of, and in relation to, another in space and time (Evans, 1967, pp. 21–22).

Since these are a hierarchy of stages, not a simple sequence, the potentials for growth and development are all present in the human organism. Out of the whole the parts arise, each component having a special time for ascendency, until all the processes have run their course and have developed into a functioning whole. Thus the human personality is seen as an evolving system comprised of potential matrices, which arise according to some sort of ground plan. Correlated with this is the interdependence of the emergent matrices; the development of a subsequent matrix is somewhat dependent on that which has gone before. Each alters the previously achieved balances. The stages are not discrete, nor are they simply an additive process.

The stages might be pictured simplistically as a set of teeterboards balanced upon each other (see Figure 4). Each level (or stage) depends upon the balance achieved in the preceding stage, and an adjustment of any level involves an adjustment of all the others. The point at which each level is balanced is the ratio of polar qualities achieved in each stage.

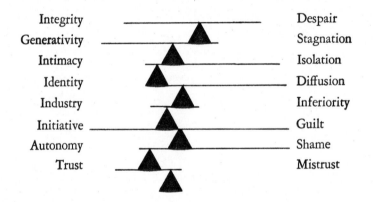

Integrity	Despair
Generativity	Stagnation
Intimacy	Isolation
Identity	Diffusion
Industry	Inferiority
Initiative	Guilt
Autonomy	Shame
Trust	Mistrust

Figure 4.   Stages of Life Cycle According to Erikson.

2. The life cycle formulation of Erikson is based on man's genetic energy, but is totally dependent on social experiences. Three principles of organization and process are: (1) physical (constitutional or somatic organization); (2) ego (the self as organizing force); and (3) social (organizing responsive to the rules and expectations of society and culture). In other words, the somatic process, the ego process, and the societal process equal the human life. The similarities and differences between this triad and the Freudian triad are important. Someone commented that Erikson's is an ego psychology and Freud's is an id psychology. Erikson has said,

"a human being, thus, is at all times an organism, an ego and a member of society and is involved in all three processes of organization" (Erikson, 1963, p. 36). In our view, of course, these are three systems levels.

Within this scheme the unfolding of the human system is seen as a combination of maturation, socialization, and education. The eight stages of the life cycle represent a synthesis of developmental (maturation) and social (learning) tasks. *Maturation* is "the process of growth for all members of the species, with predictable characteristics." *Learning* is "individual growth, new behavioral acquisitions based on the organism's experience rather than its structure" (Church and Stone, 1957, p. 38). Growth, then, derives from the constant interaction of maturation and learning. The organisms's *readiness* is determined by maturational considerations, while its *learning* is a function of social experiences.

3. The idea of *crisis* is central to Erikson's theory. His use of this term is quite similar to the idea of crisis in *crisis intervention* and refers to a time of necessary change. The crises during growth and development, as Erikson uses the term, connote a heightened potential for development (or change) accompanied by greater vulnerability. Crisis is not necessarily a negative state of affairs, but rather an unavoidable occasion requiring coping of some variety. In Erikson's view the crises occur at their proper time out of the interaction of the organism's maturation and society's expectations. The outcome (not *resolution* necessarily) is dependent upon the personality resources the individual has accrued up to that point *and* the opportunities and resources available in his social situation.

Erikson has written extensively and thoroughly on two of the eight crises of development—the first crisis, basic trust vs basic mistrust, and identity vs diffusion. Attention to these particular periods of child development is not unique to Erikson, since infancy and adolescence have attracted the attention of much of child development research. His theories about the first critical task of life, trust vs mistrust, are compatible with the work of René Spitz in his studies of the establishment of an initial object relationship (Spitz, 1965). Erikson's formulation is also consistent with the extensive literature on maternal deprivation and even with the work on imprinting. His ideas about adolescence are compatible with a host of theorists including Friedenberg (1962), Keniston (1971), Paul Goodman (1960), and Allen Wheelis. In fact, one gets the impression that infancy and adolescence are indeed the two most critical phases of personality development.

The critical developmental tasks that Erikson has enumerated and described are expressed as bipolarities. This formulation is consistent with general systems theory that the dynamism of life derives from the fact of negative and positive charges with tension, and therefore movement, existing between them. It is most

Figure 5. The Adolescent Crisis, "Identity vs Identity Diffusion."

	1.	2.	3.	4.	5.	6.	7.	8.
I. INFANCY	Trust vs Mistrust				Unipolarity vs Premature Self-Differentiation			
II. EARLY CHILDHOOD		Autonomy vs Shame, Doubt			Bipolarity vs Autism			
III. PLAY AGE			Initiative vs Guilt		Play Identification vs (oedipal) Fantasy Identities			
IV. SCHOOL AGE				Industry vs Inferiority	Work Identification vs Identity Foreclosure			
V. ADOLESCENCE	Time Perspective vs Time Diffusion	Self-Certainty vs Identity Consciousness	Role Experimentation vs Negative Identity	Anticipation of Achievement vs Work Paralysis	Identity vs Identity Diffusion	Sexual Identity vs Bisexual Diffusion	Leadership Polarization vs Authority Diffusion	Ideological Polarization vs Diffusion of Ideals
VI. YOUNG ADULT					Solidarity vs Social Isolation	Intimacy vs Isolation		
VII. ADULTHOOD							Generativity vs Self-Absorption	
VIII. MATURE AGE								Integrity vs Disgust, Despair

SOURCE: Reprinted with permission from Erik H. Erikson, "Identity and the Life Cycle: Selected Papers," *Psychological Issues* (Monograph). New York: International Universities Press, 1959, Volume 1, p. 120.

important to bear in mind that these bipolarities are not achievement scales to serve as measurable criteria of growth and development. One does not achieve *complete* trust and then move on to the next plateau, autonomy. The outcome of each of the developmental crises is a relative mix of the polar qualities, and the developing person must cope with the subsequent task at its proper time as dictated by maturation and social expectations. In one sense these critical tasks of development are present at all times in each person's life and are directly related to one another. They are sequential as to when they emerge as crises.

Figure 5 illustrates the interrelatedness of the various crises. This figure focuses on the crisis of adolescence, identity vs identity diffusion, and illustrates how each of the earlier crises contributes to the readiness to cope with this one and how it in turn influences the subsequent crises. Theoretically it should be possible to take any of the crises represented on the diagonal and fill in the related boxes to show the relationship of that crisis to the preceding and the following steps.

Erikson's worksheet (Figure 6) illustrates his eight stages of man on five dimensions. The second dimension (B: radius of significant relations) indicates the progression of interrelationships from the dyad of the infant and maternal person through the ever-expanding hierarchy of social systems. The eighth stage includes all of mankind. Columns C, D, and E have to do with social order, psycho-social modalities, and psychosexual stages, and indicate the relatedness of these dimensions.

Erikson's life cycle scheme can validly be described as a systems viewpoint based in the "natural" epigenetic principle. As the individual's life cycle unfolds he has the maturational potential and the social necessity to involve himself in ever-wider social systems and ever-changing social conditions. To fulfill his functional destiny, the person must of necessity be engaged in transactions with these other social systems.

In summary, then, Erikson's eight ages of man represent the necessary occasions for the individual uniting biological, psychological, and social forces. He stresses the adaptive and creative power of the person and respects each individual's unique capacity to forge his own way of life. His faith in man's social creativity is reflected in his optimistic comment, "there is little that can not be remedied later, there is much that can be prevented from happening at all" (Erikson, 1950, p. 164).

B. Behavioral Theory

That which is here labeled *behavioral theory* is not properly considered a theory of growth and development. The term *behavioral* refers to those schools of thought and theory construction that concern themselves with how behavior is learned and how behavior can be modified. This, of course, is a mainstream in the discipline of psychology. Included are behaviorism, learning theory, action therapy, and behavior modification.

The basic tenet of this approach was stated by J. B. Watson early in this

	A Psychosocial Crises	B Radius of Significant Relations	C Related Elements of Social Order	D Psychosocial Modalities	E Psychosexual Stages
I	Trust vs Mistrust	Maternal Person	Cosmic Order	To get To give in return	Oral-Respiratory, Sensory-Kinesthetic (Incorporative Modes)
II	Autonomy vs Shame, Doubt	Parental Persons	"Law and Order"	To hold (on) To let (go)	Anal-Urethral, Muscular (Retentive-Eliminative)
III	Initiative vs Guilt	Basic Family	Ideal Prototypes	To make (=going after) To "make like" (=playing)	Infantile-Genital, Locomotor (Intrusive, Inclusive)
IV	Industry vs Inferiority	"Neighborhood," School	Technological Elements	To make things (=completing) To make things together	"Latency"
V	Identity and Repudiation vs Identity Diffusion	Peer Groups and Outgroups; Models of Leadership	Ideological Perspectives	To be oneself (or not to be) To share being oneself	Puberty
VI	Intimacy and Solidarity vs Isolation	Partners in friend- ship, sex, competi- tion, cooperation	Patterns of Cooperation and Competition	To lose and find oneself in another	Genitality
VII	Generativity vs Self-Absorption	Divided labor and shared household	Currents of Education and Tradition	To make be To take care of	
VIII	Integrity vs Despair	"Mankind" "My Kind"	Wisdom	To be, through having been To face not being	

Figure 6. Worksheet.

SOURCE: Reprinted with permission from Erik H. Erikson, "Identity and the Life Cycle: "Selected Papers," Psychological Issues (Monograph). New York: International Universities Press, 1959, Volume 1, p. 164.

century. Watson first expressed the firm belief that the only proper study of mankind, the purpose of psychology, is the study of behavior through empirical observation and experimentation. This belief rejects the notion that psychology is the study of the mind, because "mind" is neither directly observable nor verifiable. Such theorists hold that their methodology is scientific, objective, and inductive as compared with the methodology of personality theorists whose methodologies are subjective, deductive, and not verifiable.

Behavioral theory is not a single theory or school of thought, but a number of approaches that are similar in attempting to account for the acquisition and the retention of new forms of behavior as well as the modification or extinction of established behavioral patterns. Problematic behavior is seen as resulting from mislearning rather than from illness. Intervention techniques based in behaviorism and learning theory use designations such as "behavior modification" rather than "therapy" to communicate the idea that problematic behavior is not to be viewed as illness.

The basic concept is S-O-R—stimulus, organism (the state of the organism, such as maturation or fatigue), and response (behavior). Behavior then is response, and any antecedent condition that produces that behavior is stimulus. Ideally stimulus-response laws would enable prediction of behavior since they specify which antecedent condition will produce a given response. Some of the more recent theories of conditioning focus attention on that which follows response, the consequences of behavior, in preference to studying the antecedents of behavior. If the consequences of behavior augur for a recurrence of the behavior, it is termed a *reinforcing stimulus,* or simply *reinforcement.* This theoretical approach is having a significant impact in the helping professions.

A term you will encounter is *operant conditioning* or *instrumental conditioning.* These terms refer to techniques that emphasize and utilize the relationship between the behavior to be learned (or desired modification) and its consequents. Operant principles derive from the work of B. F. Skinner and are found in the following two propositions.

1. An organism will learn to repeat a behavior for which it is rewarded, and will avoid one for which it is ignored or punished. *Positive reinforcement* refers to a reward, *negative reinforcement* refers to punishment, and *nonreinforcement* refers to behavior being ignored. Recent writers stress the efficacy of nonreinforcement as a technique to extinguish behavior.

2. Complicated behavior patterns, particularly those that can be described as skillful, are gradually learned in small steps that come progressively closer and closer to some optimal level of performance (London, 1964, pp. 110 ff.).

Given these two propositions, a person's behavior can be understood if it is possible to discern what the person finds rewarding through watching overt acts and their consequences.

Operant conditioning is a clearly stated procedure for modifying behavior. The four operations of corrective conditioning are:

1. Analyze the nature of the organism and the environment with respect to the problem behavior.

2. Determine which features of the environment are sustaining or reinforcing this behavior. Decide what new patterns of behavior would be desirable.

3. Identify objects or situations in the environment that will function as positive or negative reinforcement. These must be subject to control.

4. Manipulate the environment to reinforce approximations of the desired behavior and negatively reinforce those behaviors that conflict with the desired behaviors. Again, the most effective negative reinforcement may well be to ignore the undesired behavior and respond only to the desired behavior.

These operations can be readily viewed from a social systems perspective. The analysis of the nature of the organism and the environment is a procedure wherein the focal system is identified. Its relationships to subsystems and its relationships to suprasystems are described in respect to the problem behavior. The linkages of the organism to its environment are made explicit and the feedback cycle is attended to. Goals are established by the suprasystem with the focal system being viewed as a component. The manipulation of the environment to reinforce approximation of desired behavior is in essence the purposeful control of the feedback cycle.

B. F. Skinner is the prototype of the action therapist, although at this time other writers are more prolific (Bandura, 1963; Eysenck, 1960; Wolpe, 1969). Skinner holds that the total measure of the man is observed in his actions. He believes strongly that it serves no purpose to "explain" behavior; what is essential is to learn how to control and modify it. *Walden Two* is Skinner's design of a utopian society based on principles of control and modification toward the fulfillment of benign goals (Skinner, 1948). In his most recent utopian work, Skinner has offered a blueprint for the construction of a culture grounded in his technology of behavior (Skinner, 1971).

The major characteristics of the behavioral approach are:

1. Indifference to the origin of symptoms and greater attention to specifying goals of modification.

2. Unconcern with what the patient thinks or says about himself except in so far as such *behaviors* have tangible value for producing change.

3. The approach is grounded in theories of learning, specifically under-standing the observable factors that operate in the acquisition of behaviors.
4. The approach is identified with the idea of conditioning of some type.
5. Learning and behavior acquisitions follow the stimulus-response model.
6. Problem behavior develops through miseducation and is not to be viewed as illness. Recognition of the fact that behavior is construed to be problematic or nonproblematic through a process of social definition.

Although the question, "What does behavioral theory have to do with social work?" has been asked, it is no longer an appropriate one. Coming down to cases, it can readily be recognized that almost all counseling or human services are designed to maintain or modify behavior. Many of the techniques used by human service professionals are conditioning techniques. They are not however so labeled nor used purposefully within the theoretical framework that has been so painstakingly developed by psychologists throughout the years. Examples can be cited in all fields of social work. The training and job placement (WIN) of AFDC parents invokes principles of operant conditioning. The program clearly states the goal of employment behavior. Reinforcements are planned through financial rewards, and society reinforces through greater acceptance in confirma-tion of worker status. Family group therapy techniques operate to reinforce desired behavior, particularly communication and expression of feeling through manipulation of reinforcement contingencies, within the family system. Many so-called "supportive" techniques are reward systems and tend to reinforce desired behavior or extinguish undesirable behavior. There is an ever-increasing attention to the goals of social work practice rather than the causation of problem behavior, with accompanying greater concern with results (changes in behavior) and less concern with the refinement of techniques.

C. Cognitive Theory

PIAGET

Phillips begins his book on Piaget by saying, "I hope that you will take from all this a conception of the human brain as a vastly complicated system for the storage and retrieval of information; a system that becomes capable of increasingly complex operations; a system that changes in ways that are at least to some degree similar to the constructions that Piaget has given us" (Phillips, 1969, p. xii). From this suggestion that Piaget is a systems theorist of sorts, we can advance to Maier's statement that:

> Piaget believes in universal order. He suggests a single unity of all things: biological, social, psychological, and ideational, in living as well as non-living systems. All science is interrelated. A theorem established in one branch of science, he feels, is directly relevant to the laws and principles of other branches. Altogether, Piaget insists upon cosmic unity.... (Maier, 1965, p. 84)

He goes on to describe how Piaget relates parts to wholes within systems.

Piaget is a systems theorist whose area of concentration has been cognitive development. Cognitive theory concentrates on the process of knowing and learning. Thus three major views of personality presented in this chapter constitute more or less of a triad of *emotion,* in Freud's theory, *behavior,* in behaviorism, and *thought,* in Piaget's theory. In comparison to the work that has been done on the first two views of the personal system, far less has been done in formal research exploration of the cognitive processes.

Much of what has been done in this field can be traced to Jean Piaget and his collaborators. Piaget, born in 1896, still lives in Switzerland. A precocious student, he published his first scientific paper at the age of 10 and was offered a museum directorship, which he declined. His early interest was in biology, but this broadened to philosophy and psychology during his training at the University of Neuchatel. He sought to combine these three fields in a "psychological and biological epistemology," or theory of knowledge. He has kept at this task constantly with thousands of research studies during the past 50 years.

Piaget has only slowly gained a reputation in the United States because he does not fit neatly into any of the established disciplines. Psychology reluctantly acknowledges him, and philosophy hardly recognizes his work. Oddly enough, and for reasons we mention later, his greatest impact has been on educational theory and practice.

Piaget's research methods have been criticized because they are not always orthodox. He uses psychoanalytic interviewing style, exploring children's responses, especially their mistakes. Piaget questions the child while the child is doing various tasks and while he is not, and also observes silently on occasion. In his career he has invented over 50 new research techniques. Here is one brief example. The child is presented with a group of coins and a bunch of flowers. He is asked how many flowers he can buy if each flower costs one coin.

> Gui (four years, four months) put 5 flowers opposite 6 pennies, then made a one-for-one exchange of 6 flowers (taking the extra flower from the reserve supply). The pennies were in a row and the flowers bunched together: "What have we done? —*We've exchanged them.* —Is there the same number of flowers and pennies? —*No.* —Are there more on one side? —*Yes.* —Where? —*There* (pennies). (The exchange was again made, but this time the pennies were put in a pile and the flowers in a row). Is there the same number of flowers and pennies? —*No.* —Where are there more? —*Here* (flowers). —And here (pennies)? —*Less.* (Phillips, 1969, p. 5)

This exchange illustrates the flexible interview style and searching for concepts in the child's thinking that is typical of Piaget's methods. In this instance, it appeared to the child that if the objects were spread out there were more of them than if they were bunched up, indicating that the concept of transferability of numbers from one set of objects to another was beyond the knowledge of this 4½ year old. Piaget has also taken the "unscholarly" approach of studying his own children, and performing small experiments to test their development.

The topics of Piaget's major work are evident in these titles: "the construction of reality," "judgment and reason," "language and thought," "logic and psychology," "moral judgment," "the origin of intelligence," and "the psychology of intelligence." His major work is *Introduction to Genetic Epistemology* (1949). He has refined and added to this work since then.

Although he is not widely known in the United States, Piaget's reputation has accelerated in recent years. In Europe he is regarded as "Mr. Child Psychology"; he is, however, something more than the Dr. Spock of the intellect. Phillips says of him and his collaborators:

> The publications of the Geneva school constitute by far the largest reposi-
> tory of knowledge about the cognitive development of children that is
> available anywhere; students of psychology should be familiar with
> Piaget's theory even if it turns out to be basically wrong, because it will
> undoubtedly serve as a base for many future studies of children's thinking.
> (Phillips, 1969, p. 11)

Piaget is regarded by some theorists as being equal to Freud in his eventual impact on personality theory. He has dealt in concrete detail with the major problems of logic, thought, and philosophy that have hindered our understanding of man, in this century. His major impact, as noted earlier, has been on education.

> Piaget has said some pretty important things about children, and anyone
> who says important things about children ultimately must be important to
> educators. Teaching is the manipulation of the student's environment in
> such a way that his activities will contribute to his development (toward
> goals whose definitions are not our present concern). It should be obvious
> . . . that the effect of a given environment on a child is as much a function
> of the child as of the environment. If a teacher knows that, his behavior
> will be affected by his conception of what students are like. Indeed, his
> very definition of teaching will be so determined. Mine was. (Phillips,
> 1969, pp. 107–108)

Piaget's emphasis on first-hand involvement, experience, and grappling with problems appropriate to the child's intellectual development are consistent with the view of John Dewey, whose influence on American education has been profound.

The implications of Piaget's work are important for the human services. He stresses invention and creativity and the ability of the person to grow rather than remain handicapped by past deficiencies or conflicts. His view of teaching is that "every time you teach a child something you keep him from reinventing it" (Phillips, 1969, p. 120).

> The principal goal of education . . . is to create men who are capable of doing new things . . . men who are creative, inventive and discoverers. The second goal of education is to form minds which can be critical, can verify, and not accept anything they are offered . . . we need pupils who are active, who learn early to find out by themselves, partly by their own spontaneous activity and partly through materials we set up for them; who learn early to tell what is verifiable and what is simply the first idea to come to them. (Elkind, 1968, p. 80)

The basic ideas of Piaget are relatively easy to understand from a systems viewpoint:

1. Equilibrium. Equilibrium, in Piaget's view, is a steady state of the cognitive processes. Specifically, he regards equilibrium as a balance between the person and his environment in which the person's knowledge adequately explains what he experiences. In Freudian theory equilibrium is an *internal* balance of physiological and psychic forces rather than an *external,* social-environmental balance as in Piaget's theory or Erikson's. In other words, Freud's is a closed system, Piaget's is open. Equilibrium as Piaget views it may be defined as a state of active compatibility between the needs of the person and the demands and supplies from the environment. That is, there is feedback which confirms and continues to reinforce the person's developing capacity to understand and master his environment. The similarity to Erikson here is obvious.

2. Intelligence. Piaget defines intelligence as a "special form of biological activity." "For Piaget, the one-time biologist, intelligence can be meaningfully considered only as an extension of certain fundamental biological characteristics" (Flavell, 1963, p. 41). Intelligence arises from the biological makeup of man and is always a part of man as a biological being. Its function is the same as that of other system processes: to preserve the organism. According to Piaget, intelligence is both the activity of coping with the environment *and* the end state of "compatibility." Intelligence, by the latter definition, is the maximum potential of the adaptive capacities; it is never fully realized.

3. Schema. The structural units in Piaget's system are called *schemata* (the plural of *schema*). Schemata are roughly equivalent to the "mediating processes" of Hebb and others (Hebb, 1949, 1966; Hunt, 1961). They form a kind of framework onto which incoming sensory data can fit—indeed must fit; but it is a framework that is continually changing its shape, the better to assimilate those data (Phillips, 1969, p. 9). The term *schema* is at the heart of Piaget's theory. Intelligence has a structure and this structure is stable and predictable. It is systematic and orderly. At any particular time, it maintains an equilibrium which changes—that is, it maintains a steady state.

Since Piaget believes that thought begins as action, he says that thought structures are patterns of internalized actions, ranging from the most elementary reflex pattern to profound philosophical thought. Schemas (we prefer this to "schemata") are organized action sequences and behavior patterns. Schemas arise by association. The reflexes become associated with other experience, and such isolated behaviors as sucking, grasping, looking, and hearing become larger and more comprehensive. For example, looking and sucking are coordinated into seeing-grasping-sucking the bottle simultaneously. Progressive refinements of schemas allow the child to see the bottle, hold it, turn it around, tilt it, lay it down, pick it back up, see that it is empty, cry, and so forth.

The later, larger schemas are more highly developed. Eventually the child will be able to *think* of these operations instead of really perform them—that is, to carry on the action internally, think it through, correct it mentally, and *then* try it, all without picking up the bottle. Piaget says that thought is nothing more than such actions and schemas, refined and modified endlessly by intelligence. He carries this a step further by stressing that reality as we know it can only be this structure of associated and coordinated experiences. In other words, reality *is* structured by the schemas we have built up. Our schemas include time and space, and are the frame for our understanding. We are bound by these frameworks except when dreaming and under the influence of drugs, when our usual schemas are loosened and other associations occur. Here the relation to Freudian "associations" seems very close.

There are two fundamental characteristics of schemas, *"organization and adaptation.* Every act is organized and the dynamic aspect of organization is adaptation" (Phillips, 1969, p. 7). These are the same in all biological processes, and are consistent with systems ideas.

Adaptation takes two forms: *assimilation* and *accommodation.* The person attempts to fit new experience into the old schemas, to accept it as similar to previous experience. This is assimilation. Accommodation refers to the person's modification of his old schema to "accommodate" the new experience. These are similar, then, to what Buckley calls *morphostasis* and *morphogenesis* (see Chapter 1 and Glossary), the maintenance or change of a system's structure in order to achieve a new steady state after the input of new energy. These two tendencies, like other polarities, never are mutually exclusive; there is always some balance of the two.

Summary of Theoretical Approaches

All three forms of personality theory; psychosocial, behavioral, and cognitive, agree on the general nature of biological functioning and genetic endowment. They seem to be complementary when approached from a systems viewpoint.

Piaget's view of the structure of intelligence is quite consistent with the systems view. Just as Freud's concepts of id, ego, and superego came from classical mechanical physics, so Piaget's concept of schema comes from Einstein's theory of relativity and from Whitehead's and Dewey's philosophies. Piaget specifically refers to physics as being analogous to his own ideas, and many of his experiments deal with children's understandings of such physics concepts as velocity, time, and distance. Piaget has explicitly acknowledged a similarity between his own theories and those of Bertalanffy, the foremost general systems theorist (Koestler and Smythies, 1969, p. 65).

Piaget stresses the organizing capacity of the intellect; Freud stressed internal conflict, but Piaget's "intellect" is similar to Freud's ego—both are the organizing principle of the personality. Piaget simply acknowledges the existence of the unconscious; Freud drew heavily on this concept. Both agree that the unconscious is orderly and related to the conscious processes.

In comparison with behaviorism, Piaget is concerned more with the organizational activities *within* the individual.

> A cognitive theory is concerned especially with central organizing processes in higher animals, and it recognizes a partial autonomy of these processes, such that the animal becomes an actor upon, rather than simply a reactor to its environment. Actually, the opposite of this, the so-called associationist doctrine, is to some extent a straw man; for excepting B. F. Skinner, who adjures all theories, there is probably no prominent psychologist today who does not explicitly recognize the importance of mediating processes. (Phillips, 1969, p. 6 n.)

II. THE CRITICAL PHASES OF THE LIFE CYCLE

A. Establishment of Primary Attachment (Dependency and Trust) in the Parent-Child Dyad

The newborn infant enters the world in a totally dependent state. The major part of the first year is devoted to the effort to survive and to the forming and elaboration of the adaptation devices directed toward survival. The infant during this early period is helpless and is incapable of surviving by his own efforts. The mothering person (or persons) compensates for and supplies his lacks. The newborn is in a state of undifferentiation. Physiological organization is rudimentary and there is no demonstrated psychic organization. In the world of the newborn there is no object or object relation. This will develop during the course of the first year (Spitz, 1965).

Erikson describes the first critical social task as "a sense of basic trust versus a sense of basic mistrust." By this he means the necessity for the development of a *feeling* of trust in others and a *feeling* of trust in one's self. Spitz refers to this first task as the initiation of an object relationship. In the Erikson formulation of the dimension of trust the following elements are of importance.

1. The mothering person becomes an inner certainty as well as an outer predictability. This is a state that has included in it the measures of consistency, continuity, and sameness of experience.

2. The infant develops a sense of being able to trust himself and the capacity of his own organs to cope with urges.
3. This sense of trust forms the basis in the child for the later development of a sense of identity.
4. Since the sense of trust is essentially social it is based on communication, particularly tactile, nutritive, and emotional, between the infant and the mother.

Since Spitz's work in the 1930s on the effects of maternal deprivation, there has been considerable controversy in the literature as to whether the primary social attachment need be formed between the infant and the mother. It is fairly well agreed that the mother in this sense does not necessarily mean the biological mother. Some authors refer to the caring person, rather than mother, holding to the necessity for continuity, consistency, and predictability but not seeing this necessarily embodied in any one particular person. Consequently there is fairly general agreement that the climate within which an infant can adapt to the first social task is of the utmost importance, but the question of who the person or persons need be to establish this climate remains controversial. This has been a basic question in the recent development of day care centers that provide care for infants.

The first infant needs to be met are the oral, nutritive needs, and the mouth is the initial receptor; it is the most sensitive and demanding tissue in the body at this time. Sensitive tissues develop in other erotogenic zones later and these form the basis of Freud's stages of oral, anal, and genital. Erikson too employs the idea of zones and refers to the zonal sensitivity of the "sense of trust versus sense of mistrust" period as oral—respiratory, sensory, kinesthetic—and stresses that these are incorporative modes. At any rate, the first social activities of the infant are concerned with incorporation, getting and learning to get. During the latter portion of the first critical stage the infant begins to give in return.

Formation of the primary social attachment is accomplished in a dyadic field wherein the infant and caring person or persons "are one." Initially, at least, we should *not* refer to the infant or the growing child as an entity in himself. He is helpless and must be cared for, is not an independent entity and is as one with the other party to the dyad. He is now *merely* a component, a component of a system—something that cannot be said of him at any later time. It is possible to think of the "connectiveness" of the human organism to other humans. In the prenatal environment the developing organism is connected through the umbilical cord; in the first months of life he is connected by a psychological "cord" that must be severed later so he can move on to social connections. To paraphrase Erikson, the child in the first months of life could well say "I am what I am given," next say, "I am what I can get," and finally say "I am what I can give."

Within the dyad the infant does not long remain a passive recipient. Quite early in life he must respond and interact through the formation of a primary social attachment. From a systems stance it can be said that the transactions between the human system and the environment are a necessary condition for the definition of boundary of self. In other words, it is through the recognition of and interaction with "other" that the boundaries of self can be defined. If this process is not sufficiently engaged in, the boundaries of self are not defined and infantile autism often results. If the latter part of this process is not forthcoming, that is, the differentiation of self within the social attachments, the resulting condition is referred to as symbiosis.

Maternal deprivation. A number of dysfunctional dyadic forms have been identified and grouped under the rubric of maternal deprivation (World Health Organization, 1962). Maternal deprivation can be described in both quantitative and qualitative aspects. The term generally refers to an insufficiency of interaction between the child and the mother persons and the conditions under which this insufficiency seems to develop. The term *maternal deprivation* should not be taken literally but as an expression of the effect on the child. Some of the conditions under which maternal deprivation become apparent are, briefly:

1. Institutionalization or hospitalization of the infant with no provision for substitute mothering. This is a circumstance where the infant is indeed deprived of a mothering agent. It has been documented by René Spitz in his writings and in the film *Grief*.

2. Circumstances where the child is with a mother or mother substitute who provides insufficient opportunity for interaction.

3. Sufficient care is available to the child but the child is unable to interact because of previous deprivations, maturational deficiencies, or unknown causes. Not infrequently parents of disturbed preschool children report that almost from birth an infant was not responsive to cuddling and "gentling." Frequently a neurological deficit is suspected by the physician.

4. Distorted relationships
   a. Situations where the child is not differentiated from the parent. The parent does not distinguish the boundary between self and child.
   b. Interlocking dependency, a symbiotic relationship wherein the mother must have a totally dependent infant and the child requires total mothering. This is the normal circumstance of the neonatal infant but prolongation is distorting.
   c. The parent may assimilate the child as being certain aspects of herself (or himself) or identify the child completely with the qualities of another person. Again a measure of this is normal, as seeing an infant as having Uncle John's eyes or Aunt Clara's hair, but when the total child is viewed as possessing the qual-

ities of another he has little chance to differentiate himself and establish himself as a separate person.

    d. The parent(s) perceive the child as the embodiment of a single quality, such as stupid, bad, or totally demanding.

5. Insufficient relationships

    a. The mothering person is unable to give emotionally because of her own isolation or coldness as a person.

    b. The parent may be narcissistic and involved with self so that no more than physical care is provided. Her (his) human system is closed to an extent that permits little or no transaction of feeling with her (his) child.

    c. Situational factors exhaust the caring person's energies and little love is available for nurturance of the child. These demands may come from within the family system or from the surrounding environment.

Another form of defective dyad that complicates the child's efforts to establish a basic sense of trust is labeled *separation*. Whereas deprivation refers to insufficiency of relationship, separation refers to interruption of an already established relationship. It has to do with the need for continuity.

John Bowlby was appointed by the World Health Organization of the United Nations to study the effects of separation (Bowlby, 1962, pp. 205–214). In his own studies he found that juvenile delinquency was highly correlated with separation experiences in the preschool years. His review of other research yielded similar results. He then suggested that early childhood separation was a causal factor in some delinquents. Although this causal relationship has been questioned by a number of critics, his general findings have been accepted and incorporated into the body of knowledge of child development. He concluded that a separation in the first three months of life is not disturbing if an adequate mother substitute is provided. By the age of three months the child has begun to form a social attachment or dyad with the mothering person and separation begins to present problems to the infant's efforts to cope with this first developmental task. Prolonged separation from the ages of six months to twelve months is most deleterious and may not be reversible (Bowlby, 1966, pp. 117–119). Bowlby described the characterological development that resulted from harmful separation as the "affectionless character," meaning a shallow and untrusting person who is unable to enter into intimate emotional transactions with other persons.

SUMMARY

As the first major task of the life cycle, the first foundation in psychological development, the cornerstone of social functioning, the child must engage in striving to establish an essential, primary social relationship. The interrelatedness of the physical, psychological, and social is most observable in this stage. The infant must survive as an organism and begin his evolution as a self, a person. The social resources available are largely centralized in his mothering person(s) and these resources must be offered to him to begin with. Later he can learn to seek them for himself. Inputs must be offered to him and he must accept them— nutritive inputs for physical survival and emotional inputs for psychological survival. He will emerge from this interaction with a sense of being able or unable to count on others and himself, a mixture of trust and mistrust, hope and hopelessness.

B. Differentiation of Self within the Family System

The family system is the scene of the second and third of Erikson's crises of psychosocial growth. The mother-child dyad of the earlier task becomes a three-or-more-person system, for these tasks. First, a brief review of these crises as Erikson presents them.

Autonomy vs Shame and Doubt carries the special requirement for the establishment of a sense of self as an entity separate from the environment. This social expectation is congruent with the maturational development wherein the child is beginning to have the physical capacity to manage certain of his functions, for example ambulation and elimination. Conflicting desires to assert himself as an autonomous being *and* to be uncertain of his capacity to do so compete within the child. He must risk relinquishing some of the comfortable dependency of the primary dyad.

He first asserts himself as separate by saying in effect, "No, I can *will* not to do what you want me to do." The well-known negativism of the two year old is expression of the assertion of will. In American culture this becomes attached to the cultural dictates about toilet habits, neatness, and respect for property. In other cultures negative behavior is responsive to other themes important to those cultures. The corollary of negative assertion is self-control and independence. If the family environment does not provide limits for assertive behavior the child may find himself out on a limb, beyond his capacity to manage himself. If the family environment overly restricts his opportunities to test his capacity to will his own behavior he will not have the chance to experience himself as a separate and sovereign entity. In case of either extreme he will develop a sense of shame and doubt about himself as a self-determining human system.

These preschool years are centered in the family system, the primary social unit of the culture. It is in this social climate that the child becomes a person, a social being. The autonomy crisis occurs in a field of experience with certain characteristics.

1. It is necessary for the developing person to differentiate himself within the nurturer-nurturee dyad. He must discover that he exists

separate from his source of nurturance. "Where does mother end and where do I begin?"

2. Sensitivity to order is characteristic of this age. Children frequently insist on sameness in their environment and become distraught when important objects are relocated. Predictability, continuity, and consistency of the physical environment assume a special meaning, analogous to these same qualities of the nurturing person in the first stage. The environment must be trustworthy because the child, partly at least, constructs himself from the environment. He learns to name objects and thus have a degree of control over them (Brown, 1965, pp. 267–276). Organization of the energies of the self-system is possible only because the suprasystem is organized.

3. The assertion of will occurs first in negation, then in positive ways. The child diligently attempts to experience himself as a self-directing entity. First physiologically, then psychologically, and finally in a social manner he finds he can will to hold on or let go. Physiologically he develops the capacity to hold on or let go of sphincter musculature.

   If toilet habits are of sensitive importance to his culture a major battle may develop around this socializing task. Often toilet training is referred to as "breaking" the child, training him in the same sense as breaking a wild mustang. To persuade the child to submit his will to that of the culture as represented by the family becomes of crucial importance. The child then is encouraged to feel his willing capacity through controlling himself according to cultural dictates.

   Psychologically he can hold on to or let go of his feelings. He has the choice of expressing frustration and anger directly through his behavior or controlling it to please "others." If others communicate to him that these feelings are too dangerous to let out he may doubt his capacity to deal with them or feel he has omnipotent powers. If others are unable or unwilling to provide any ground rules he may feel internal anarchy and shame.

   Socially he can hold on or let go of self in relation to other systems. In holding on he may not engage in enough transactions with others and have insufficient feedback to enable him to establish his self within a social context. In letting go he may not establish self-boundaries and the environment continues to be indistinguishable from self.

4. Dichotomies of feeling, ambivalences, are a characteristic of this crisis. Polarities are a part of a process of differentiation. A child may alternately express a sense of love and hate, a sense of inde-

pendence and total dependence, or a sense of pleasure and dis-pleasure. This proximity of opposites must be coped with for the first time now, and how this is resolved will serve as the prototype for later life tasks. Erikson states that the cultural solution for this dilemma is embodied in the culture's approach to law and order.

5. Although language development has begun, much communication continues to be on a nonverbal level. Approval and disapproval are important reinforcers of behavior and are conveyed by feeling more than word. The prohibitive "no-no" may convey prohibition or permission, approval or disapproval, challenge or censure. The sensitive two or three year old may well be more responsive to parental feeling than to word meaning. Piaget finds the child's thought processes to be concrete and fragmentary, the concepts he does grasp are specific and often literal in their interpretation. At any time he may feel all "good" or all "bad."

The child who does not develop a sufficient sense of autonomy may have little or no sense of self. Manifestations of this include cloying dependency, general anxiety, foolhardy behavior, expecting others to control him, or severe withdrawal. Severe and pervasive negativism may also indicate lack of sufficient autonomy. A sense of autonomy is manifest in a measure of self-regulation and a ca-pacity to enter into social transactions as a discrete entity.

In the latter preschool years the child's primary social system continues to be the family but he is beginning to establish linkages outside the family, such as playmates, neighbors, and extended family or family friends.

Initiative vs Guilt refers to the second social task that must be coped with, in and through the family system. The child now must concern himself with defining *who* he is qualitatively. With his sense of autonomy, shame, and doubt as to his capacity to will his behavior, he must next explore who he is. The oedipal conflict is central, as is the introjection of right and wrong. As Erikson views this task, the modalities are "to make" (to get) and "to make like" (to play). The bisexuality of the child, which has been apparent up to this time, is directed toward a gender as his culture defines it. The masculine "making" is intrusive, the insertion of self into the social world to accomplish purposes. The feminine form of "making" is inclusion of the social world to accomplish purposes. The genital tissue is hypersensitive at this stage, consistent with Freud's phallic stage.

Active insertion of self or inclusion behavior brings anticipated rivalry and threat of punishment. Identification, in the imitative sense, is a frequent method of coping with the child's inner compulsion to define himself as a person and the culture's expectations that the boy be like his father and the girl be like her mother. Erikson states that the child could say to himself, "I am what I can imagine

I will be" (Erikson, 1968, p. 122). The outcome of this crisis will be a mixture of a sense of initiative and a sense of guilt. The person with a goodly measure of sense of initiative will have purpose and direction as a part of his character, will be self-motivating and able to initiate social behavior and transactions.

The "initiative" crisis has certain common characteristics.

1. The essential psychosocial task is to create a qualitative sense of self. This exploration begins in the family and then expands outward into other social systems. Because of the arousal of awareness of genital sensations and the cultural expectations of sex differentiation, much of this is played out in the oedipal context. The child of each sex forms identification with the cultural role for that sex as represented by the parent of his same sex. Furthermore each relates sexually to the parent of the opposite sex. The outcome of the oedipal complex (the complex refers to the sets of relationships) is, ideally, the child's relinquishment of the sexual interest in the parent of the opposite sex and identification with the parent of the same sex. This situation is complicated by the absence of cultural clarity about sex-differentiated behaviors, which affects the parents as well as affecting the child. Sometimes the child identifies with the "stronger" parent regardless of sex, and sometimes the child does not know whom to identify with. Sometimes the child continues to wallow in the complexities of this task into the periods of subsequent crises. Energies are preempted and the later crises are inadequately dealt with. Ideally, however, a solution is reached and the child expands his field of activity beyond the family and occupies himself somewhat in other social transactions.

2. Play becomes an important mode during this crisis. Cognitive development has progressed to the extent that imagination can be controlled and used in various ways. Erikson considers play as "autotherapeutic" in the sense that it is a rudimentary form of the adult capacity to create models and experiment with alternative behaviors without committing oneself to those behaviors. There are three stages in the hierarchical forms of play.

    a. autocosmic—the child's play begins with and centers on his own body,

    b. microspheric—the small world of manageable toys, and

    c. macrospheric—the sharing of play with others, first in parallel fashion and then in concert. (Erikson, 1963, pp. 220–221)

    In this phase two kinds of play are important. One is the solitary, day-dreaming variety wherein the child can experiment with his fantasies and try out his imaginings of what he would like to do and be. The second is peer play, wherein children together can work on solving their common concerns. Occasionally play may carry fantasy beyond control or comfort and be very frightening. Pretending is a reassuring way to help establish the boundaries of reality, especially when adults occasionally enter into the "let's pretend" activities.

3. This crisis is a time of transitional consolidation and integration. The exertion of self into environment with hope and expectation of influencing environment involves a measure of trust in the predictability of environment and one's own predictability, as well as a measure of control or will. To be able to do this enables the child to imagine how he might eventually influence the world. Because he is concerned about his intactness and bodily integrity, he may be sensitive to anything that threatens this. He may be frightened by his fantasies of power and hold himself responsible for any calamity that befalls his close others.

Again it is well to mention that the outcome of this particular crisis is a balance between initiative and guilt. This is the critical time for the development of conscience, which can be a tolerant guide or a punitive slavemaster, but a conscience there will be. The initiative hopefully will be directed toward "making" things work, people and objects, in the sense of integrated behaviors. But it can be "making" things and people in the exploitative sense. If the child can emerge from these family-centered growth tasks with a degree of trust in others and himself, a sense of separateness as a person linked to others, and a sense of purpose, he is well on the way to a fulfilling life plan congruent with his nature as a human being.

C. Definition of Self within Secondary Social Systems

The next labeled crisis occurs in interaction with the organized components of the community, formal organizations such as the school and church, informal organizations such as the neighborhood and the peer group. Physiological and cognitive maturation provide the capacities, and the culture furnishes the expectations. This is the period of development that Freud labeled *latency,* and that Piaget calls the phase of *concrete operations.* Erikson describes this fourth bipolarity as a sense of "Industry vs Inferiority." There are certain dominant characteristics of this particular crisis.

1. The theme is mastery. Mastery is sought over physical objects, one's physical self, social transactions, and ideas and concepts. It is the time to get about learning the technology and ways of one's culture. Institutionalized means are supplied by the culture whose investment is its own survival. The school is an institution charged

with transmission of the cultural technology. The Future Farmers of America and 4H are organizations for communicating the culture of the agricultural community, and the block gang exists to transmit the ways of another specialized culture. Games, contests, and athletics are also examples of institutionalized culture carriers. The school-aged child participates in various of these organizations and in the process creates a sense of himself as competent and incompetent.

2. Peer group experience is a necessary element in the crucible of testing mastery. It provides a social system parallel to the adult society with its own organization, rules, purposes, and activities. It is with the peer group that the child can test himself and grow to mastery in social relationships with equals.

3. The outcome is again a mixture or balance of the two polar feelings. A dominant sense of inferiority may result from a lack of ability, but most frequently it derives from either insufficient accrual from previous crises or unclear or unreasonable adult expectations and criteria of mastery. The idea of *sense* of industry or inferiority is important. It is the *feeling* the child has about his own competence that is crucial, not his *actual* competence as measured by parental or adult standards. The person who embarks into adolescence with a feeling that he can do at least one thing very well is in a favorable position indeed.

The child's entry into school is an important step to him, to his parents, and to his culture. One of the very few clearly demarked way stations on the long trail to adulthood, it is the occasion when society insures that each of its young members becomes a participant in an organized, institutionalized culture bearer. The recently popular phrase "Kindergarten Roundup" well conveys the cultural investment in collecting together the mavericks and commencing the long process of acculturation to technological society. An arbitrary age is set for such entry, two years younger than the legal requirement for compulsory school attendance in most states, and the social expectation is that the child will be ready. If he is indeed ready he is eager and looking forward to entry into this new world. If he is unready because his energies are still devoted to defining himself in the family system *or* his maturation is lacking, he will have "problems." He and his mother may not be ready for the separation, he may not be able to distinguish his teacher from his mother, or he may not have himself organized enough to comply with expectations for settled and cooperative behavior.

If the culture transmitted by the school is alien or oppositional to the culture of the child's family he finds himself in a difficult, indeed untenable position. The technology and ways of doing things he has familiarized himself with and developed his emerging sense of self and other within has by this time been incorporated as a part of self. To accept a differing way may be felt as an act of betrayal of self and family. If so, his efforts toward mastery may well be invested outside of the school, seeking mastery of his own culture, not that of others. Recent writers have documented this in respect to ghetto blacks and American Indians (Baratz and Baratz, 1971; Cahn, 1969, pp. 175–185).

The school has evolved as an overinvested carrier of culture as changes in technology and family functions have occurred. As society has been bureaucratized, so too has the school. On the one hand the school has taken on the form of a bureaucratic organization because it is a highly complex institution. On the other hand the school has the charge of preparing the young for participation in the existing cultural ways. The child in the school is experiencing himself as a functioning participant in a bureaucratic organization. His success is seen as predictive of later success in adult life, while his unsuccess is seen as predictive of adult unsuccess. All of the current program-planning of a preventive nature is based on this premise and aimed at earlier identification of difficulty (Goertzel and Goertzel, 1962).

Society then expects the child to demonstrate his mastery and competence primarily in the single institution of the school. This includes not only the technology of literacy but also physical mastery (gym class, intramurals, and athletic teams), arts and music, social mastery (social dancing, family life education), and domestic skills. There can be little wonder that the public schools find it very difficult to fulfill all the assignments the culture delegates. The school has even been required to deal with this society's primary problems, racism and poverty.

The culture expects the child to proceed with his construction of a sense of competence primarily in the school. His next available secondary social system is the peer group. During latency the child's primary connections continue to be within his family system; it is later in adolescence that the peer group may well take precedence over the family. The peer group of latency is modeled after the culture within which it exists. At its best it is not very visible to the adult world, and has its own parallel culture passed from generation to generation (two or three years to a generation) with continuity, but frequent innovations as well. The peer group is likely to be strongest in direct relation to the stability of the population it draws from. The peer group of suburbia is likely to be weak and transitory, while the the peer group in the small town or city neighborhood probably will be stronger. In recent years there has been a progressive undermining of the latency peer groups through adult take-over of them. In large sectors of the American culture peer activities are increasingly organized and conducted by adults. The wider scope of school functions is a part of this, Little League baseball exemplifies another part, and the day camp and "away camp" are yet others. The attention to individual fulfillment manifested by lessons in swimming, driving, tennis, golf, dancing, music, skiing, and so on has also served to diminish the availability of the child-run peer group. These adult managed and supervised activities undoubtedly serve to enable children to develop competence in a range of skills, but in the process minimize the child's opportunities to find out about himself by interacting freely in a peer culture. Maybe this is why some disgruntled offspring of upper middle class America head for communes and other experiments in peer living, and why such experimentation continues later and later into the adult years.

Mastery of the ground rules of life seems important to the latency-age child. Piaget has investigated the development of moral judgment in the child and found that children of this age are quite occupied with justice and accept arbitrary or expiatory punishment as warranted (Piaget, 1932). As they grow older the idea of retribution connected to the offending act and its natural consequences is favored. Grasp of the schema for moral judgment forms the basis for organized social relations.

Problems of latency-age children can be grouped under three general headings. The one-word description most often heard is "immaturity." The largest portion of children referred to child guidance clinics and school special services are aged 8 to 11. The reasons for referral are:

1. Poor school performance. Achievement of mastery of cultural technology does not measure up to the standards of school and/or parents. The child's school behavior disrupts his learning or the learning of others.

2. Symptoms not unsual in a younger child but not expected at this age. Some of these are enuresis, fears, short attention span, hyperactivity, daydreaming, and not assuming expected responsibilities.

3. Social inferiority. This might be the isolated child or the child who consistently associates only with younger children. A sense of social inferiority might be manifested by over-compensatory behavior, for example bullying or braggadocio. In the event societal expectations are excessive or opportunities for development of competence are too limited, a kind of cultural inferiority may result.

The middle years of childhood are the years for development of a sense of competence—to master self, social relationships, and the technology of the culture. The human system is relatively open to inputs from and transactions with the institutions of the community beyond the family system while retaining a primary linkage to the family. The growing person emerges from this with a sense of himself somewhere on the continuum from industry to inferiority. Erikson opines that the child's expression of his sense of competence could be stated, "I am what I can learn to make work" (Erikson, 1968, p. 127).

D. Transitional Self: Identity beyond Social Systems

This is the pivotal growth crisis in the Eriksonian formulation. It is the time when the biological and social imperatives demand that the evolving person pull himself together and create an identity that goes beyond his accumulation of social roles. In our culture this more or less coincides with that period of life referred to as adolescence. We prefer to use the term *adolescenthood* to convey the idea of more than a transitionary hiatus. The adolescent span of life has become a distinct life phase with its own culture, role expectations, and style.

The concept of identity has entered into the conventional wisdom and references are replete to individual "identity," group "identity" and even national "identity." Erikson's use of this concept is precise and applies primarily to the individual. He sees the social psychological task as one of integration, or more precisely reintegration, of the various components of the person into a whole. It is a process of ego synthesis that culminates in ego identity, meaning an internal consistency and continuity of meaning to others. This goes beyond the sum of childhood identifications and is not merely a synthesis of social roles.

Again the concept is that of *sense* of identity. It is not a state of being that can be objectively evaluated by observers. "An optimal sense of identity . . . is experienced merely as a sense of psychosocial well being. Its most obvious concomitants are a feeling of being at home in one's body, 'a sense of knowing where one is going' and an inner assuredness of anticipated recognition from those who count" (Erikson, 1968, p. 165).

Erikson first labeled the opposite pole *identity diffusion,* later *role confusion,* and in later writings (Erikson, 1968) he settled on *identity confusion.* This term conveys the antithesis of integration, the dispersion of selves, the alienation of the self. From a systems viewpoint one could say that internal and external tensions press the human system to reintegrate its component parts to undertake new purposes and responsibilities. If the components of personality are not brought together the person is fragmented and has no sense of self. His energy is incapable of being put to concerted use—he is entropic. Schizophrenia with its disorganization of personality components and particular disparity between thought and feeling, is the extreme form of such fragmentation. Interestingly the earlier term for schizophrenia was *Dementia Praecox,* meaning "insanity of the young." Some theorists, Erikson among them, hold that true schizophrenia cannot appear until adolescence, since it is foremost a condition of pathology of identity and identification. A sensitive expression of this condition is:

> I am learning peacefulness, lying by myself quietly
> As the light lies on these white walls, this bed, these hands.
> I am nobody; I have nothing to do with explosions.
> I have given my name and my day-clothes up to the nurses
> And my history to the anesthetist and my body to surgeons.
> (Plath, 1966, p. 10)

Erikson has focused much of his study and writing on the adolescent crisis, and the reader is presumed to be familiar with this from any of the available sources, especially *Identity: Youth and Crisis, Childhood and Society,* or "The Problem of Ego Identity." Two of the characteristics of adolescence he identifies, the moratorium and negative identity, are particularly worthy of emphasis.

The idea of moratorium refers to a socially sanctioned period of delay wherein the person is allowed to, or forced to, postpone assumption of the full responsibilities of adult commitments. The culture relaxes its expectations and is more permissive. It is then a time when the person can try out a variety of identifications, modes of behavior, and roles without a total commitment to see them through. The moratorium is both necessary and desirable to allow for integration, regrouping of forces, and the setting of life goals. The extension of adolescence in America can be viewed as a socially imposed moratorium that may be of an unnecessarily long duration for some. Moratoria may occur at times other than adolescence on a highly individualized basis. Often they are a part of the making of decisions or major changes in life goals. If the individually determined moratorium is more prolonged than societal expectations allow there is reason for concern—for example, Biff in *Death of a Salesman.*

Negative identity is another important Eriksonian concept. Negative identity *is an identity* that occurs in a situation in which available positive identity elements cancel each other out. This can occur because any identity is better than no identity at all. Negative identity is "an identity perversely based on all those identifications and roles which, at critical stages of development, had been presented to them as most undesirable or dangerous and yet also as most real" (Erikson, 1968, p. 174). The confirmation of the person's identity comes from within (this is what I feel like) and from without (this is what you say I am). This confirming feedback cycle operates in like manner for any identity. Although one's sense of identity can and does change subsequent to adolescence, this is the crucial time for identity formulation, the greatest opportunity for such development, and the time of greatest vulnerability.

ADOLESCENCE

There are more definitions of adolescence than there are definers. For a time adolescence was synonymous with the teen years, but no longer is that an adequate definition. The idea of the "between years" is frequently encountered, but that has an implication of "floating." For our purposes at this time we will employ the following definition, recognizing that it, too, is open to dispute. "Adolescence is probably in all societies that period which comes after the biological and hormonal changes of puberty have set in but before the individual's incorporation into society as an independent adult," (Ktsanes, 1965, p. 17).

Adolescence then begins with biology and ends by social definition. The commencement is organism, the process is organism interacting with culture, and the termination is culturally determined. The seemingly unique element in American adolescenthood is the increasing evidence of adolescence becoming a distinct cultural phase of life in the same sense as childhood and adulthood.

Rather than reviewing all the elements of this crisis, we will approach it from one angle. Freud has been widely quoted as holding the belief that the two elements of a successful life were the capacities to love and work. The task of identity formulation can be viewed as the prerequisite for loving and working. We will discuss briefly some of the characteristics of the adolescent and the culture that are important to development of these capacities.

1. The Peer Group. The associations of the adolescent with his peers are extremely necessary experiences. The peer groups take over some of the parental roles of support and value givers. Peers absorb much of the available social energy of the youth and become a primary reference group. The person can use his peers to find himself, through the mechanism of projecting his ego fragments onto others. He can experience and express his feelings of tenderness toward others, beyond the family system, on new planes. Various roles are available to be tried and either accepted or discarded. Friedenberg finds an attitude of respect for competence developing in the peer group (Friedenberg, 1962, p. 39) and experience wherein power and influence can be tasted (p. 59). In the peer society the adolescent can begin to be a lover and a worker in close interaction with others. He has earlier had this experience within the family system but only in the role of the child. Adulthood requires more of the person than continuance as a loving, working child within the primary family system. For some youths the peer group becomes of overriding importance, totally replacing the family. Such substitution of one kind of childlike dependency for another does not suffice for the creation of a unique identity. Some youths remain largely separated from a peer group and still manage to pull together an identity. Peers are, however, an essential part of the adolescent's struggle to find out who he is, what he values, and what he wants to become.

2. Education. The school continues to be the primary social institution as it was during latency. Increasingly, occupational choices are centered in the school experience. As occupational choice has become broader and minimally determined by father's occupation, it also has become more imbedded in the school. Curricula are constructed to expose the youth to a range of potential occupations, his performance is evaluated by himself, parents, and guidance counselors, and he is guided in certain directions. A number of factors enter in determining the "real" possibilities for any given youth. Some of these are race, sex, socioeconomic status, and "intelligence." In a society where persons are signified by what they do rather than by who they are, one's choice of work role or, more precisely, occupational aspiration takes on great meaning to one's sense of who one is and what one might become. (See the discussion of bureaucracy and personality in Chapter 3.) While Paul Goodman, Erich Fromm, and others have commented on the absurdity of this institutionalization of identity development, it continues to be the almost sole situation in which a youth gains a sense of himself as a "worker" and a potential worker.

ADOLESCENTHOOD AND CULTURE

The adolescent (a person between puberty and full adult status in matters of love and work) is an important person in our culture. There are certain evident manifestations of this importance.

Economically the adolescent has the status of a part-time worker and a full-time consumer. The jobs allotted to youth are service rather than production and often are substitutive of parental role performance—for example, babysitting, food preparation and serving, carrying grocery bags, and home maintenance. This age group is a primary target of advertising and merchandising. Whole industries in fashion and leisure time facilities cater to an adolescent market. Television's "Mod Squad," "American Bandstand," and "Room 222" indicate that one network has discovered this market. Pop culture, fashion, food, and music styles originate in the youth culture and permeate the broader culture through the impetus of the advertising and distribution industries.

There is a dual ambivalence that exists between the world of adulthood and the world of adolescenthood. This appears in the family system where parents and youth are both torn between wanting the youth to grow up and be independent and wanting him to remain a child. The ambivalence appears in the community and broader culture as the adult envies the vitality of youth, while youth envies the power and control possessed by the adult. It may be that the adult covets youthfulness as a denial of death, while increasing evidences of age cause this denial to be more difficult to maintain. Similarly, youth may covet power and control because of the prolonged dependence the culture dictates. This dual ambivalence complicates the forming of a sense of identity, because the separation into camps may contribute to the foreclosure of one's adolescent identity rather than an adult identity.

As Erikson views this, adolescence requires the culture to make adjustments because the generation coming up has absorbed the past, lives in the present, and must confront the future with new forms of living constructed of material not available to his parents. Margaret Mead has pointed out that youth in fact is the arbiter of our culture. Youth thus finds this construction of both its own life styles and those of the culture a bewildering task. Mead helps to explain why youth experiments widely in life styles and countercultural activities (Mead, 1970).

As many writers have said, each generation has a wide range of characteristics from which the culture can select those best suited to cultural survival. Considering culture as a social system, youth can be considered a component of that system and as such a source of energy and tension. As the system seeks steady state this component must stand in working relationship to other components. In order for this to happen the system will change (accommodate) or seek to maintain the status quo (assimilate). Within this dynamic interaction the individual must seek his identity, and the culture its survival.

Ideology is a special concern of the person in the throes of the identity crisis. The adolescent has a special sensitivity toward, as well as a particular vulnerability about, ideology. As Erikson puts it so clearly, "it is through their ideology that social systems enter into the fiber of the next generation and attempt to absorb into their lifeblood the rejuvenative power of youth" (Erikson, 1968, p. 134). Erikson's psychohistorical studies of Martin Luther and Gandhi demonstrate how individual solution of ideological aspects of their personal identity crises provided creative innovations that profoundly affected the total culture. Certainly Malcolm X might be a more recent example of personal identity crises transmuted into the ideology of a subculture.

The special virtue attached to identity is fidelity. The proclivity of youth to invest self and substance in a belief, an idea, or a person with total commitment and faith is generally acknowledged. The search for the Holy Grail, the Crusades, the willingness to follow the knight in shining armor be he Arthur Pendragon or Eugene McCarthy are examples. To experience total and complete volitional commitment seems a necessary element of an emerging identity.

The characteristic troubles of the adolescent identity crisis are legion. For convenience they may be grouped under the following headings.

1. Psychosis, usually in the form of schizophrenia. This is a condition of identity confusion in the extreme. The traits may be considered as exaggerations of "normal" traits.
   a. feelings of dislocation and estrangement;
   b. total docility or exaggerated rebelliousness;
   c. emotional lability, rapid mood swings;
   d. feelings of everyone being against one;
   e. idealism that seems to be a denial of reality;
   f. confused body image and sexual identification;

2. Neurosis can also be described as identity confusion in that there is a conflict between the ideal self and other selves. Stone and Church define neurosis as "a state of conflict between antagonistic and often unformulated inner tendencies that drains his energies and hampers his functioning" (Stone and Church, 1968, p. 550). The alternating excitability and lethargy of adolescents may well be examples of this tendency.

3. Delinquency is a socially defined deviant adaptation to inner demands and outer expectations. It may be the result of particular internal conflicts ("acting out" behavior) or it may be an individual or group rejection of cultural values of a larger system. The negative identity previously referred to may be manifested by delinquent behavior. While delinquency may be pathological, it may, as said earlier, be better than no identity at all.

In summary it can be said that the growth crisis of adolescence is the necessity of trying to pull together who one is. "To be or not to be, that is the question" states part of the issue confronting the adolescent. *What* to be or *what* not to be is the second part of the question. The later tasks of adulthood are to a large degree dependent on the outcome of this crisis. A person must be fairly certain and comfortable with self before he can enter into a sustained intimate relationship with another.

E. Perpetuation and Sharing of Identity

This is the phase of the life span generally referred to as the adult years. Adulthood as a period of life development (personality growth) is seldom dealt with in theories of personality development. Erikson is notable for his attempt to conceptualize the adult "productive" period as an integral part of his life cycle formulation. Pertinent here are the sixth and seventh growth crises.

A sense of "Intimacy and Solidarity vs Isolation" is the outcome of the first of these two tasks. The critical task is to enter in an involved, reciprocal way with others sexually, occupationally, and socially. One's sense of identity is merged with another to form a new primary social system. To put it another way, the person completes the transition from the family of origin to the family of procreation. This social crisis addresses itself to the activities of love and work. If one is unable to merge an intact sense of self with others, the outcome is a sense of isolation and polarization of affect. The concept of alienation (discussed later in this section) is another expression of a sense of isolation. The theme of love, genital and reciprocal, is central to this crisis.

The two adult crises Erikson delineates are closely related, and the second results in "Generativity vs Stagnation." This involves the task of active participation in establishing the next generation. In his discussion of this crisis, Erikson explains why he chose to express the quality of feeling as *generativity* rather than creativity or productivity (Erikson, 1959, p. 97). He sees the term *generativity* as being derived from "genitality" and "genes." This particularly emphasizes responsibility for perpetuation of the species and the culture. The theme of this task is *caring,* caring in the sense of nurturance and caring in the sense of concern for others. The polar sense of stagnation refers to caring primarily and essentially for one's self, with pseudointimacy with others and indulgence of one's self. Stagnation can be viewed as the "closed" human system, defending its equilibrium and minimally engaged in transactions of feelings with others.

The adult period, then, requires the person to perpetuate his own ego identity while sharing his sense of identity with others. The culture establishes social institutions, particularly procreative and child rearing, through which this task can be accomplished. At stake is a sense of well-being for the person, continuity for the culture, and survival for the species.

Other approaches to describing personality development in the mature years generally take one of two forms: either an idealized definition of maturity or a listing of the problems to be overcome. Stone and Church opt for the former alternative and furnish a list of the qualities of the healthy, mature adult. They rely on their own experiences and on Maslow and Erikson for their formulation of the characteristics of maturity.

    a. The person can live with his past without being bogged down in it. He remains adaptable, *capable of continued change.*

    b. He has developed a species of *self-determination.* He can, within certain inescapable limitations, be the master of his own destiny.

c. He has *wisdom* in the sense he not only knows things but can use his knowledge wisely to solve the problems of living.

d. He is at *home with reality,* aware of rampant ambiguities but able to tolerate them.

e. He is also at *home with himself,* able to know and tolerate his own strengths and weaknesses.

f. *Human relationships* are held at high priority. He is able to give and receive affection without embarrassment of fear for his own integrity.

g. He has a sense of responsibility and *concern with social problems* and ways of alleviating them.

h. He embraces a *democratic code of ethics,* not only ideologically but also in a deeply personal sense.

i. He not only can tolerate, but requires a certain amount of *solitude.*

j. He tries to rise above the proscriptions of his culture and *does not accept values ready made.*

k. With perspective he can live in *consciousness of his own mortality.* (Stone and Church, 1968, pp. 511–523, *passim*)

A psychiatry text, which is excellent for human services professions, gives this definition:

> The mature adult is one who has developed a clear personal identity, demonstrated by an ability for an intimate, satisfying and loving relationship with a mature member of the opposite sex and a personal assumption of the responsibility of rearing children. He is able to both assume personal responsibilities when necessary and to accept the decisions of those with competent authority for the general good. He independently pursues his own goals, with recognition of his own limitations and with willingness to seek advice from others, making due allowance for their deficits with an understanding tolerance. The healthy adult is one who is absorbed in achievement relative to his family, vocations and avocations rather than in personal self-assertions. (Noyes and Kolb, 1963, p. 29)

These definitions reflect cultural attitudes in regard to sexual orientations, independence, authority, achievement, and work. It is possible to group the central social expectations under four headings.

1. Sexuality. Adult sexuality is an important aspect of intimacy and the sharing of identity. Genitality, in the sense of the capacity for full and mutual consummation of sexual potential, is only characteristic of adulthood. Sexual mutuality forms the foundation of the procreative family system. Erikson says, "love then, is mutuality of devotion forever subduing the antagonisms inherent in divided function" (Erikson, 1964, p. 129).

2. Generativity and Child Rearing. The assumption of responsibility for transfer of the culture and nurturance of the young fulfills the destiny of the adult of a species. This requirement is particularly stressful for those without a firm sexual identity and the capacity to merge self-interest with the interest of others. This, of course, is not confined to being a biological and rearing parent. It includes a participatory generative role that is gratifying to self and others, such as child care, teaching, or a role that benefits future generations.

3. *Participation in Social Processes* to further the purposes of society and culture. This requires a measure of subordination of personal needs to the needs of others. This is particularly stressful to those who isolate and retain a primarily self-indulgent orientation. An additional complicating factor here is the omnipresent dilemma of the conflict between the values of individualism and social responsibility. Milton Mayer has formulated a provocative position statement on this dilemma (Mayer, 1969).

4. *Work.* A work function is required that is gratifying to self and to society. In our culture work has become a major organizing theme and we construct our life styles around it. The usual response of the adult to a "Who am I?" kind of question is more often than not an occupational response. When we meet a person who does not work it is usually difficult to relate to him until it is determined *why* he does not work. Something must be "wrong" with him. Recent writings on the rehabilitation of schizophrenics have emphasized the necessity of employment if there is to be hope of continued remission. Work provides an identification, represents social usefulness, and is the means of organizing a life.

Certain work identifications are still tied to the place of work ("I work in the mines" or "I work in the quarry"), but other designations are also used. Now most people express work identification as either "I do" or "I am." Traditionally the "I am" designation belonged to the classical professions of law, the clergy, and medicine. The "I do" description is usually a shorthand job description ("I sell shoes" or "I wire circuit boards"). The press toward professionalization in a wide variety of occupations is an attempt to establish a work identification of the "I am" type. One example is the historical shift from "I do social work" to "I am a social worker."

Erich Fromm presents a clear and concise exposition of the idea that the marketplace orientation of our society determines and maintains work identity (Fromm, 1962). Fromm suggests that the person is valued not for what he *is* but for what he *seems to be;* this is then related to supply and demand. "Image" becomes crucial and the person must project the "right" image to be successful. Advertisers are concerned with product image, campaign managers with candidate image, NASW with social work image, and N.E.A. with teacher image. One's value as a person is not self-defined but is dependent on value definitions by others within the criteria of the marketplace. Fromm describes how this has led to the cult of adaptability, with the prime value invested in changeability. Work then has permeated our social systems to an extent we seldom recognize. The "problem" segments of society are defined and labeled by work status.

1. The *nonworkers* include the age groups of youth and the aged. These are not unemployed persons; they are clearly identified as nonworkers, not eligible for work identification. The aged are in a

worse plight than the young since school is viewed as a kind of pseudowork and "student" serves as a work status.

2. The *unemployed* are society's greatest concern. The able-bodied unemployed person violates social prescriptions. He is without a work identification—in fact, his primary social identity may well be *unemployed*. Since the idea of "right to work" holds sway, such unemployment is attributed either to lack of opportunity or to individual deficiency.

3. The *unemployable* present a particular problem because of the humanitarian values held by society. Changing the ground rules and expectations of the worker as Goodwill Industries and sheltered workshops do, makes it possible to remove some people from this classification. This fulfills the promise of the right to work and provides an opportunity structure wherein this right can be realized. Even so, there remains an irreducible residue of unemployables. Although they are "pitied rather than censured," the lack of work identification is judged an important personality deficiency by the person and his significant others.

All of the foregoing is indicative of the exceedingly high premium on an adult having work function that is gratifying to himself and others. Dostoyevsky once wrote, "If it were desired to crush a man completely, to punish him so severely that even the most hardened murderer would quail, it would only be needed to make his work absolutely purposeless and absurd." (Zwerling, 1968, p. 52.)

Alienation

Alienation is a concept that provides some insight into many of the manifest psychological and social difficulties of adulthood. In this context Webster defines alienation as "the withdrawing, diverting or estrangement, as of affections." The word alienation "takes in all washing"; it conveys the general idea of a person or group being in a state of normlessness, powerlessness, meaninglessness, and self-estrangement. Alienation as an idea is applicable to all of man's systems, the intrapsychic system as well as the range of social systems.

Social scientists concerned with this theme universally acknowledge their indebtedness to Emile Durkheim's description of *anomie* in his work on suicide (Durkheim, 1951). Leo Srole formulated five operational elements in anomie (Srole, 1956). The most familiar exposition of the behavioral manifestations of alienation is contained in Robert Merton's essay "Social Structure and Anomie" (Merton, 1957, pp. 131–160). Merton focuses on "normlessness" as the component of focal interest in the alienation complex. He classifies adaptations to alienation by five categories based on the various combinations of and the acceptance or rejection of the goals of the culture, and the acceptance or rejection of the institutionalized means of achieving those goals.

SUMMARY OBSERVATION

The crises of adulthood are focused in the socially defined expectations for the person to intimately involve himself with others in the creation and maintenance of the social systems that enable the culture and species to survive. An adult who does not do this will be isolated, self-seeking, and stagnant. To paraphrase Erikson, the adult might say, "I am what I can love and care for and about."

F. Conservation of Identity

This is the concluding task of the life cycle and as such can be characterized as the crisis of aging. *Conservation* refers to consolidation, protection, and holding on to the ego integrity one has accrued over a lifetime, in the midst of loss and divestment of usual roles and functions. The theme of aging is *loss*. The positive sense of conservatism is that identity passes from one social context to another and yet remains the same. The self maintains its continuity and consistency from one social system to another.

Erikson's polarity during the waning years of life is "Ego Integrity vs Disgust and Despair." This is the culmination of the previous seven crises. Integrity refers to "the ego's accrued assurance of its proclivity for order and meaning—an emotional integration faithful to the image-bearers of the past and ready to take, and eventually to renounce, leadership in the present" (Erikson, 1968, p. 139). It is the capacity of a person to accept his life history, to see the effect he has had on the world through his relationships, and to accept his mortality. The other pole, the sense of disgust, is characterized by bitterness and refusal to accept death as the finite boundary of the personal life cycle.

A definition of "aging" or "age" is difficult to formulate to everyone's satisfaction. In one sense the aging process begins at birth. Socially, age is defined by function. For example, most professional athletes are old by the time they are 35 (an exception is football's George Blanda, still an active player, who illustrates the elasticity of aging). Some industries consider the 50-year-old worker as too old to be employed. Social Security currently sets the age of retirement as 65 for men and 62 for women. A utilitarian definition is suggested by Birren.

> A person is "old" or, better perhaps, "aging" when he is so regarded and treated by his contemporaries and by the younger generation and when he himself has read the culturally recognized individual and social signs symbolic of membership in the generation of elders. The only matter of individual choice open to the old person has to do with whether he wishes to accept or postpone belief in his new identity and act accordingly. (Birren, 1959, p. 280)

Erikson has commented that "it is perfectly obvious that if we live long enough, we all face a renewal of infantile tendencies—a certain childlike quality, if we're lucky, and senile childishness, if we're not. The main point is again a developmental one: only in old age can true wisdom develop in those who are thus 'gifted'" (Evans, 1967, pp. 53–54).

The tasks of aging in our culture are nicely summarized by Birren in quoting Simmons's cross-cultural studies (Simmons, 1946). These are:

1. To live as long as possible, at least until life-satisfaction no longer compensates for its privation, or until the advantages of death seem to outweigh the burden of life.
2. To get more rest, relief from the necessity of wearisome exertion at humdrum tasks, and protection from too great exposure to physical hazards—opportunities, in other words, to safeguard and preserve the waning energies of a physical existence.
3. To remain active participants in personal and group affairs in either operational or supervisory roles—any participation, in fact, being preferable to complete idleness and indifference.
4. To safeguard or even strengthen any prerogatives acquired in long life, i.e., skills, possessions, rights, authorities, prestige, etc.
5. Finally, to withdraw from life, when necessity requires it, as honorably as possible, without too much suffering, and with maximum prospects for an attractive hereafter. (Birren, 1959, pp. 864–865)

As earlier stated, aging is characterized by the theme of loss. It involves relinquishment of certain patterned investments of self. The nature of transactions with other human systems is curtailed. These disengagements can be discussed under a few general headings.

1. Loss of Work Role and Occupational Identification. This has a more profound effect on those with the "I do" work identification than it does on those with an "I am" identification. The retired doctor continues to be seen as a doctor, but the retired shoe salesman is no longer a salesman. Willy Loman in *Death of a Salesman* is an example of a man faced with such a loss of identity. The relinquishment of the work role is particularly difficult for such a man because so much feedback about his worth is tied to this role. Loss of work role usually is accompanied by a marked reduction in income and the necessity of readjustment in standard of living. The person is deprived of membership in his former work system. The situation is somewhat different for women, who may face losses of roles (children leave home, or husband dies) earlier.

2. Loss of Intimate Ties. As the person's friends, acquaintances, and spouse die, he is again faced with separation experiences he faced as a child or young adult. Those who were part of his personality system are gone. He must undergo the painful process of withdrawing (decathecting) his attachments to them at a time when it is most difficult to establish new linkages to replace the former ones. He may not be able to modify his own structure sufficiently to accommodate new attachments. His environment narrows, and perhaps the intensity of the remaining attachments is increased. Such attachments may become "overinvested"; for example, a pet or a formerly casual acquaintance may suddenly become all-important. If no replacements or reinvestments are accomplished, the person may turn inward, seeking energy internally, or he may "bank the fires," attempting less and seeking equilibrium on a lower level of interaction with the environment.

3. Loss of Sexual Interests. Research on the sexual activity of the aged, limited as it is, indicates a gradual decline in frequency over the entire adult period. There is no sharp decline at any particular age. As overt sexual engagement declines, the aged may find it difficult to express or receive tenderness or affection in other ways; grandchildren frequently serve this function for grandparents. Because socially our stereotype of the aged indicates that such needs somehow disappear, we are often unrealistic about the behavior of the aged. For example, probably many of the aged men who have been arrested for "molesting" young children may well be expressing tenderness in the only manner available to them, without intending to harm the children. Unfortunately, society's understanding of this is blocked by our tendency to deny sexuality in the elderly person. The available evidence indicates that sexual companionship (with or without sexual activity) is as important to most elderly persons as it is to younger persons.

4. Loss of Physical Abilities, Particularly Sensory and Motor. Physiologically, the number of taste buds declines with age, eyesight and hearing may suffer impairment, and walking may become difficult. These limitations necessarily handicap the aged person in maintaining contact with his social environment. His world may be narrowed to the walls of his own home, and to his television set.

His self-concept may be threatened by these losses. An example is the 60-year-old who refuses to be beaten at tennis. The person's reaction may be to deny the losses and to demand of himself what he was capable of at a younger age, or his reaction may be depression and unrealistic refusal to do what he is still capable of. It is common among the aged to make reasonable adjustments to less acute faculties —to read larger type, to be more accurate rather than fast—in other words, to make the best use of one's abilities. Such realistic adjustments are part of the person's integrity and maintenance of self.

5. Intellectually, the Person May Become a More Closed System. Borrowing from Piaget, it could be concluded that as one's schemas multiply and more adequately account for one's experience, they become progressively less modifiable. Accommodation declines, while assimilation increases. The person may exclude stimuli from awareness, to limit the energy interchange with those in his environment. He may become less concerned with interpreting and storing new information and more concerned with preserving previous information, sometimes literally in the form of scrapbooks, possessions of a deceased spouse, or a house that was the family dwelling. Either of these intellectual patterns, becoming more closed or remaining open, may be performed so as to allow integrity. Erikson's "wisdom" implies, in one's past, the accrued identity of a lifetime. "Despair and disgust" implies closure, but might well include feedback that indicates the person's alienation from his environment. Thus it implies openness as well.

6. *"Despair and Disgust."* These also include the feeling that time is running out. There are no alternatives possible "at this late date." In *Death of a Salesman,* Willy depends upon his son Biff to reassure him of his own integrity, but Biff has neglected to write to his father:

> BIFF: I was on the move. But you know I thought of you all the time.
>   You know that, don't you, pal?
> LINDA: I know, dear, I know. But he likes to have a letter. Just to know
>   that there's still a possibility for better things. (Miller, 1955,
>   p. 55)

The aged person as a human system must find his steady state, his identity, among the social systems to which he is related. Erikson says that "man as a psychosocial creature will face, toward the end of his life, a new edition of an identity crisis which we may state in the words, "I am what survives of me" (Erikson, 1968, p. 141). What survives are the human systems one has been related to and part of: persons, families, groups, organizations, communities, societies, cultures. These human systems in turn affect other persons who are being born and who are developing. This is why Erikson calls it a *life* cycle—not the life cycle of an individual, alone, but the cycle of life itself: the human system.

> Webster's Dictionary is kind enough to help us complete this outline in circular fashion. Trust (the first of our ego values) is here defined as "the assured reliance on another's integrity," the last of our values. . . . It seems possible to further paraphrase the relation of adult integrity to infantile trust by saying that healthy children will not fear life if their elders have integrity enough not to fear death. (Erikson, 1963, p. 269)

SUGGESTED READINGS

Erikson, Erik. *Identity: Youth and Crisis.* New York: Norton, 1968. In this book Erikson expands on the critical task of identity formation within the context of contemporary issues. It is also one of many of his writings to discuss the total life cycle. (This book has been used as the small-map text for this chapter.) For a thorough explanation of his life cycle formulation see *Childhood and Society,* 2nd ed. (New York: Norton, 1963).

Freud, Sigmund. *Outline of Psychoanalysis.* New York: Norton, 1949. The last book that Freud wrote, it is a concise explanation of the principles derived from his life's work. It is *strongly* recommended that the reader be familiar with Freud's own expression of his ideas rather than relying on the interpretations of latter-day critics.

Goodman, Paul. *Growing Up Absurd.* New York: Random House, 1960. One of the first and probably the best polemic on the topic of growing up in a technological society.

Maier, Henry W. *Three Theories of Child Development.* New York: Harper & Row, 1965. The author, a social worker, examines, compares, and contrasts the theories of Erikson, Piaget, and Sears. He further looks at them as base for social work practice.

Phillips, John L., Jr. *The Origins of Intellect: Piaget's Theory.* San Francisco: W. H. Freeman, 1969. This is an excellent source for anyone wishing to read further about the contributions of Piaget. Especially good are the Preface, Chapter 1, and Chapter 5.

Pincus, Allen. "Toward A Developmental View of Aging for Social Work," *Social Work* 12, 3, July, 1967, 33–41. Pincus has written the most pertinent articles on aging, for social work practice. This one summarizes his view of aging as a dynamic process.

Stone, L. Joseph, and Joseph Church. *Childhood and Adolescence.* 2nd ed. New York: Random House, 1968. This is an excellent text for any student who has not had the opportunity to study child development. It is comprehensive and thorough, with a host of illustrative examples.

World Health Organization. *Deprivation of Maternal Care.* Geneva: World Health Organization, 1962. This reassessment of maternal deprivation was a follow-up to John Bowlby's WHO monograph of 1951. The contributors are acknowledged authorities for a number of disciplines. Anyone interested in early child care should be familiar with this material.

Literary Sources

Golding, William. *Lord of the Flies.* New York: Capricorn Books, Putnam, 1959. (Other editions, exist, as well as a film version.) Illustrates the effects of culture, processes of social organization, group dynamics, and symbolic meanings in a group of boys in their middle years.

Miller, Arthur. *Death of a Salesman.* New York: Bantam Books, 1955. Miller's classic play of everyman caught up in a world of change and attempting to live in the past.

Bergman, Ingmar. "Wild Strawberries," in *Four Screenplays.* New York: Simon and Schuster, 1960. An elderly man reminisces about the past as a means of dealing with the present.

Malcolm X (with the assistance of Alex Haley). *The Autobiography of Malcolm X.* New York: Grove Press, 1966. This moving autobiography exemplifies all levels of human systems and a person's interaction with them. It highlights how systems affect the person and how a person can influence systems.

Powers, Thomas. *Diana: The Making of a Terrorist.* New York: Bantam Books, 1971. This traces the evolution of an upper middle class girl from her girlhood in a small town to her death as a member of the Weathermen in a New York bomb explosion. Powers intricately interweaves social class, alienation, culture, ideology, personality development, and group and organizational change. In addition, the topical nature of the book makes it excellent teaching material.

GLOSSARY

Readers are also referred to the Index for usage of terms as they occur in the text.

ACCOMMODATION. Modification of the system to adapt to environmental conditions. See ADAPTATION, ASSIMILATION.

ADAPTATION. Action by the system to secure or conserve energy from the environment. Parsons's use of this term includes this as well as the achievement of goals in the environment. See ACCOMMODATION, ASSIMILATION, FUNCTIONAL IMPERATIVES.

ALIENATION. This term has a wide variety of definitions. We consider that fundamentally it describes a state in which a person experiences no synergistic linkage with any system (or component) he judges significant to him.

ASSIMILATION. A form of adaptation in which incoming information is interpreted as similar to previous information—that is, it is fitted into old schemas. See ACCOMMODATION, ADAPTATION.

AUTONOMY. Independence from other components within a system. The components are related to a common suprasystem but are largely or entirely separate from each other.

BEHAVIOR. Short-term exchanges between components or systems that accomplish specific goals for the system. This includes socialization, communication, and social control. See EVOLUTION, STRUCTURE.

BODY LANGUAGE. Communication of a nonverbal nature expressed through touch, posture, facial expression, and movement.

BOND. The common interest, identification, or feeling of "we-ness" among members of a group which permits the group to exist as a system. See BOUNDARY.

BOUNDARY. The limits of the interaction of the components of a system with each other or with the environment. It is usually defined by intensity or frequency of interaction between systems and components.

BUREAUCRACY. A distinct form of organization in which there is administrative centralization, hierarchical control, specificity of rules, and clearly identified role expectations. This form of organization is usually found in cultures that are highly elaborated, and usually serves social control functions in the society.

CLASS. A system of stratification of a given society. Usually ordered by indices such as income, occupation, and education. See ROLE, STATUS.

COMMUNICATION. In a narrow sense, the transportation of information between or within systems; in a broader sense, the transportation of energy, also. In this broader sense, information is considered a special form of energy. (See Monane, 1967, Chapter 2, for his use of these terms.)

COMPONENT. Synonymous with *part*—a part of a system. It may or may not be a system in itself, in contrast to a subsystem, which *is* a system. See SUBSYSTEM.

DIFFERENTIATION. Assignment or allocation of functions to separate parts. "Division of labor" is one example. See SPECIALIZATION.

DISINTEGRATION. "Disintegration means systemic death. With it, components *de*-systematize. It is a movement away from organization into entropy and randomness" (Monane, 1967, p. 159). See ORGANIZATION.

ECOLOGICAL SYSTEMS. A term used by some systems writers in the broad sense of systems that are hierarchically related. In biology and ecology, the term refers to living organisms in the earth's biosphere that are hierarchically related.

ENERGY. Capacity for action, action, or power to effect change. We use this term much as Parsons uses *action*. See ENTROPY, POWER.

ENTROPY. "The quantity of energy *not* capable of conversion into work" (Isaac Asimov, "In the Game of Energy and Thermodynamics You Can't Break Even," *Smithsonian,* August, 1970, p. 8). Entropy is the tendency of systems to "run down," to distribute energy randomly so that it becomes less available; the system therefore becomes more chaotic and less capable of organized work. Some argue that open systems are not subject to the law of entropy.

ENVIRONMENT. Anything not included within the interaction of the components of a system. It may also be considered as anything that affects the system but over which it has no control (Churchman, 1968, p. 50).

EQUIFINALITY. The term derives from systems theory; it means that in the event that the inputs are the same, two different systems may arrive at similar steady states, even though they had different initial conditions. One illustration is that although two children may grow differently, one overshooting and the other undershooting initially, they both will arrive at adulthood in good health and normal size *if* they are fed similarly and adequately.

EQUILIBRIUM. Fixed balance in a closed system, characterized by little interchange with the environment and avoidance of disturbance. See HOMEOSTASIS, STEADY STATE.

ETHOLOGY. The study of animal behavior, especially of innate patterns. In the last decade writings of ethologists, including Konrad Lorenz, Desmond Morris, and Lionel Tiger and Robin Fox, have gained popular renown. See TERRITORIALITY.

EVOLUTION. Change in a system's structure and behavior from one time to another. This term describes which relationships have altered and in what manner a system's functions are being performed differently at some particular time. See BEHAVIOR, STRUCTURE.

FEEDBACK. The process in which a system monitors internal or environmental responses to its behavior and accommodates itself to the information (or energy). See ADAPTATION, COMMUNICATION.

FOCAL SYSTEM. This is the system that is the focus of attention at the moment. It is specified to be consistent with the demand that the perspective of the viewer should be stated. Systems analysts frequently label this the *target system*, if the focal system is the system in which change is to be achieved. See HOLON, PERSPECTIVISM.

FUNCTIONAL IMPERATIVES. Parsons specifies four functions that are imperative in a system. These are ADAPTATION, GOAL ATTAINMENT, INTEGRATION, and PATTERN MAINTENANCE. We identify other energy functions that we consider more descriptive.

GOAL. A desired steady state to be achieved by fulfilling a specific function of the system within some short term. See PURPOSE.

GOAL ATTAINMENT. (GE and GI functions). One of two kinds of major systems functions, the other being SECURING AND CONSERVING ENERGY. The process is the expenditure of energy to achieve system goals, either internally or externally.

HIERARCHY. A form of organization that characterizes all viable systems. Hierarchy is a relationship between subsystems, systems, and suprasystems in which any unit is dependent upon its suprasystem for performance or energy functions and must provide direction to its subsystems.

HOMEOSTASIS. Fixed balance in an open system, characterized by a degree of interchange with the environment and maintenance of the system's structure. See EQUILIBRIUM, STEADY STATE.

HOLON. Arthur Koestler's term, denoting that a system is both a part of a larger suprasystem and is itself a suprasystem to other subsystems. See FOCAL SYSTEM, SUBSYSTEM, SUPRASYSTEM.

IDENTITY. Erikson defines this in several variations. The central idea is integration of the components of personality, along with validation through interaction with the social environment. The result of these is ego identity, which is inner assurance of congruence between one's own feelings about self and others' feelings about oneself. The concept has been loosely applied to other systems, such as "national identity," "racial identity." Identity is a steady state of the personality system, but is richer in its meaning than steady state. See STEADY STATE, SYNERGY.

INFORMATION. The content of feedback and communication. In a narrow sense, information includes signs and symbols communicated. In a broader sense, information could include energy interchange itself. See COMMUNICATION, FEEDBACK.

INSTITUTIONALIZATION. One form of differentiation in which some sanctioned component or system is delegated and formally recognized as performing specific system functions. The differentiated system may have exclusive responsibility for the performance of this function. A new subsystem may be created for this purpose, or the assignment may be given to an existing subsystem. See DIFFERENTIATION, SPECIALIZATION.

INTEGRATION. One of Parsons's four FUNCTIONAL IMPERATIVES. The system must ensure the harmonious interaction of its components, in order to secure and conserve internal energy resources.

LINKAGE. Energy interchange between systems.

LOOP. This term is from engineering and cybernetics. It is a specific form of feedback in which a system's output becomes input that modifies the system's functioning. That is, the system's own behavior supplies stimuli for system modification. See FEEDBACK.

MISSION. See PURPOSE.

MORPHOGENESIS. A system tending toward structural change. In actuality all systems must simultaneously maintain and change, a shifting balance between morphogenesis and morphostasis.

MORPHOSTASIS. A system tending toward maintenance of the status quo, structurally. See MORPHOGENESIS.

OPEN or CLOSED SYSTEM. OPEN denotes energy exchange across a system's boundary. CLOSED denotes lack of energy exchange across boundaries.

ORGANIZATION. The process of patterning and articulation of energy exchange in a system. Persistent regularities of relationship between components are the organization, or structure, of the system. See DIFFERENTIATION, SPECIALIZATION.

PATTERN MAINTENANCE. One of Parsons's four FUNCTIONAL IMPERATIVES. This refers to the necessity of the system to regulate and enforce legitimized behaviors in order to conserve energy and achieve goals. We view this as including our SI and GI functions.

PERSPECTIVISM. In the systems approach, this means that any description or definition must include some statement as to one's own position in relation to a system, or some statement as to the system one chooses as the focal system. Philosophically, the term denotes that any viewpoint is relative to one's own perceptions and relations to the system being described, and to its environment.

POLARITIES. Opposite or contrasting qualities. Many of the systems ideas are conceived as polarities on a continuum, with any system at any time being in a state of mixture or ratio of two polar qualities, such as task vs sentiment, adaptation vs integration, basic trust vs basic mistrust.

POWER. The capacity to achieve goals by the application or deprivation of energy to another system so as to affect its functioning. Bredemeier and Stephenson note that "power may be exercised effectively whenever one party can grant or withhold what another needs and cannot get elsewhere" (*The Analysis of Social Systems*. New York: Holt, Rinehart and Winston, 1962, p. 50).

PSYCHOSEXUAL. Generally refers to the Freudian stages of personality development, that is, oral, anal, phallic and genital.

PSYCHOSOCIAL. Generally refers to the Eriksonian life cycle formulation of personality development. This is a modification and extension of the psychosexual with emphasis on the social and cultural influences.

PURPOSE. A desired steady state of a system achieved by assignment of goal(s) to a subsystem, and completion of the goal(s). *Goal* denotes that the system itself will be the object of change; *purpose* that the suprasystem will be the object of change. Systems analysts frequently use *mission* to mean the same as purpose. See GOAL.

ROLE. A position that can be filled by a person. It carries with it expectations of behavior that are defined and sanctioned by significant environmental systems.
The role occupant generally has some leeway in interpretation of assigned
behaviors. (This is analogous to the theater where the playwright prescribes
the role expectation but the artist interprets through his role performance.) See
ROLE, STATUS.

SCHEMA. Precisely used, this is Piaget's term for a single complex, or nexus, of associated responses a person is capable of making. The plural is *schemata*, or
schemas. We use the term in a broader sense to emphasize its transferability to
systems other than a person—for example, the repertoire of responses which an
organization or community is capable of making. We also use the term to
mean the integrated knowledge, experience, and interpretations that underlie a
system's responses.

SECURING AND CONSERVING ENERGY. We designate this as one of two major kinds
of functions in a system (the other is GOAL ATTAINMENT). The process is
one of expending energy to secure further energy, or to reduce the expenditure
of energy, as in minimizing intrasystem conflict.

SOCIAL CONTROL. The use of energy by a system to assure that its components fulfill
assigned functions (see PURPOSES). Such activity includes socialization and
enforcement of norms of behavior. Enforcement may entail persuasion, authority, or force. The purpose of social control is to permit continued functioning
of the system through reducing or preventing deviance among the components.
See SOCIALIZATION.

SOCIALIZATION. One form of social control, intended to assure the availability of
components' energies to the system. The means of achieving this are primarily
through assimilating the culture. Hence education, indoctrination, and encultura-
tion are forms of socialization. See SOCIAL CONTROL.

SPECIALIZATION. The assignment of a system activity to one and only one component.
See DIFFERENTIATION.

STATUS. A vertical dimension of ranking. May be ascribed (assigned by society) or
achieved (attained by dint of individual and group activity). See CLASS, ROLE.

STEADY STATE. A total condition of the system in which it is in balance both internally
and with its environment, but which is in change. The word *steady* fails to
connote the dynamic nature of systems, while the word *state* fails to connote a
succession of conditions of the system. Used fairly loosely and somewhat inter-
changeably with EQUILIBRIUM and HOMEOSTASIS, but distinct from them.

STRUCTURE. The most stable relationships between systems and components—that
is, with the slowest rate of change. This states which components or systems
are related to each other within a given time period, but not necessarily the
manner in which they are related to each other or the functions being performed
for each party to the relationship. See BEHAVIOR, EVOLUTION.

SUBSYSTEM. A component of a system that is in itself a system. It is one kind of component. See COMPONENT, SUPRASYSTEM, SYSTEM.

SUPRASYSTEM. A larger system that includes the focal system we are concerned with—
the "whole" of which the focal system is a "part." See SUBSYSTEM, SYSTEM.

SYMBOLIC INTERACTION. A theoretical perspective within social psychology that
seeks to understand human behavior through study of the "social act." Such
study attends to overt behavior and what the act symbolizes within the social
context.

SYNERGY. Increasing the amount of available energy in a system through increased
interaction of the components. Loosely, it may be described as the creation of

new energy through compounding the actions of the parts, but this is a moot point in systems theory. See ENERGY, ENTROPY.

SYSTEM. An organized whole made up of components that interact in a way distinct from their interaction with other entities, and which endures over some period of time. See COMPONENT, SUBSYSTEM, SUPRASYSTEM.

TERRITORIALITY. Refers to the proclivity of organisms, including man, to seek, obtain, and defend an area of space or action. This serves to order and stabilize behavioral space. See ETHOLOGY.

BIBLIOGRAPHY

Adams, Margaret. "The Compassion Trap—Women Only," *Psychology Today*, November, 1971, 71 ff.

Albee, Edward. *Who's Afraid of Virginia Woolf?* New York: Pocketbook Cardinal, 1963.

Ardrey, Robert. *The Territorial Imperative.* New York: Atheneum, 1966.

Argyris, Chris. "Personal *vs.* Organizational Goals," in *Human Relations in Administration,* Robert Dubin, 3d ed. Englewood Cliffs, N.J.: Prentice-Hall, 1968 pp. 80–89.

Bales, Robert F. *Interaction Process Analysis.* Cambridge: Addison-Wesley, 1950.

Bandura, Albert. *Social Learning and Personality Development.* New York: Holt, Rinehart and Winston, 1963.

Banfield, Edward. *Political Influence.* New York: Free Press, 1961.

Baratz, Stephen, and Joan Baratz. "Early Childhood Intervention: The Social Science Base of Institutional Racism," in *Majority and Minority,* Norman R. Yetman and C. Hoy Steele, eds. Boston: Allyn and Bacon, 1971, pp. 470–479.

Barnard, Chester I. "Dilemmas of Leadership in the Democratic Process," in *Human Relations in Administration,* Robert Dubin, ed. 3rd ed. Englewood Cliffs, N.J.: Prentice-Hall, 1968, pp. 390–394.

Barnard, Chester I. "Education for Executives," in *Human Relations in Administration,*

Robert Dubin, ed. 3rd ed. Englewood Cliffs, N.J.: Prentice-Hall, 1968, pp. 19–25.

Barnett, Lincoln. *The Universe and Dr. Einstein.* London: Gollancz, 1948.

Bell, John Elderkin. *Family Group Therapy.* Public Health Monograph, 1964.

Bennis, Warren G. "Post-Bureaucratic Leadership," *Trans-Action* 6, July/August, 1969, 44 ff.

Bennis, Warren G., and Herbert A. Shepard. "A Theory of Group Development," *Human Relations* 9, 4, November, 1956, 415–437.

Berne, Eric. *The Structure and Dynamics of Organizations and Groups.* New York: Grove Press, 1966.

Berrien, F. K. "A General Systems Approach to Human Groups," in *Man in Systems,* Milton D. Rubin, ed. New York: Gordon and Breach, 1971, pp. 119–137.

Bertalanffy, Ludwig Von. *Robots, Men and Minds.* New York: Braziller, 1967.

Bierstedt, Robert. "Power and Social Organization," in *Human Relations in Administration,* Robert Dubin, ed. Englewood Cliffs, N.J.: Prentice-Hall, 1961, pp. 238–247.

Billingsley, Andrew. *Black Families in White America.* Englewood Cliffs, N.J.: Prentice-Hall, 1968.

Bird, Caroline. *The Invisible Scar.* New York: David McKay, 1966.

Birdwhistell, Ray L. *Kinesics and Context: Essays on Body Motion Communication.* Philadelphia: University of Pennsylvania Press, 1970.

Birren, James E., ed. *Handbook on Aging and the Individual: Psychological and Biological Aspects.* Chicago: University of Chicago Press, 1959.

Blau, Peter M. *Bureaucracy in Modern Society.* New York: Random House, 1956.

Blumer, Herbert. "Society as Symbolic Interaction," in *Symbolic Interaction,* Jerome G. Manis and Bernard N. Meltzer, eds. Boston: Allyn and Bacon, 1967, pp. 139–148.

Boehm, Werner. "Relationship of Social Work to Other Professions," in *Encyclopedia of Social Work.* New York: National Association of Social Workers, 1965.

Boguslaw, Robert. *The New Utopians.* Englewood Cliffs, N.J.: Prentice-Hall, 1965.

Boulding, Elise. "The Family as an Agent of Social Change," *The Futurist,* Vol. VI, No. 5, October 1972, pp. 186–91.

Bowlby, John. "Child Care and the Growth of Love," in *Human Development,* Morris L. Haimowitz and Natalie Reader Haimowitz, eds. 2nd New York: Crowell, 1966.

———. *Deprivation of Maternal Care.* Geneva: World Health Organization, 1962.

Breuer, Joseph, and Sigmund Freud. *Studies in Hysteria.* Trans. A. A. Brill. New York: Nervous and Mental Disease Publishing Co., 1936.

Brown, Lester R. "New Supranational Institutions," *The Futurist,* October 1972, 197–202.

Brown, Roger. "How Shall a Thing Be Called"? in *Readings in Child Development and Personality,* Paul Mussen et al., eds. New York: Harper & Row, 1965.

Bruner, Jerome. *Toward a Theory of Instruction.* New York: Norton, 1968.

Buckley, Walter. *Sociology and Modern Systems Theory.* Englewood Cliffs, N.J.: Prentice-Hall, 1967.

Cahn, Edgar S. *Our Brother's Keeper: The Indian in White America.* Cleveland: World Publishing Company, 1969.

Campbell, D. T. "Common Fate, Similarity and Other Indices of the Status of Aggregates of Persons as Social Entities," *Behavioral Science,* 3, 1958, 14–25.

Cartwright, Darwin, and Alvin Zander. *Group Dynamics.* Evanston: Row, Peterson, 1960.

Chatterjee, Pranab, and Raymond A. Koleski. "The Concepts of Community and Community Organization: A Review," *Social Work* 15, 3, July, 1970, 82–92.

Christaller, Walter. *Central Places in Southern Germany.* Trans. Carlisle W. Baskin. Englewood Cliffs, N.J.: Prentice-Hall, 1966.

Churchman, C. West. *The Systems Approach.* New York: Dell, 1968.

Coles, Robert H. *Erik H. Erikson: The Growth of His Work.* Boston: Little, Brown, 1970.

Constantine, Larry, and Joan Constantine. "Where is Marriage Going?" *The Futurist* 4, 2, April, 1970, 44–46.

Cooley, Charles Horton. "'Looking-Glass Self," in *Symbolic Interaction,* Jerome G. Manis and Bernard N. Meltzer, eds. Boston: Allyn and Bacon, 1967, pp. 139–148.

Coser, Lewis. *The Functions of Social Conflict.* New York: Free Press, 1964.

Coyle, Grace. *Group Work with American Youth.* New York: Harper & Row, 1948.

Dahl, Robert A. "The Concept of Power," *Behavioral Science* 2, July, 1957, 201–215.

———. "A Critique of the Ruling Elite Model," *American Political Science Review,* June, 1958.

———. *Who Governs?: Democracy and Power in an American City.* New Haven: Yale University Press, 1961.

Dewey, John. *Democracy and Education.* New York: Free Press, 1966.

Domhoff, G. William. *Who Rules America?* Englewood Cliffs, N.J.: Prentice-Hall, 1967.

———. *The Higher Circles.* New York: Vintage Books, 1971.

Domhoff, G. William, and Hoyt B. Ballard, eds. *C. Wright Mills and the Power Elite.* Boston: Beacon Press, 1968.

Dubin, Robert, ed. *Human Relations in Administration.* Englewood Cliffs, N.J.: Prentice-Hall, 1961, 1968.

Durkheim, Emile. *Suicide.* Trans. John A. Spaulding and George Simpson. Glencoe, Ill. Free Press, 1951.

———. "Division of Labor and Interdependence," in *Human Relations in Administration,* Robert Dubin, ed., Englewood Cliffs, N.J.: Prentice-Hall, pp. 42–45.

Elkind, David. "Giant in the Nursery—Jean Piaget." *New York Times Magazine,* May 26, 1968, pp. 25–80.

Engels, Friedrich. *The Origin of the Family, Private Property and the State.* Chicago: C. H. Kerr, 1902.

Erikson, Erik H. in *Symposium on the Healthy Personality,* M. J. E. Senn, ed. New York: Josiah Macy Jr. Foundation, 1950, pp. 91–146.

———. "The Problem of Ego Identity," in *Psychological Issues,* George S. Klein, ed., New York: International Universities Press, 1959, pp. 101–167.

———. *Young Man Luther.* New York: Norton, 1962.

———. *Childhood and Society.* 2nd ed. New York: Norton, 1963.

———. *Insight and Responsibility.* New York: Norton, 1964.

———. *Identity: Youth and Crisis.* New York: Norton, 1968.

———. *Gandhi's Truth.* New York: Norton, 1969.

Etzioni, Amitai. *Modern Organizations.* Englewood Cliffs, N.J.: Prentice-Hall, 1964.

Evans, Richard I. *Dialogue with Erik Erikson.* New York: Harper & Row, 1967.

Farb, Peter. *Man's Rise to His Civilization as Shown by the Indians of North America from Primeval Times to the Coming of the Industrial State.* New York: Dutton, 1968.

Fast, Julian. *Body Language.* New York: Lippincott, 1970.

Feldman, Frances Lomas, and Frances H. Scherz. *Family Social Welfare.* New York: Atherton, 1967.

Flavell, John H. *The Developmental Psychology of Jean Piaget.* Princeton: Van Nostrand, 1963.

French, Robert Mills. *The Community.* Itasca, Ill.: Peacock, 1969.

Freud, Sigmund. *Introductory Lectures on Psychoanalysis.* Trans. Joan Riviere. London: Allen and Litwin, 1933, pp. 32–36.

————. "Three Contributions to the Theory of Sex," in *The Basic Writings of Sigmund Freud,* A. A. Brill, ed. New York: Modern Library, 1938a, pp. 551–629.

————. "The Interpretation of Dreams," in *The Basic Writings of Sigmund Freud,* A. A. Brill, ed. New York: Modern Library, 1938b, pp. 179–549.

————. "The Psychopathology of Everyday Life," in *The Basic Writings of Sigmund Freud,* A. A. Brill, ed. New York: Modern Library, 1938c, pp. 31–178.

————. *An Outline of Psychoanalysis.* Trans. James Strachey. New York: Norton, 1949.

Friedenberg, Edgar Z. *The Vanishing Adolescent.* New York: Dell, 1962.

Fromm, Erich. "Personality and the Market Place," in *Man, Work, and Society,* Sigmund Nosow and William H. Form, eds. New York: Basic Books, 1962, pp. 446–452.

Galper, Jeffry. "Nonverbal Communication Exercises in Groups," *Social Work* 15, 2, April, 1970, pp. 71–78.

Garland, James A., et al. "A Model for States of Development in Social Work Groups," in *Explorations in Group Work,* Saul Berstein, ed. Boston: Boston University School of Social Work, 1965, pp. 12–53.

Gehman, Richard. "TV in Amishland," *TV Guide,* July 18, 1970, pp. 8 ff.

Goertzel, Victor, and M. B. Goertzel. *Cradles of Eminence.* Boston: Little, Brown, 1962.

Goffman, Erving. *The Presentation of Self in Everyday Life.* Indianapolis: Bobbs-Merrill, 1961.

Golembiewski, Robert T., and Arthur Blumberg. *Sensitivity Training and the Laboratory Approach.* Itasca, Ill.: Peacock, 1970.

Goode, William J. *The Family.* Englewood Cliffs, N.J.: Prentice-Hall, 1964.

Goodman, Paul. *Growing Up Absurd.* New York: Random House, 1960.

Gordon, Robert A., and James E. Howell. "Current Opinions about Qualifications for Success in Business," in *Human Relations in Administration,* Robert Dubin, ed. 3rd ed. Englewood Cliffs, N.J.: Prentice-Hall, 1968, pp. 164–169.

Gouldner, Alvin W. "Organizational Analysis," in *The Planning of Change,* Warren G. Bennis et al., eds. New York: Holt, Rinehart and Winston, 1961, pp. 393–400.

Green, Philip S. "Group Work with Welfare Recipients," *Social Work* 15, 4, October, 1970, pp. 3 ff.

Hall, Calvin S., and Lindzey, Gardner. *Theories of Personality.* New York: Wiley, 1957.

Hall, Edward T. *The Silent Language.* Greenwich, Conn.: Fawcett, 1961.

————. *The Hidden Dimension.* Garden City, N.Y.: Doubleday, 1969.

Hamilton, Gordon. *Theory and Practice of Social Casework.* New York: Columbia University Press, 1944.

Hearn, Gordon, ed. *The General Systems Approach: Contributions Toward an Holistic Conception of Social Work.* New York: Council on Social Work Education, 1969.

Heraud, Brian J. *Sociology and Social Work.* Oxford: Pergamon Press, 1970.

Hill, Reuben, and Donald A. Hansen. "The Identification of Conceptual Frameworks Utilized in Family Study," *Marriage and Family Living* 22, November, 1970, 299–311.

Hillery, George A., Jr. *Communal Organizations: A Study of Local Societies.* Chicago: University of Chicago Press, 1968.

Hollingshead, August. *Elmtown's Youth.* New York: Wiley, 1969.

Hollis, Florence. *Casework: A Psychosocial Therapy.* 2nd ed. New York: Random House, 1972 (especially pp. 185–201).

Homans, George. *The Human Group.* New York: Harcourt, Brace & World, 1950.

Hostetler, John A., and G. Huntingdon. *The Hutterites in North America.* New York: Holt, Rinehart and Winston, 1967.

Hunter, Floyd. *Community Power Structure.* Chapel Hill: University of North Carolina Press, 1953.

Huxley, Julian. *Man in the Modern World.* New York: Mentor Book, 1964.

Ichheiser, Gustav. "Misunderstandings in Human Relations: A Study in False Social Perception," *American Journal of Sociology* 55, 2, September, 1949.

Jackson, Don. "The Study of the Family," in *Family Process,* Nathan W. Ackerman, ed. New York: Basic Books, 1970, pp. 111–130.

Kahn, Alfred J. *Theory and Practice of Social Planning.* New York: Russell Sage Foundation, 1969.

Kanter, Rosabeth Moss. "Communes," *Psychology Today* 4, 2, July, 1970, 53 ff.

Keniston, Kenneth. "Youth: A 'New' Stage of life," *The American Scholar* 39, 4, 1970, 631–654.

Knowles, Louis L., and Kenneth Prewitt, eds. *Institutional Racism in America.* Englewood Cliffs, N.J.: Prentice-Hall, 1969.

Koestler, Arthur. *The Act of Creation.* New York: Dell, 1967a.

————. *The Ghost in the Machine.* London: Hutchinson, 1967b.

Koestler, Arthur, and J. R. Symthies, eds. *Beyond Reductionism: New Perspectives in the Life Sciences.* Boston: Beacon Press, 1971.

Ktsanes, Thomas. "Adolescent Educational Values and Their Implications for the Assumption of the Adult Role," *Adolescence: Pivotal Period in The Life Cycle,* Tulane Studies in Social Welfare 8, 1965, 17–27.

Kvaraceus, William C. *Delinquent Behavior.* Washington, D.C.: National Education, 1959, Vol. 1: *Culture and the Individual.*

La Barre, Weston. *The Human Animal.* Chicago: University of Chicago Press, 1954.

Landsberger, Henry A. "Parsons' Theory of Organizations," *The Social Theories of Talcott Parsons,* Max Black, ed. Englewood Cliffs, N.J.: Prentice-Hall, 1961, pp. 214–249.

Laszlo, Ervin. *The Systems View of the World.* New York: Braziller, 1972.

Lenski, Gerhard. *Human Societies.* New York: McGraw-Hill, 1970.

Leslie, Gerald. *The Family in Social Context.* New York: Oxford University Press, 1967.

Levine, Naomi. *Schools in Crisis.* New York: Popular Library, 1969.

Lidz, Theodore. *The Family and Human Adaptation.* New York: International Universities Press, 1963.

Linton, Ralph. *The Cultural Background of Personality.* New York: Appleton-Century-Crofts, 1945.

Litwin, George H. "Climate and Behavior Theory," in *Organizational Climate: Explorations of a Concept,* Renato Tagiuri and George H. Litwin, eds. Boston: Harvard University Press, 1968, pp. 35–61.

Loeb, Martin. "Social Class and the American Social System," *Social Work* 6, 2, April, 1961, 12–18.

London, Perry. *The Modes and Morals of Psychotherapy.* New York: Holt, Rinehart and Winston, 1964.

Loomis, Charles P., and Zona K. Loomis. *Modern Social Theories.* Princeton: Van Nostrand, 1961.

Lorenz, Konrad. *On Aggression.* New York: Harcourt, Brace & World, 1963.

Lyman, Stanford M., and Marvin B. Scott. "Territoriality: A Neglected Sociological Dimension," *Social Problems* 15, Fall, 1967, 236–245.

Lynd, Robert S., and Helen Merrell Lynd. *Middletown.* New York: Harcourt, Brace, 1929.

———. *Middletown in Transition.* New York: Harcourt, Brace, 1937.

Mabee, Bryan. "The Facts about Lesbianism: A Special Inquiry into a Neglected Problem," *The New Statesman* 69, March, 1965, 491–493.

Maier, Henry W. *Three Theories of Child Development.* New York: Harper & Row, 1965.

Malcolm X. *The Autobiography of Malcolm X.* New York: Grove Press, 1966.

March, James G., and Herbert A. Simon. "Significance of Organizations," in *Human Relations in Administration,* Robert Dubin, ed. 3rd ed. Englewood Cliffs, N.J.: Prentice-Hall, 1968, pp. 31–33.

Marrow, Alfred J. *The Practical Theorist: The Life and Work of Kurt Lewin.* New York: Basic Books, 1969.

Marshall, T. H. *Class, Citizenship, and Social Development.* Garden City, N.Y.: Doubleday, 1964.

Maruyama, Magorah. "Monopolarization, Family and Individuality," *Psychiatric Quarterly* 40, 1, 1966, 133–149.

Maslow, Abraham. "Synergy in the Society and in the Individual," *Journal of Individual Psychology* 20, 1964, 153–164.

———. *Toward a Psychology of Being.* Princeton: Van Nostrand, 1968.

May, Rollo. *Love and Will.* New York: Norton, 1969.

Mayer, Milton. *On Liberty: Man vs The State.* Santa Barbara: The Center for the Study of Democratic Institutions, 1969.

Mayo, Elton. *The Social Problems of an Industrial Civilization.* Boston: Harvard University Press, 1945.

McGregor, Douglas. *The Human Side of Enterprise.* New York: McGraw-Hill, 1960.

McLuhan, Marshall. *Understanding Media: The Extensions of Man.* New York: McGraw-Hill, 1965.

Mead, Margaret. *Culture and Commitment.* Garden City, N.Y.: Natural History Press
—Doubleday, 1970.

Meenaghan, Thomas M. "What Means 'Community'?" *Social Work* 17, 6, November,
1972, 94–98.

Menninger, Karl. *The Vital Balance.* New York: Viking, 1963.

Merton, Robert K. "Social Structure and Anomie," in *Social Theory and Social Structure.* rev. ed. Chicago: Free Press, 1957a, pp. 131–160.

————. *Social Theory and Social Structure.* Glencoe, Ill.: Free Press, 1957b.

Miller, Arthur. *Death of a Salesman.* New York: Bantam, 1955.

Miller, James G. "Toward a General Theory for the Behavioral Sciences," *American
Psychologist* 10, September, 1955, pp. 513–531.

————. "Living Systems: Basic Concepts," *Behavioral Science* 10, July, 1965, pp.
193–237.

————. "Living Systems: The Organization," *Behavioral Science* 17, 1, January,
1972, 1–182.

Mills, C. Wright. *The New Men of Power.* New York: Harcourt, Brace, 1948.

————. *The Power Elite.* New York: Oxford University Press, 1951.

Mills, Theodore. *The Sociology of Small Groups.* Englewood Cliffs, N.J.: Prentice-
Hall, 1967.

Moe, Edward O. "The Nature of a Community," in *The Planning of Change,* Warren
G. Bennis et al., eds. New York: Holt, Rinehart and Winston, 1961, p. 400.

Monane, Joseph H. *A Sociology of Human Systems.* New York: Appleton-Century-
Crofts, 1967.

Moore, Barrington. *Political Power and Social Theory.* Cambridge: Harvard University Press, 1958.

Morris, Desmond. *The Naked Ape.* New York: McGraw-Hill, 1967.

Mumford, Lewis. *The City in History.* New York: Harcourt, Brace & World, 1961.

————. *The Myth of the Machine: II. The Pentagon of Power.* New York: Harcourt
Brace Jovanovich, 1970.

Neuman, Krystyna, and Henry Wilhelm. "A Radical Commune: An Approach to
Revolution," *The Modern Utopian* 4, 1, 3.

Nimkoff, Meyer. *Comparative Family Systems.* Boston: Houghton Mifflin, 1965.

Nisbet, R. A. *The Sociological Tradition.* New York: Basic Books, 1966.

Northen, Helen. *Social Work with Groups.* New York: Columbia University Press,
1969.

Noyes, Arthur P., and Lawrence C. Colb. *Modern Clinical Psychiatry.* Philadelphia:
W. B. Saunders Co., 1963.

Nye, F. Ivan, and Felix M. Berardo. *Emerging Conceptual Frameworks in Family
Analysis.* New York: Macmillan, 1968.

Olmsted, Michael. *The Small Group.* New York: Random House, 1959.

Olsen, Marvin. *The Process of Social Organization.* New York: Holt, Rinehart and
Winston, 1968.

O'Neill, Nena, and George O'Neill. *Open Marriage.* New York: M. Evans and Co.,
1972.

Papademetriou, Marguerite. "Use of a Group Technique with Unwed Mothers and
Their Families," *Social Work* 16, 4, October, 1971, 85–90.

Park, Robert E. *Race and Culture.* Glencoe, Ill.: Free Press, 1950.

Park, Robert E. *Human Communities.* Glencoe, Ill.: Free Press, 1952.

Parsons, Talcott. *Structure and Process in Modern Societies.* Glencoe, Ill.: Free Press, 1960.

———. "The Normal Family," *Family Mental Health Papers,* Los Angeles, County Bureau of Public Assistance, 1964a.

———. *The Social System.* New York: Free Press, 1964b.

Parsons, Talcott, R. F. Bales, and E. A. Shils. *Working Papers in the Theory of Action.* Glencoe, Ill.: Free Press, 1953.

Pei, Mario. *The Story of Language.* New York: Mentor Book, 1966.

Perlman, Helen Harris. *Persona.* Chicago: University of Chicago Press, 1968.

Phillips, John L. *The Origins of Intellect: Piaget's Theory.* San Francisco: W. H. Freeman, 1969.

Piaget, Jean. *The Moral Judgment of the Child.* Trans. Marjorie Gabain. London: Kegan Paul, 1932.

———. *Genetic Epistemology.* Trans. Eleanor Duckworth. New York: Columbia University Press, 1970.

Plath, Sylvia. "Tulips," in *Ariel.* New York: Harper & Row, 1966, pp. 10–12.

Pollak, Otto. "Contributions of Sociological and Psychological Theory to Casework Practice," *Journal of Education for Social Work* 4, Spring, 1968, 49–54.

Presthus, Robert. *The Organizational Society: An Analysis and a Theory.* New York: Vintage Books, 1962.

———. *Men at the Top.* New York: Oxford University Press, 1964.

Ramsoy, Odd. *Social Groups as System and Subsystem.* Oslo: Norwegian Universities Press, 1962.

Reik, Theodor. *Listening with the Third Ear.* New York: Farrar, Strauss, 1948.

Rodman, Hyman, ed. *Marriage, Family and Society.* New York: Random House, 1966.

Roethlisberger, F. J., and W. L. Dickson. *Management and the Worker.* Cambridge: Harvard University Press, 1947.

Rogers, Carl. *Carl Rogers on Encounter Groups.* New York: Harper & Row, 1970.

Rose, Arnold M. *The Power Structure.* New York: Oxford University Press, 1967.

Rose, Reginald. *Twelve Angry Men.* Chicago: Chicago Dramatics Publications Company, 1955.

Ross, Murray G. *Community Organization.* New York: Harper & Row, 1955.

Sager, Clifford, and Helen Singer Kaplan, eds. *Progress in Group and Family Therapy.* New York: Brunner/Mazel, 1972.

Sanders, Irwin T. *The Community.* New York: Roland Press, 1958.

Sarri, Rosemary C., and Meade J. Galinsky. "A Conceptual Framework for Group Development," in *Readings in Group Work Practice,* Robert D. Vinter, ed. Ann Arbor: Campus Publishers, 1967.

Satir, Virginia. *Conjoint Family Therapy.* Palo Alto, Calif.: Science and Behavior Books, 1964.

Scheflen, Albert E. *Body Language and the Social Order.* Englewood Cliffs, N.J.: Prentice-Hall, 1972.

Shepherd, Clovis R. *Small Groups.* San Francisco: Chandler, 1964.

Simon, H. A. *Administrative Behavior.* New York: Macmillan, 1945.

Simon, Paul. "I Am A Rock." New York: Charing Cross Music Inc., 1966.

Skinner, B. F. *Walden Two.* New York: Macmillan, 1948.

————. *Beyond Freedom and Dignity.* New York: Knopf, 1971.

Sommer, Robert. *Personal Space.* Englewood Cliffs, N.J.: Prentice-Hall, 1969.

Sorokin, Pitrim A. *Fads and Foibles in Modern Sociology.* Chicago: Regnery, 1956.

Southey, Robert. "The Doctor," quoted in the *Oxford Dictionary of Quotations.* 2nd ed. London: Oxford University Press, 1959, p. 508.

Spitz, Rene. *The First Year of Life.* New York: International Universities Press, 1965.

Srole, Leo. "Social Integration and Certain Corollaries: An Exploratory Study," *American Sociological Review* 21, 1956, 709–716.

Stein, Maurice R. *The Eclipse of Community.* Princeton: Princeton University Press, 1960.

Stone, Irving. *The Passions of the Mind.* Garden City, N.Y.: Doubleday, 1971.

Stone, L. Joseph, and Joseph Church. *Childhood and Adolescence.* New York: Random House, 1957.

————. *Childhood and Adolescence.* 2nd. ed. New York: Random House, 1968.

Strean, Herbert. "Application of the 'Life Model' to Casework," *Social Work* 17, 5, September, 1972, 46–53.

Teicher, Morton I. "The Concept of Culture," *Social Casework* 39, October, 1958, 450–455.

Thibaut, John W., and Harold H. Kelley. *The Social Psychology of Groups.* New York: Wiley, 1959.

Tillis, Mel. "Detroit City." Capitol Records.

Toffler, Alvin. *Future Shock.* New York: Randon House, 1970.

Tonnies, Ferdinand. *Community and Society.* Trans. Charles P. Loomis. East Lansing: Michigan State University Press, 1957.

Townsend, Robert. *Up the Organization.* New York: Knopf, 1970.

Trecker, Harleigh. *Social Group Work Principles and Practices.* New York: Whiteside, 1955.

Ullman, Edward L. "A Theory of Location for Cities," *American Journal of Sociology* 46, May, 1941, pp. 853–864.

Urofsky, Melvin, ed. *Why Teachers Strike.* Garden City, N.Y.: Anchor Books, 1970.

Vattano, Anthony J. "Power to the People: Self-help Groups," *Social Work* 17, 4, July, 1972, 7–15.

Vidich, Arthur J., and Joseph Bensman. *Small Town in Mass Society.* Princeton: Princeton University Press, 1958.

Vogel, Ezra, and Norman Bell. *A Modern Introduction to the Family.* New York: Free Press, 1960.

Voiland, Alice L., and Associates. *Family Casework Diagnosis.* New York: Columbia University Press, 1962.

Warren, Roland L. *The Community in America.* Chicago: Rand McNally, 1963.

Washburne, Norman F. *Interpreting Social Change in America.* New York: Random House, 1964.

Watts, Alan. *The Book: On the Taboo Against Knowing Who You Are.* New York: Pantheon Books, 1966.

Weisman, Celia B. "Social Structure as a Determinant of the Group Worker's Role," *Social Work* 8, 3, July, 1963, 87–94.

West, D. J. *Homosexuality.* Chicago: Aldine, 1967.

Whittaker, James C. *We Thought We Heard the Angels Sing.* New York: Dutton, 1943.

Whorf, Benjamin Lee. *Language, Thought and Reality*. New York: Technology Press and Wiley, 1956.

Whyte, Lancelot Law. *The Unconscious Before Freud*. Garden City, N.Y.: Doubleday, 1962.

Whyte, William Foote. *Street Corner Society*. 2nd ed. Chicago: University of Chicago Press, 1955.

Wolpe, Joseph. *The Practice of Behavior Therapy*. New York: Pergamon Press, 1969.

Zaleznik, Abraham, and Anne Jardim. "Management," in *The Uses of Sociology*, Paul F. Lazarsfield et al., eds. New York: Basic Books, 1967.

Zimmerman, Carle. *Outline of the Future of the Family*. Cambridge: The Phillips Book Store, 1947.

Zwerling, Israel, *Alienation and the Mental Health Professions*. Richmond School of Social Work, Virginia Commonwealth University, 1968.

NAME INDEX

175

SUBJECT INDEX

Human Behavior in the Social Environment
by Ralph E. Anderson and Irl Carter

Publisher, Alexander J. Morin
Manuscript Editor, Christine Valentine
Production Editor, Nanci Oakes Connors
Production Manager, Mitzi Carole Trout

Designed by Christine Valentine
Composed by Typoservice Corporation,
Indianapolis, Indiana
Printed and Bound by George Banta Company, Inc.
Menasha, Wisconsin